Teaching Criminal Justice *Ethics*

Strategic Issues

edited by

John Kleinig

Margaret Leland Smith

John Jay College of Criminal Justice
Institute for Criminal Justice Ethics
The City University of New York

anderson publishing co.
2035 Reading Rd.
Cincinnati, OH 45202
1-800-582-7295

Teaching Criminal Justice Ethics: Strategic Issues

2035 Reading Rd.
Cincinnati, OH 45202

Phone 800.582.7295 or 513.421.4142
Web Site www.andersonpublishing.com

ISBN 0-87084-831-3
Library of Congress Catalog Number 97-72026

Editor Elizabeth A. Shipp
Acquisitions Editor Michael C. Braswell

Contents

Acknowledgments

The contributions to this volume were first presented at a workshop on criminal justice ethics education held 6-8 June 1996 at John Jay College of Criminal Justice, City University of New York. Sponsored by the Institute for Criminal Justice Ethics, the workshop followed a successful one-day national conference on criminal justice education that was held on 20 October 1995 and was generously supported by a grant from the City University of New York.

Preparation for the workshop was preceded by a national survey of criminal justice ethics education, coordinated by Margaret Leland Smith, the Institute's researcher, assisted by Valerie West and Mary Hapel.

In presenting the revised papers from the workshop, we acknowledge the assistance received from Gerald W. Lynch and Basil W. Wilson, respectively president and provost of John Jay College, and their staffs.

Introduction

The Development of Criminal Justice Ethics Education

John Kleinig and Margaret Leland Smith

College-level criminal justice programs, now widely available in the United States, represent a relatively new development in higher education. Fifty years ago, the theoretical and practical questions about crime and public safety that underpin a criminal justice curriculum would, to the extent that they had been identified, have been subjects for discussion in criminology, political science, criminal psychology, or law courses. The development of criminal justice as an interdisciplinary field of inquiry did not occur until the late 1960s,[1] and, although linked courses in law and ethics have long been available, criminal justice ethics courses are only now coming of age.

The development of criminal justice was driven in large measure by government funding. In 1965, President Johnson set up a Commission on Law Enforcement and Administration of Justice. Its report, *The Challenge of Crime in a Free Society*, issued in 1967, recommended increased training for law enforcement personnel, including a college education for police recruits.[2] In the same year, the National Advisory Commission on Civil Disorders was formed, and its Report, published in 1968, was sharply critical not only of the police response to urban disturbances, but also of the administration of justice in poor communities.[3] As a result of these Reports, Johnson set up a new agency within the Department of Justice, the Law Enforcement Assistance Administration (LEAA). Within that agency, there was a further structure, the Law Enforcement Education Program (LEEP), devoted to the upgrading of police education. LEEP injected massive funds into police education. In 1969, LEEP grants amounted to $6.5

million, shared among 485 institutions. By 1975, 1065 colleges were receiving grants totaling $40 million. Money that was initially distributed to "police science" programs was subsequently distributed more generally to the new criminal justice programs, spurring growth in the study of corrections and the administration of justice.

By the mid-1970s, there was dissatisfaction with the implementation of a variety of LEAA initiatives, and specifically with the use of LEEP funds. Expansion of academic and training programs had been accomplished at the expense of quality. LEEP funding was phased out in 1978, just as Lawrence Sherman, with the support of the Police Foundation, issued *The Quality of Police Education*, a critical review of current police higher education. One of the recommendations of that review was the inclusion within the required curriculum of undergraduate police education programs of "a thorough consideration of the value choices and ethical dilemmas of police work."[4] Noting that "there are no adequate texts and materials presently available in this important area," Sherman recommended support for "the development of curricular materials on police ethics."[5]

Sherman was subsequently commissioned to expand on this need, and in 1981 produced a report, *The Teaching of Ethics in Criminology and Criminal Justice*,[6] a revised version of which was subsequently circulated more widely by the Hastings Center under the title, *Ethics in Criminal Justice Education*.[7] By the time he wrote, a good number of criminal justice programs had begun to include separate courses on criminal justice ethics or police ethics, despite the absence of texts and other teaching materials. Sherman's monograph remains a significant statement of the strategic issues to be confronted in a criminal justice ethics education.

A 1995 survey conducted by the Institute for Criminal Justice Ethics found that criminal justice ethics courses are being offered by slightly less than half of the undergraduate criminal justice programs.[8] The locus of criminal justice teaching—itself the residue of earlier struggles and negotiations—has had some bearing on the likelihood of a specialized interest in criminal justice ethics. Where criminal justice programs have developed an interdisciplinary autonomy of their own, they have been twice as likely to mount courses in criminal justice ethics as programs that have remained under the general aegis of the social sciences, such as sociology or criminology. The reasons for this may be complex.[9] Not only have independently administered criminal justice programs been more alert to the need for ethics education, but they often have strong ties to the vocational field of criminal justice. In a significant number of cases, representatives of the criminal justice agencies to whom schools send their graduates have actively lobbied for the inclusion of criminal justice ethics in the curriculum. Programs that have remained under the umbrella of a research-oriented social science department have demonstrated less concern with the ethical dimensions of criminal justice. The burgeoning interest in professional ethics is reflected not only in the increased number of research ethics courses, but in the refocusing of criminal justice ethics courses on the needs of practitioners.

John Jay College of Criminal Justice was founded in 1964 as an experiment in police education, though its mission broadened gradually to provide an environment in which research interests in the fields of criminology and criminal justice could be combined—sometimes uneasily—with general vocational preparation. The College's mission encouraged a more detailed exploration of ethical issues in criminal justice. In 1981, the Institute for Criminal Justice Ethics was founded by William C. Heffernan and Timothy Stroup, and in 1982 the first issue of a biannual journal, *Criminal Justice Ethics*, was published. In some ways the publication of *Criminal Justice Ethics* established a new domain of interdisciplinary discussion, and *Criminal Justice Ethics* remains the only specialized journal in its field. The Institute's first monograph, *Police Ethics: Hard Choices in Law Enforcement*,[10] coincided with the 1985 publication of Frederick Elliston and Michael Feldberg's *Moral Issues in Police Work*.[11] For several years, the two books, along with *Criminal Justice Ethics*, served as texts for courses in police ethics and for more professionally-oriented courses in criminal justice ethics.[12] More philosophically-oriented instructors have used general texts in ethics, along with supplements from law and criminal justice journals. Since 1989, however, a number of texts specifically tailored to criminal justice ethics courses have appeared, testimony to the increasingly significant place of ethics in the criminal justice curriculum.[13] These texts address questions in corrections and justice administration as well as in policing.

As opportunity arose, it became clear to the executive members of the Institute that the time had come for another strategic review of ethics education in criminal justice. Out of this concern—and with generous support from the City University of New York—there came three interlocking projects. First, the Institute conducted a national survey of criminal justice ethics education to gauge the growth, character, and problems of ethics teaching in criminal justice programs. Second, the Institute constructed a working bibliography of materials relating to the teaching of criminal justice ethics.[14] And third, the Institute sponsored an intensive two-day workshop on the teaching of criminal justice ethics. The revised papers from that workshop have been made available in this volume, along with the updated results of the first two projects, which are included as appendices.

The national survey showed, in addition to the 45 percent of programs that offered courses exclusively dedicated to criminal justice ethics, that in some 65 percent of programs, courses were given in which ethical issues figured significantly. These ethics courses are popular. Many students have a direct practical interest in criminal justice: they are active and aspiring law enforcement and corrections personnel seeking to enhance work-related credentials. For such students, criminal justice ethics has vocational significance, as professional or occupational ethics, and hence it focuses on issues that are likely to be encountered "on the job." Although significant numbers of these students have a primary concern with policing, there is also a growing number whose vocational interests are in corrections, security, and juvenile justice.

But there is also a sizeable population of students for whom the concern with criminal justice is related to a more general concern of citizens with public safety, or a more critical interest in social justice. For these students, criminal justice ethics has a difference focus—that of the consumer, not the practitioner. Their focus on the role of the state, the rights of citizens, suspects, accused persons, and those who have been convicted, as well as on issues of equality of access to criminal justice services, is likely to be distinct from that of the more vocationally oriented students.

Yet another group sees the criminal justice system institutionally, as a complex of organizational structures or focus of activities that generate issues of ethical significance—the conduct of forensic science laboratories, the manufacture of firearms and security equipment, private prison enterprises, and so on.

And there will also be those for whom the criminal justice system is mainly a focus of research, and for whom the ethical questions will center on the treatment of subjects, the meaning of informed consent, the confidentiality of information, and the social implications of choices in funded research.

Our review of the criminal justice ethics education literature revealed significant gaps, both in classroom materials and in strategic aids to teaching. Although ethics education has made significant advances in some of the traditional and newer professional disciplines—medicine, law, engineering, and business—in criminal justice the development has been much slower. It is true that the ethical issues that confront legal practitioners within the criminal justice system have been addressed at some length, and—for historical reasons—there is a fairly extensive literature relating to the work of police ("law enforcement"); nevertheless, there is very little that focuses on the concerns of those working in probation and parole and, except for broader issues of penology, relatively little to assist those who work as prison officers and administrators.

In 1991 the Association for Practical and Professional Ethics was formed as an umbrella organization for those individuals and institutions concerned with the ethical dimensions of public life, but criminal justice ethics is barely represented in its strongly philosophical membership. Where criminal justice ethics is taught, it does not generally appear to be taught by people who have acquaintance with the organization that is most likely to keep them abreast of developments in the teaching of practical and professional ethics. Most of those who teach criminal justice ethics have been recruited from the ranks of sociology or criminology. The Institute's executive body therefore took the decision to construct a workshop which, though directed to the concerns of criminal justice, and sensitive to some of the issues highlighted by the survey, would infuse the teaching of criminal justice ethics with ideas and approaches that had been found valuable in other areas of practical and professional ethics.

We believed that at least four general issues needed to be canvassed—the aims of criminal justice ethics education, the ways in which it might be incorporated into the criminal justice curriculum, some general techniques for teaching it effectively, and methods of evaluating its teaching. These issues cannot be sharply separated, and those we invited often moved their focus from one area to another. In constructing the conference, we did not see it as our task to produce a criminal justice ethics syllabus, for we recognized that different programs, with somewhat different aims and student bodies, would want to approach criminal justice ethics in rather different ways, and would therefore need to construct appropriate and distinctive syllabi.

I AIMS IN CRIMINAL JUSTICE ETHICS EDUCATION

What are we trying to achieve in teaching criminal justice ethics? William Heffernan contrasts two goals, which he embeds in a wider understanding of a liberal education. We can view the purpose of criminal justice ethics education as one of providing guidance—a commonplace of nineteenth-century western education, with its morally homogeneous world. Or we can see it—more appropriately for a morally-plural twentieth-century world—as familiarizing students with a wide literature, providing them with the critical skills that will enable them to appraise it. Heffernan recoils from the idea of the university as a purveyor of doctrine and suggests that the autonomy-enhancement function of a liberal university requires that no educational judgments be made on the basis of conformity to social or professional orthodoxies.[15] Not that students should be prevented from expressing their own views, only that they should not be judged on the basis of those views. In his response to Heffernan, John Kleinig questions the sharpness of the distinction that Heffernan draws between his two models, and suggests that the very project of reflecting on the ethical dimensions of criminal justice might require more substantive commitments than those suggested by Heffernan's formal concerns. However, that leaves the important question about where the line should be drawn. Should a student be marked down if he displays blatantly sexist/racist attitudes in an ethics essay? Does his work manifest a failure of reason as well as of morality? Heffernan's essay shows how the teaching of criminal justice ethics raises fundamental questions about the idea of a university.

Some of the same concerns resurface in Joan Callahan's paper. In her discussion of the ways in which ethics might be integrated into the criminal justice curriculum, she argues that the applied or practical turn in moral philosophy is as old as moral philosophy itself. The great moral theorists—those whom Heffernan would encourage students to study for foundational theory—were themselves often concerned to advocate or guide. Callahan regards the view that moral philosophy is, and that the teaching thereof should remain, neutral as a peculiarity of mid-twentieth-century philosophy. Although she believes that a certain kind of moral theorizing can be of the sort that Heffernan advocates, she notes—as he does, that this is to be distinguished from what goes on in practical ethics. The latter, she believes, has several aims, aims which overlap with but extend beyond those acknowledged as legitimate by Heffernan: (1) the recognition of moral issues; (2) the development of moral imagination; (3) the sharpening of analytical/critical skills; (4) the sorting out of disagreements; and (5) the influencing of decisions and behavior.

Michael Davis, before focusing more narrowly on what might be aimed at in a course on police ethics, first observes that "criminal justice ethics" might be understood either as a form of institutional ethics or as a species of professional ethics. That is, it might review ethical questions that emerge out of the social practice of criminal justice, or it might focus specifically on the ethical concerns faced by its professional practitioners. His own focus is on the latter, and specifically on police as its most visible practitioners. Davis details a number of general aims that he believes to be achievable through teaching occupational or professional ethics: (1) increased ethical sensitivity; (2) increased knowledge of relevant standards of conduct; (3) improved ethical judgment; and (4) improved ethical willpower. There is an interesting overlap with and divergence from Callahan here. Although he does not want to suggest that courses or programs that include a substantial ethical component will ensure optimal behavior, he clearly thinks that the goal of improving ethical performance is legitimate.

Charles Claxton offers a third perspective on the aims of criminal justice ethics education. For Claxton, the focus should not be on the "telling" or the content to be taught in an ethics classroom, but on the activity of learning—on the students' active construction of meaning. Claxton sees the aim of ethics teaching to be that of helping "learners increase their capacity of thought so that they can deal more effectively with ethical issues."[16] Working from the research of Sharon Parks, he argues that students need to be supported as they move from a process in which their thinking is dominated by external ("interpersonal") authority to one in which their thinking is much more autonomous or "inner-dependent." Much of Claxton's paper is directed to ways of achieving this goal. It is the task of teachers to present their materials in a manner that allows learners to grasp what is presented, and to transform the material into something that has increasingly complex meaning for them. This is not a simple transfer of information, but a collaborative venture involving students, teacher, and text. Claxton models this recursive approach using two examples drawn from criminal justice. Students will come to think about the thinking process, become more aware of their assumptions or "mental models," and develop a sense of responsibility for their own judgments.

In her response to Davis and Claxton, Dorothy Roberts speaks of the need to address a problem that is hinted at by the "informal codes" that characterize some police behavior—codes that seem to stand in some sort of tension with both their formal codes and ordinary morality. Does police ethics allow *exceptions* to ordinary morality (as these informal codes seem to suggest) rather than just the *additions* to which Davis draws attention? Roberts links this question to a larger debate in professional ethics about role morality and, implicitly, the problem of dirty hands. Roberts also notes a shortfall in Claxton's discussion, seeing in his view of education as a creative, self-transformational process the beginnings, but only the beginnings, of a more radical transformation. Drawing on the work of Paulo Freire, she notes the "liberating" possibilities of an education that elicits the student construction of knowledge and draws on their own repositories of experience. Where minority students are involved in an engagement with criminal justice concerns, the result might well be a powerful critique of the status quo.

II INTEGRATING CRIMINAL JUSTICE ETHICS INTO THE CURRICULUM

How should ethical concerns be incorporated into a criminal justice program? Michael Davis suggests eight compatible and mutually supportive ways in which ethics might be integrated into a program: (1) independent study; (2) an event that focuses on ethical issues; (3) making code observance an institutional requirement; (4) guest lectures on ethics; (5) a course on professional ethics taught outside the department (by, say, the philosophy department); (6) a course on professional ethics taught by a member of the profession; (7) an in-house course on professional ethics; and (8) a pervasive approach.

Much of the debate has involved a comparison of freestanding courses in criminal justice ethics [Davis's options (5) through (7)] with various methods of "pervasive" ethics education, in which an ethical component constitutes a constant thread in the criminal justice curriculum. Davis himself sees most merit in (8): it reinforces what is taught elsewhere; it makes ethical reflection a natural part of practical decision making; because of limited resources and constrained curricula, it may be the only way in which students will be confronted by ethical questions during their training; it can keep alive some of the original motivation for entering the criminal justice field; and it is appealing to students.

But Davis, like Callahan, recognizes the difficulties involved in successfully planning integration of this kind.[17] He notes three barriers to implementing the pervasive approach—a lack of ethical training on the part of teaching personnel; a lack of fit between what is being asked of personnel and what they are oriented to provide; and a paucity of text materials that offer the integrated approach required by the pervasive method.

Joan Callahan provides an overview of the freestanding and pervasive approaches. She spells out the strengths and drawbacks of each, and argues for an approach that will allow some place for both. Davis seems to agree, although he prefers the pervasive method, whereas Callahan gives more weight to the freestanding approach. She offers several reasons in support of her contention: (1) if ethics is not given the status of a separate course, it will be seen as unimportant; (2) if it is tacked on to other courses, it will be edged out as other course demands increase; and (3) that if it is not given its own place in the curriculum, and is seen instead as everyone's responsibility, it will become no one's responsibility.

Nevertheless, Callahan believes that a significant problem is associated with teaching a freestanding course: When should it be taught? At the beginning, when it is too early, or at the end, when it may be too late? She sees some merit to what Samuel Gorowitz has termed an "intermittent" approach, but recognizes that this will add to the pressure to extend the length of professional training.

Michael Davis has more time for what Callahan refers to as "weaving" ethical issues into routine courses on criminal justice administration, psychological issues in criminal justice, and so on. But he recognizes that there are several problems with this. An expert on police administration will not necessarily be an expert on the ethical questions that are encountered in that area. Some retraining may be necessary. It may also need to include some sharing between "practitioners" and "mere academics." Further, many of the standard texts fail to give an appropriate place to ethical questions in their treatments of issues. Nevertheless, he believes that despite the significant restructuring that might be necessary to implement a pervasive approach, it will have the additional values of (a) reminding students of one of the factors that has drawn them to the profession (service), and (b) giving students something with which they can engage. The pervasive approach does not meet with student resistance.

Even so, Davis believes that there might still be something to be said for a noncompulsory freestanding course. It provides a foundation on which others may build, and offers a more systematic introduction to ways of thinking about ethical questions.

Caroline Whitbeck comes at the issue of integration of ethics into the curriculum in a different way, one that understands ethical inquiry as a problem-solving activity. She argues that the most productive approach to ethics teaching is that of the practical agent, not that of the judge. Whitbeck urges the use of actual professional cases and standards, and a refocusing of moral deliberation from the top-down application of principles to the use of analogical reasoning. She believes that the use of case studies, in which discussants take the point of view of participating agents, constitutes an important part of professional ethics education, whether such cases are used in the context of a pervasive approach, which she appears to favor, or as part of a freestanding course.

A valuable caveat is entered by Frances Kamm. Though Kamm is supportive of a combined approach to practical ethics of the kind that Callahan outlines, she sees a certain danger where general moral theory is abandoned for an exclusive focus on case studies. A good grasp of such theory contributes to one's ability to reflect productively on practical ethical issues, including cases.

III STRATEGIES IN TEACHING CRIMINAL JUSTICE ETHICS

When we move from a consideration of broad questions about the way in which criminal justice ethics might be incorporated into the criminal justice curriculum to some of the ways in which it might be taught—whether in a separate course, or as part of some other course, say, on investigatory techniques or prison administration—several factors need to be taken into account. We must take into account certain general presumptions about the capacities of students vis-à-vis their grasp of ethical issues, and more specific data about techniques that will allow them fruitfully to reflect on ethical questions.

Elizabeth Reynolds Welfel focuses on the first of these factors. In her paper on the contribution that psychology might make to the teaching of criminal justice ethics, Welfel draws on the work of Jean Piaget, Lawrence Kohlberg, and James Rest to make two general points: first, that the teaching of ethics (and that includes the teaching of professional ethics) needs to take into account the level of moral development that students have reached, and second, that any teaching of ethics should recognize and accommodate the various constitutive elements of moral reflection.

One would hope that by the time college students engage with issues in criminal justice ethics, they would have progressed beyond the earlier stages of Piagetian/Kohlbergian moral development, and would be prepared to reflect on issues in a principled, if not autonomous manner. But, as Rest notes, and Welfel endorses, moral education involves more than the development of an ability to reason about moral issues, it includes nurture of a capacity to identify issues as moral growth in resolution and will.

Without disagreeing with Rest's enriched account of moral development, Robin Flaton suggests that further articulation needs to be given to the reasoning component. Following Kuhn, she suggests that the quality of reasoning about social problems is related to the conception a person has of the epistemological status of such inquiries. Those who adopt either of two extreme views—one holding that absolute certainty can be achieved, and one that holds that all views are equally valid—do not develop as good reasoning skills as those who take the view that knowledge, albeit revisable knowledge, is possible. This, she believes, constitutes an argument for the moral value of continuing moral education.

Once we turn from generalities about the moral capacities of students to specific techniques, there is strong backing for a pedagogy that centers on, or at least has a significant place for, case studies. Whitbeck notes the increasing importance given to case materials in professional education. She distinguishes and illustrates five kinds of case materials—open-ended scenarios, cautionary tales, news stories, stories of exemplary conduct, and the judgments of authoritative bodies. In her discussion she draws attention to the different kinds of skills needed for each kind of case.

An in-depth exploration of the value that real cases have for moral development and the deepening of moral insight, especially when a lengthy narrative is presented, is offered by Kenneth Winston. Drawing on the resources of the Harvard Case Study Program, Winston shows how reflection on a particular incident, when embedded in its larger social context, can provide an extremely rich moral resource. Real-life cases do not usually highlight the single issues favored by most teachers, but involve a complex amalgam of concerns, which need to be considered in their inter-connectedness if appropriate and wise decisions are to be made. Like Whitbeck, Winston uses his discussion to make a more general point about the direction of moral reflection—not so much from general theory to particular case as from particular case to general theory, thus reversing the trend in many texts on practical ethics. However, Gary Seay, his respondent, is not so sure about this reversal, and believes that it may obscure the implicit workings of theory when particular cases are reflected upon. Perhaps there is no simple either/or here, but something more complex, such as Rawls' appeal to a process of seeking and reaching "reflective equilibrium."[18] Both Winston and Seay seem to be attracted to this strategy.

Frances Kamm also has several comments to make on strategies of moral reasoning when confronted by cases. She takes Callahan and Whitbeck to task for offering step-by-step approaches to the resolution of moral dilemmas that do not comport with those that we are likely to find the most productive. It may be better to follow through with a naturally appealing solution than to canvas as many solutions as possible; alternatives can then be introduced as possible objections when justificatory reasons have been assembled. What is more, the thinking up of options and the evaluation of alternatives cannot be separated in the manner that step-by-step approaches appear to suggest. Even though Callahan and Whitbeck eschew the algorithmic approach to moral decision making that sees practical decision making as a straightforward application of moral theory, Kamm's remarks suggest that even their own alternatives may be too formulaic.

IV EVALUATING THE TEACHING OF CRIMINAL JUSTICE ETHICS

The final session of the Conference was given over to a roundtable discussion of a topic that is all-too-rarely considered in discussions of ethics teaching: What constitutes successful ethics teaching? How can one tell whether one has succeeded as a teacher of criminal justice ethics?

These questions are obviously complicated by the existence of competing conceptions of what is to be aimed at in teaching criminal justice ethics —whether it is, minimally, a familiarity with and understanding of certain materials in the field, or, maximally, moral strengthening or transformation. The more minimal the expectations, the easier it will be to assess the success of the teaching. Grander expectations—such as a marked improvement in moral performance—can hardly be assessed at the end of a course, but must await the "test" of life. Several of the contributors believed that although course assessments would necessarily be limited in what they could show, it could nevertheless be expected that a well-executed course could provide measurably heightened sensitivity, improved reflection, and better performance.

In the end, consensus was not possible. But this should not be seen as failure, but rather as an indication of the need for continuing reflection on the issues that were raised. For all its importance, criminal justice ethics education offers no easy answers.

NOTES

1. For a valuable detailed history of the development of criminal justice education, see Frank Morn, *Academic Politics and the History of Criminal Justice Education* (Westport, CT: Greenwood Press, 1995).

2. President's Commission on Law Enforcement and Administration of Justice, *The Challenge of Crime in a Free Society* (Washington, DC: U.S. Government Printing Office, 1967).

3. National Advisory Commission on Civil Disorders, *Report* (Kerner Report) (New York: Bantam Books, 1968).

4. Lawrence W. Sherman and the National Advisory Commission on Higher Education for Police Officers, *The Quality of Police Education* (San Francisco: Jossey Bass, 1978), pp. 4, 89.

5. Ibid., p. 4.

6. Lawrence W. Sherman, *The Teaching of Ethics in Criminology and Criminal Justice* (Washington, DC: Joint Commission on Criminology and Criminal Justice Education and Standards, LEAA, 1981).

7. Lawrence W. Sherman, *Ethics in Criminal Justice Education* (Hastings-on-Hudson, NY: Hastings Center, 1982). This appeared as Volume X of the Center's Monographs on the Teaching of Ethics.

8. See Appendix I in this volume: "Survey of Criminal Justice Ethics Education."

9. Ibid.

10. William C. Heffernan and Timothy Stroup (eds.), *Police Ethics: Hard Choices in Law Enforcement* (New York: John Jay Press, 1985).

11. Frederick A. Elliston and Michael Feldberg (eds.), *Moral Issues in Police Work* (Totowa, NJ: Rowman & Allanheld, 1985).

12. They were not the only books. Police academy-oriented courses could make use of Don L. Kooken, *Ethics in Police Service* (Springfield, IL: C C Thomas, 1957); David A. Hanson, *Police Ethics* (Springfield, IL: C C Thomas, 1973); or Alan P. Bristow, *You . . . and the Law Enforcement Code of Ethics* (Santa Cruz, CA: Davis Publishing Co., 1975). More recently, see Patricia Haggard, *Police Ethics* (Lewiston, NY: Edwin Mellen Press, 1994). See also Appendix II, in this volume.

13. Joycelyn Pollock, *Ethics in Crime and Justice: Dilemmas and Decisions*, second edn. (Pacific Grove, CA: Brooks/Cole, 1994); Frank Schmalleger (ed.), *Ethics in Criminal Justice: A Justice Professional Reader* (Bristol, IN: Wyndham Hall Press, 1990); Howard Cohen and Michael Feldberg, *Power and Restraint;The Moral Dimension of Police Work* (New York: Praeger, 1991); Michael C. Braswell, Belinda R. McCarthy, and Bernard J. McCarthy (eds.), *Justice, Crime, and Ethics*, 2nd edn. (Cincinnati, OH: Anderson, 1996); Sam S. Souryal, *Ethics in Criminal Justice: In Search of the Truth* (Cincinnati, OH: Anderson, 1992); Daryl Close & Nicholas Meier (eds.), *Morality in Criminal Justice: An Introduction to Ethics* (Belmont, CA: Wadsworth, 1994); John Kleinig, *The Ethics of Policing* (Cambridge: Cambridge University Press, 1996). See also Appendix II, in this volume.

14. A duplicated in-house version was circulated in January, 1996. An updated version is included as Appendix II, in this volume. An early duplicated bibliography, which focused mainly on law enforcement, was compiled by Frederick Elliston: *Police Ethics: Source Materials* (Washington, DC: Police Foundation, n.d.[1983]).

15. He allows that the situation might be very different within a training academy, where questions that might appropriately be asked within a university setting have been practically foreclosed.

16. Charles S. Claxton, "Teaching and Learning in Criminal Justice Ethics," in this volume, p. 59.

17. In 1991 the Wharton School at the University of Pennsylvania undertook to develop a curriculum in which ethics was pervasively incorporated. The large-scale planning and preparation that this involved is usefully detailed in *Integrating Ethics into the Wharton Undergraduate Curriculum* (Philadelphia, PA: The Wharton School, University of Pennsylvania, 1993).

18. John Rawls, *A Theory of Justice* (Cambridge, MA: Belknap/Harvard University Press, 1972), pp. 48-51.

PART I

Aims in Criminal Justice Ethics Education

Chapter 1

The Aims of Criminal Justice Ethics Education

William C. Heffernan

A recent conversation I had with a colleague at John Jay led me to think more carefully than I had before about the aims of courses on ethical issues in criminal justice. The conversation was triggered by a newspaper article about a New York City police officer, and John Jay graduate, who had just been indicted for killing someone he was trying to arrest. My colleague said he had had the officer in his criminal justice ethics class. The officer had done exceptionally well, my colleague said. He had subtly analyzed the theories discussed in the course; he had shown a rare ability to synthesize ideas; and he had demonstrated outstanding writing ability as well. He had gotten an "A," my colleague told me—and now he stood charged with choking someone to death during the course of an arrest.

As I thought about our exchange in the days that followed, it occurred to me that if the officer was actually convicted, then his grade should be changed retroactively. You flunk criminal justice ethics, I mused, if you engage in egregious conduct as a criminal justice official—and you flunk it no matter how much you shine in your written work and class comments. Or, taking a different tack, I wondered if *the course* could be said to have failed: success in criminal justice ethics instruction, I thought, can be judged in terms of behavioral outcomes, not the polish of a student's prose.

In considering these points, I of course grasped the practical difficulties they posed—for example, the difficulty in finding out how course-graduates have actually behaved. But changing behavior, I realized, lies at the heart of outsiders' demands for courses in criminal justice ethics. When agency chiefs or newspaper editorial writers say that there should be an ethics component in criminal justice education, they are not suggesting that exposure to different views about the foundations of ethics is a good thing in itself. Rather, they expect ethics courses to have a payoff—to lead to a decline in police assaults on arrestees, to a decline in bribe taking, and so on.

With six months' hindsight on the conversation, I can now see that two different models must be considered in thinking about criminal justice ethics courses in particular and occupational ethics courses in general. On the one hand, such courses can be analyzed in terms of a guidance model. The aim of such courses, it could be said, is not to stimulate debates about what is right but rather to apply well-established ethical principles to particular criminal justice settings ("police officers should not club already-shackled arrestees," "corrections officers should not take bribes to provide inmates with drugs," and so on). An advocate of the guidance model would argue that it is not enough for students simply to *say* these things. According to an advocate of this model, students should also leave the course imbued with the motivation to do what is right. Ultimately, the advocate would maintain, a criminal justice ethics course can be called successful only if students act on this motivation when out in the field.

We can contrast this guidance model with one that emphasizes the contested issues in a discipline. Under the contested-issues model, instructors in criminal justice ethics courses carry out their duties in much the same way that instructors in a broad range of liberal arts courses do: that is, they expect students to become familiar with a wide range of readings, to contrast ideas and develop distinctions, and to analyze clearly the issues that confront them in the course. Instructors following the contested-issues model do not grade students on the substantive correctness of the positions. Like instructors in, say, history or sociology courses, they employ formal criteria in assessing students' work, asking not whether a student was right or wrong in her positions but whether the positions were skillfully presented.

In this essay, I use these two models to comment on the aims of criminal justice ethics courses. I advance three arguments with respect to the models. First, I argue that the contested-issues model defines the sole acceptable approach to university-based instruction in ethics. No compromise with the guidance model is possible, I suggest: instructors who take the contested-issues model seriously should not offer covert guidance while pretending to teach a course taught in terms of subject-mastery aims.

My other arguments are related to this one. The second point I make is that criminal justice ethics courses, like other occupational ethics courses, have benefited from a blurring of their aims. While most instructors in such courses tend to adhere to the contested-issues model, public support for such courses tends to be based on the misimpression that they have a guidance function. Instructors have a vested interest in preserving this misimpression; I argue, though, that they should declare frankly that their courses cannot be expected to, and do not, aim at producing better criminal justice officials, at least as the public understands this term. Finally, I contend that the indignation the public feels about conduct such as bribe taking and assaults on suspects can indeed find some relief in university-based instruction. The relief, I suggest, is not, however, to be found in ethics but in public administration courses, where instructors can consider ways to restructure criminal agencies so as to reduce the incidence of the behavior that distresses the public.

I THE TWO MODELS

Until the modern era, universities throughout the western world functioned as authoritative moral institutions for the cultures they served. Students who wished to enroll in Oxford or Cambridge were required to subscribe to the Anglican Church's thirty-nine articles. Even those who subscribed to church doctrine could later be expelled for deviating from it; Percy Bysshe Shelley, for example, was sent down from University College, Oxford for advocating atheistic beliefs.[1] And instructors who deviated from orthodoxy were expected to resign their university positions, as John Henry Newman did when he converted from Anglicanism to Roman Catholicism.[2]

In the pre-modern college or university, ethics instruction usually conformed to the guidance model. Consider, for example, the course Mark Hopkins, president of Williams College in the mid-nineteenth century, taught for the college's seniors. Three characteristics of the course deserve particular attention. First, it took the content of ethics to be uncontroversial. As Frederick Rudolph has noted, "Although [Hopkins's] course was everywhere accepted as philosophy, it was, both in purpose and practice, a mixture of Congregational orthodoxy and personal opinion."[3] Second, the course assumed without question that the term "ethics" refers solely to norms of personal conduct. It did not question the justness of social distributions; its purpose was to insure student conformity to norms established by a social order whose legitimacy was not to be questioned. And third, in teaching the course Hopkins did not simply advance formal definitions of right and wrong, he also offered each of his students concrete advice about how to conduct his life. Hopkins—quite wisely, given his guidance aim—did not teach in a catechistic fashion. His classroom style was avuncular and undogmatic. He followed up classroom instruction with conversations on the college walkways, in his study, and even in student rooms. As James Garfield, twentieth president of the United States and an 1854 graduate of Williams College, remarked, the ideal education was one in which Mark Hopkins sat at one end of a log and a student at the other, with the student thus having an extended opportunity to talk to Hopkins about the great issues of life.[4]

Hopkins's course was by no means unique in American higher education. During the middle of the nineteenth century, Timothy Dwight of Yale and Eliphalet Nott of Union, to name two of the more prominent college presidents of the time, taught similar courses at their institutions.[5] These senior courses gave a reassuring answer to the question Socrates addresses in *Meno* of whether virtue can be taught.[6] They taught ethics not simply by formal instruction but by integrating the discussion of ethical norms into communal life: chapel services, athletics, and impromptu conversations between the president and his students all became occasions for reinforcing the subject-matter of classroom analysis. The courses also were grounded in what today would be called a "cult of personality"; Hopkins, Dwight, Nott, and the other presidents who taught them were believed to exemplify all that is good and true in human nature and so to provide models for students as to how to conduct their lives. It was through a fusion of cognitive and conative elements that the courses offered guidance. Had the courses attempted only an analaysis of ethics, their graduates would not have remembered the courses with the vividness that they did.

A veteran of a contemporary ethics course will immediately recognize the difference between what she experienced and what mid-nineteenth century students went through. A contemporary course that deals generally with ethics (I shall turn later to courses in criminal justice ethics) answers the question of whether ethics can be taught by focusing on contested issues in the discipline. Such a course deals with disagreements about:

the *content* of ethical norms (for example, what actually is right and wrong or good and evil),

the *orientation* of ethics (for example, whether ethics should concentrate on theories of the right or theories of the good), and the *foundation* of ethics (for example, whether it is possible to demonstrate that ethical norms are binding on others).

Because of the importance of these issues, most instructors in contemporary ethics courses, even those who take stands on specific questions themselves, tend to adhere to the contested-issues model when evaluating students: they assess student work on the basis of formal criteria (breadth of research, overall coherence, development of argument, and so on) and not on the substantive "correctness" of the positions they take. It is hard to imagine how Hopkins would have reacted to a student who disagreed with the code he taught. Hopkins quite possibly would not have expelled the student or given him an "F" for the course but instead would have looked for some way to enlighten him about the true nature of morality. What Hopkins would not have done, though, is evaluate the student's work in light of the formal criteria mentioned above.

My aim, however, is not to examine the distance travelled between the creedal instruction that, until relatively recently, dominated university education and the modern approach to ethics instruction. Rather, my aim is to show that college ethics teachers *ought to* adhere to the contested-issues model of instruction. In my opinion, there are three reasons why this model is desirable. The first is straightforward: instructors should take seriously the fact of moral disagreement. Central to the guidance model is an indifference to the fact of contest over the nature and content of ethics. Hopkins did not emphasize moral disagreement in his senior course: to have done so would have undercut his guidance aim. But the cost of Hopkins's approach was to impose an extraordinary limitation on his students' understanding of morality—to cut them off not simply from anti- and nonchristian approaches to ethics but also from alternative versions of christian ethics that differed from the one Hopkins was propounding. Only by emphasizing the contested nature of ethics, I believe, can instructors alert students to the full richness of past reflections on morality.

The second reason why the contested-issues model should be adopted has to do with the importance of promoting moral autonomy. If, as I believe to be desirable, students should be encouraged to construct their own moral frameworks for conducting life, then they have broad leeway in ethics courses to explore ideas without fear of sanction for the positions they take. In state-supported universities, students have constitutionally-protected free speech rights to do this. Students in private universities do not enjoy this constitutional protection. However, the best rationale that can be advanced for the constitutional right of free speech in this context is to be found in the moral consideration I have mentioned—that ethics courses provide students with an occasion to reflect on their moral identities and so to become well-informed authors of their own moral fate. This rationale sustains free speech protection in public and private universities.

The third reason dovetails with this. Instructors, too, have a morally significant interest in being able to take stands on controverted ethical issues. They can do so only if they do not have reason to fear being sanctioned by their institutions for the stands they take. To say that instructors should be able to take a stand *in class* on ethical issues does not undercut the contested-issues model, for provided an instructor reviews with students other positions besides her own and makes clear to her students that their work will not be evaluated in light of their agreement with her substantive positions, the aims of the contested-issues model can be realized.

Taken together, these three reasons provide a justification for what can be called the liberal approach to ethics instruction. This approach is not to be confused with moral nihilism. On the contrary, it provides morally signficant reasons for employing morally neutral criteria in the evaluation of student work. Under the guidance model, institutions claiming authoritative moral wisdom determine what is to be taught and who is to teach it. Under the contested-issues model, liberal institutions issue one important substantive injunction—emphasize the contested nature of ethical issues —but otherwise insist only on a procedural approach to evaluating students and teachers. The result under the guidance model is thus a replication of authoritative doctrine. The result under the contested-issues model is diversity in the best sense of the term. Under the contested-issues model, Professor Immanuel Kant will evaluate the essay *On the Genealogy of Morals* by his precocious student Fred Nietzsche in light of morally neutral criteria despite the fact that the essay repudiates Kant's moral thought as well as that of most other moralists. In time, Nietzsche might even become a colleague of Kant's, making their philosophy department a microcosm of contests over the nature of ethics.

Should the contested-issues model also be employed in criminal justice ethics education? Two reasons, neither one of which is convincing, might be advanced against its adoption. First, it could be contended that a criminal justice ethics course deals with "applied" ethics, thus making it appropriate for instructors in such a course to establish a framework of moral precepts that gives general guidance to students and to use this framework to examine issues of special relevance to criminal justice. The difficulty with this argument is that it sacrifices the values I mentioned earlier—exposing students to the fact of moral disagreement, encouraging them to construct their own moral framework, and allowing instructors to develop a moral framework that differs from socially orthodox ones. These values do not recede in importance just because the focus of a course changes from general issues in ethics to the specific issues that arise in a given occupation. On the contrary, an instructor can accord them the importance they deserve while also doing justice to the different focus of an occupational ethics course. That is, an instructor can summarize succinctly general disagreements about ethical theory and clarify those disagreements by showing their relevance to specific issues in the criminal justice system.

Alternatively, it could be argued that criminal justice ethics courses are preprofessional in nature, that many students enrolled in them intend careers in law enforcement or else to have already embarked on such careers, and that instructors should thus avoid moral theories that run counter to their professional norms. I think the empirical component of this argument—that is, the component about the composition of students in criminal justice courses—is correct. But I do not see why it follows from this that criminal justice ethics instructors should concentrate on moral theories consistent with professional norms. To say this is to make these into second-class courses, to treat them as the equivalent of police academy courses. The preferable approach is to say that students in criminal justice ethics courses cannot be subjected to any substantive limitations in the positions they can take. Such courses are subject to a content-limitation: students taking them can properly be expected to talk primarily about issues that arise in the operation of the criminal justice system. Like students in general ethics courses, though, they should not operate under viewpoint-limitations as to the arguments they can advance.

II CONVENIENT MISUNDERSTANDINGS ABOUT THE AIMS OF CRIMINAL JUSTICE ETHICS EDUCATION

I contended earlier that ethics courses in fact adhere to the contested-issues model of instruction. Can the same be said of *criminal justice* ethics courses? While I believe that such courses *should* adhere to this model, my suspicion is that they *tend toward* the contested-issues model while incorporating some elements of the guidance model. Few criminal justice ethics instructors, I believe, take guidance to be their primary pedagogical aim. Moreover, most would agree that, even were this to be their overriding aim, they probably could not realize it given their students' age and other experiences. But this does not mean that criminal justice ethics courses are as open-ended as those in general ethics. Instructors in these courses sometimes have not been trained as professional philosophers, and even when they have, they may be more persuaded than I am by either of the arguments I have just dismissed—the argument that an "applied" ethics course should provide students with a single framework in which to resolve disputed issues and the argument that such courses should limit their content to approved professional norms. I shall thus assume that criminal justice ethics courses adhere mostly to the contested-issues model but that they incorporate some elements of the guidance model as well.

Even this blend of approaches stands in sharp contrast with what agency chiefs and college administrators *believe* to be the aim of such courses. In my conversations with agency chiefs and administrators, I have never met one who did not assume that there are straightforward ethical rules and that the business of criminal justice ethics courses is to inspire students to act on these in their professional lives. Outsider support for criminal justice ethics courses—that is, support from agency chiefs and academic administrators—is grounded not in the thought that such courses will inform students about the cross-currents of ethical theory but in a concern with the history of assaults and bribe taking on the part of police and corrections officers. It is public indignation with this behavior that provides the larger context for colleges' adoption of these courses. Agency chiefs support the adoption of such courses as part of a package of measures designed to demonstrate their commitment to reform. Academic administrators support the adoption of such courses to show that universities are relevant to social concerns, that they can offer services that will tangibly improve the quality of life.

Indeed, the addition of criminal justice ethics courses to the curriculum must be viewed in light of a larger trend in which universities have tried to prove their social relevance. Recently, Harvard Business School accepted a $25 million gift from John Shad, a former chairman of the Securities and Exchange Commission, to develop an ethics program at the school. Gifts have also been made to law schools to upgrade ethics instruction in those institutions. The gifts have been scandal-driven: insider trading has provided the impetus for business schools; Abscam, among other things, for law schools, and so on. In mounting occupational ethics courses, academic administrators have been quite willing to let donors and agency chiefs believe that such courses can play the same role Mark Hopkins assigned to his senior ethics course at Williams College. My impression is that academic administrators actually *believe* that occupational ethics courses can play this role. In the final analysis, though, it does not matter what they believe. What matters is that they respond to incentives—fund-raising and public relations incentives—by *creating the impression* that occupational ethics courses can contribute to eliminating the behavior that so distresses the public.

If administrators operate under a strong incentive to make it seem as if criminal justice ethics courses will guide students toward "better" professional performance, instructors in these courses operate under an equally strong incentive not to disabuse them of this notion. It is for this reason that I have used the term "convenient misunderstandings" in the title for this section. Each side has a great deal to lose through a clarification of the other's position. If an administrator were ever to ask the instructor in the criminal justice ethics course I mentioned at the beginning of this essay whether he thought the course *should have* aimed at providing guidance for its students, I am sure the instructor would say that the course should not have tried to achieve this. And if the instructor were to ask the administrator whether he was talking to agency chiefs as if the course actually did aim at guiding officers toward socially approved behavior, I am sure the administrator would concede that this was his line. But I am also sure that both sides have avoided direct questions such as these. I think many instructors know that they benefit from administrators' misunderstandings. I suspect, though I am not sure, that administrators do not even realize that they are operating under a misunderstanding.

Should criminal justice ethics instructors try to clear up this misunderstanding? My unequivocal answer is that they should. Criminal justice ethics courses can accomplish what general ethics courses can: each can expose students to a broad range of moral argument and so give them an opportunity to construct moral frameworks of their own. Even if they actually did aim at changing behavior—at reducing assaults and bribery, for example—they would contribute very little to realizing that aim. The guidance model is likeliest to succeed in a "total institution" (to use Erving Goffman's term) such as the nineteenth-century college; it has a far lower likelihood of success in a pluralistic institution such as the late-twentieth-century college. But, in any case, very few instructors would say that their courses aim at providing guidance. Because of the misunderstandings that surround these courses, it is thus urgent that instructors defend these courses for what they can actually accomplish. I readily concede that the public-at-large and even academic administrators are skeptical about the benefits of courses that stimulate reflection but do not result in immediate social benefits. This does not alter the obligation of candor, though. If courses on occupational ethics are to be conducted on an honest basis, instructors must clear up outsiders' misimpressions about their actual aims.

III HOW UNIVERSITIES SHOULD RESPOND TO THE PUBLIC'S INDIGNATION

How, then, *should* universities respond to the public's indignation over police behavior such as assaults and bribetaking? The answer to this is to be found, I think, not in ethics courses but in courses and research devoted to public administration—in reflections on how to design an agency structure in which behavior such as assaults and bribe taking is discouraged and in which it is rapidly detected and punished when it does occur. Academic administrators have, I believe, foolishly touted ethics courses as a response to police misconduct when they should instead be supporting research and training in public administration. Let me elaborate on this proposal by noting first its implications for university education in general and second the division of labor it presupposes for public administration and ethics courses.

If the modern university played the same role in contemporary society that the authoritative institutions of the pre-modern world played in theirs, one could simply say that ethics courses should reinforce social orthodoxy and that public administration courses should identify the type of organizational structure that will sustain this orthodoxy. But the modern university now plays two roles. On the one hand, it has broken with the past by offering a wide array of courses, ethics courses among them, that aim at producing independent-minded individuals. On the other hand, the university continues to support the social order in its technical courses: in engineering courses, for example, and in courses on public administration. These courses are concerned with means rather than ends. Their instructors take certain social ends as a given and ask how these can most efficiently be achieved.

Is it appropriate for the modern university to offer even this degree of support for the social order? I think it is. The division of labor that has developed within the modern university is one that assigns to liberal arts courses an autonomy-enhancement function while assigning to technical courses a social-support function. Admittedly, in performing this latter function, universities can carry out research that people, on reflection, later consider to be inappropriate. But universities are too valuable to limit themselves to the promotion of the long-range benefit associated with an independent-minded citizenry. Provided the boundaries between autonomy-enhancement and social-support are carefully policed, universities can helpfully perform both functions, offering long-range benefits through the first function and benefits in the here-and-now through the latter one.

The division of labor I propose for public administration and criminal justice ethics courses provides a helpful illustration of how a university can simultaneously perform each function. Criminal justice ethics courses stimulate student reflection on the nature of morality. Provided such courses are not based on the guidance model, students' reflections can challenge the current social order, making it possible for them to imagine a different code of conduct for officers or perhaps alternative approaches to justice in the legal system. Public administration courses, by contrast, take current social norms as a given. In doing so, they are likely to focus on settings in which police conduct provokes substantial public alarm. A public administration course devoted to the criminal justice system is thus likely to concentrate on identifying the measures that can reduce incidents such as bribe-taking and assaults on arrestees.

In my opinion, such a course will almost surely have a greater impact on brutality and corruption than will a course in criminal justice ethics. A person's propensity to violate widely accepted norms, such as those prohibiting corruption and excessive force, is unlikely to be affected by an ethics course, even one that is artfully structured to guide students toward socially approved behavior. When bribe taking and corruption loom as serious possibilities, public administration experts are in a much better position to comment on the structure of incentives that will discourage such conduct than are ethics instructors. Thus when academic administrators are asked whether there is a contribution their universities can make to reducing police misconduct, I think they can say that there is. The answer, they can say, is not to be found in ethics courses. These courses (I hope the administrators will note) can make a long-range contribution to society by encouraging students to consider critically the nature of morality. For immediate results, though, the administrators can recommend the courses and research of their public administration instructors.

NOTES

1. See Richard Holmes, *Shelley: The Pursuit* (New York: Dutton, 1974), pp. 54-55.

2. See entry on John Henry Newman in *The Dictionary of National Biography* (Oxford: Oxford University Press, 1882), vol. 14, p. 345.

3. Frederick Rudolph, *Mark Hopkins and the Log* (New Haven: Yale University Press, 1956), p. 48.

4. Ibid., p. vii.

5. See George P. Schmidt, *The Old Time College President* (New York: Columbia University Press, 1930), p. 109. As Schmidt notes, the senior course in moral philosophy "became as common a feature of the average American college as the president's house and the treasury deficit."

6. In *Meno*, Meno asks Socrates, "Can you tell me, Socrates—is virtue something that can be taught?" (*Meno* 70a). Socrates answers, "The fact is that far from knowing whether it can taught, I have no idea what virtue is" (*Meno* 71a, trans. W.K.C. Guthrie).

Response to Heffernan: Moral Neutrality in Criminal Justice Ethics Education

John Kleinig

I

I am sure Professor Heffernan appreciates that just as one swallow does not make a summer, so one incident involving an ex-student does not show very much about either the student's moral capacities or the success of an ethics course in bringing about significant moral progress. Parity of reasoning might lead us to reverse the grades of doctors and lawyers who misuse their skills, or economists and political scientists who offer disastrous advice. What we really want to do in such cases is to ensure that such people do no further damage. As for the success or otherwise of a course that seeks to raise moral awareness or sensitivity, it is to be judged probabilistically—by whether, *overall*, those who complete it are less likely to come to moral grief.[1] That, surely, is true of any college or university course: its success is likely to be called into question if it does *nothing* to raise the quality of decision making in the area it covers.

The thrust of Heffernan's paper, however, is that such pleading is not required, for it is not—or at least should not be—the purpose of a university ethics course to improve the moral quality of a person's conduct. His distinction between *guidance* and *contested issues* models is intended to favor the latter, in which the purpose is stated to be an analysis of contested issues in ethical theory without any prescription of conduct.

I wish to challenge Heffernan's dichotomy of approaches, not because it cannot be made, but because I think it is more complex than he makes it out to be, and because even what he makes it out to be is freighted with presumptions that are only contingently related to it.

Heffernan's "two models" are developed via a contrast between the nineteenth and twentieth centuries—the former possessing a moral homogeneity lacking in the latter. "Ethical guidance" might well appear acceptable in a world that is morally homogeneous, in much the same way as it is still considered appropriate in the experimental sciences and, indeed, to draw on his later argument, in much the same way as institutional prescriptions are still considered appropriate in the field of public administration. But now that moral homogeneity has been lost, and our social and religious universe has become a multicultural one, "ethical guidance" has become morally problematic, and those in colleges and universities are advised to restrict their teaching ends to the analytical ones that are characteristic of the contested issues model. That is, it is the task of teachers to ensure that students are "familiar with a wide range of readings," that they be able "to contrast ideas and to develop distinctions," and that they "analyze clearly the issues that confront them in the course."[2]

Even though the contested issues model is not intended to be prescriptive, neither is its adoption meant to *prevent* people from expressing particular moral outlooks. Indeed, the model is itself the expression of a moral standpoint, and its commitment to the moral autonomy of teachers and learners provides that each participant in the educative process be permitted to express his or her own moral perspective.

The fact that the contested issues model is not itself morally neutral should alert us to the possibility that the contrast between the two models is not quite as exclusive as is initially suggested. Indeed, the contrast here is not dissimilar to that which exists between legal positivists and legal moralists. Positivistic writers, such as H. L. A. Hart, who argued strongly against the so-called "enforcement of morals," nevertheless believed that the legal system still needed to conform to and to reinforce the norms of what he called "critical morality"—those moral presumptions about human beings that undergird the possibility of a law and morality worth having.[3]

My point here is not merely technical. Those of us who hold no brief for the guidance approach, at least in its nineteenth-century version, nevertheless do not see our acceptance of a contested issues approach as neutral philosophical analysis or values clarification. The student who went out and choked someone to death did not do so because the course he had taken remained neutral about such things. Assault, rape, murder, extortion and racial discrimination were not contested issues from which so-called "guidance" had been eliminated, but moral touchstones that allowed for the sensitive analytical exploration of discussions of contested issues such as offender profiling, the reasonable use of force, the nature of sexual harassment, and so on, these latter being issues about which reasonable people may and do disagree. Had my erstwhile student seriously argued that it was OK to vent his anger in a lethal fashion, I am not so sure that I—or, indeed, any teacher who adopted the contested issues model—would have viewed it with the same equanimity as I would have toward someone who argued that police should be provided with hollow-point bullets. Someone who seriously defends assault, rape, murder, and so forth has failed to grasp what the moral enterprise is about. We would be dealing with a moral "flat-earther."

We do not, of course, live in the nineteenth century, and we cannot and should not try to get away with the moralizing that was common in universities and university courses at that time. But I do not think that the inapplicability of *this version* of the guidance model should lead us to adopt a prescriptively neutral contested issues model. Indeed, as I have indicated, and as I think Heffernan partially agrees, the contested issues model is not altogether neutral in its own presumptions and aims. It places considerable moral store on the value of autonomy.

I think that one of the problems with Heffernan's approach is the way in which he uses a discussion of the teaching of ethical theory as his entrée to a discussion of the teaching of criminal justice ethics. Whether one approaches ethical theory from the side of Kant, and seeks to find the transcendental structure of morality without appealing to moral cases, or, as is more usually done, one seeks to extract from the paradigmatic judgments of normative morality some general theoretical structure or pattern of justification, the engagement in ethical theorizing is, essentially, that. It is an intellectual inquiry into the framework of our moral world, something like atomic theory in chemistry. Its foci are interpretation and comprehension rather than practice and action. It is not altogether neutral, but neither is its intention prescriptive. Despite its attractions for some philosophers, it provides a very poor basis for moral decision making. And approaches to practical ethics that seek to derive moral judgments from the outer reaches of moral theory show precious little understanding of what is involved in moral decision making. Moral judgment is a much more complex enterprise.

Practical ethics, unlike theoretical ethics, is generated by the practical concerns of citizens, professionals, and occupants of social roles—their need to make decisions about or in response to concrete cases and practices—and is specifically oriented to providing some kind of guidance, albeit not of the kind that properly bothers Heffernan.

If, as part of a course on police ethics, I discuss the morality of using informants, I do not grade my students on the basis of their agreement with views that I may hold on the matter. This is an issue on which we may expect reasonable people to disagree. Yet there are considerations relevant to the discussion of the issue—for example, the need to balance crime control and due process concerns, the need to avoid exploitation and the exercise of inappropriate discretion, the moral relevance of risk, the value of intimate trust relationships, and so on, that I think it important that my students take into account and which, *if they leave out of account*, may well affect their grade. Although—in cases such as this—the position they finally take (*qua* position[4]) is indeed irrelevant to their grade, the kinds of considerations to which they appeal in getting there, and even the way in which they get there, are not. If a student says that because informants are scum anyway, it is OK to subject them to risk as part of the information-gathering process, or that because they represent a very economical source of police intelligence, they should be exploited as much as possible, then he is going to have some pretty significant marginal comments to deal with, and is unlikely to be seen to have shown any considerable grasp of the *moral* dimensions of the topic.

I have no wish to deny that there is scope for argument about the kinds of things that I am claiming should be taken into account. What I deny is that we are dealing with a blank page of possibilities. What is more, the kind of structured thinking that practical ethical inquiry demands and which, I believe, is necessary to ethical development, is very similar to the kind of structured thinking that is essential to a course in literature or law and that is necessary to the development of literary and legal skills. Of course I do not deny that people may sometimes choose the bad or even subvert the processes of the practices into which they have been initiated. But that is not to deny that it is the purpose of these courses to give people an appreciation for literature or the law; nor is it to imply that if some of those who do well in them still make bad choices, the course is shown to have been a failure.

I appreciate that what I am advocating here involves a certain form of judgment, and that the task of teaching ethics has to be engaged in with a degree toleration and open- (not empty-) mindedness. Heffernan carefully chooses his examples—Percy Bysshe Shelley was expelled from University College, Oxford, because of his advocacy of atheism, and John Henry Newman also quit Oxford when he converted to Roman Catholicism. Today we would want nothing of that. But what about the faculty member who *openly* advocates Nazism or racism or Stalinism or genocide or paedophilia? Is it Heffernan's view that if we take the view *now* that such people are not really fit to teach criminal justice ethics, in a century's time we may come to view their exclusion in the same way and with as little justification as we now view the exclusion of atheists and Catholics?

Of course, Heffernan might argue that those nineteenth-century scholars who were excluded were excluded because the model of teaching that operated was different. Then, guidance was expected. But now guidance is no longer expected, and those people, along with Nazis and racists, can take their place as teachers of the kind envisaged by the contested issues model. But I am not so sure that we or he would be comfortable with that. And we would not be comfortable, I believe, because the contested issues approach does not operate with "morally neutral criteria." It does not say "everything is contested or contestable."[5] Indeed, were it to do so, it would undermine the very claims that Heffernan makes for it. Heffernan's appeal to moral autonomy as a basis for accepting the contested issues approach loses its power if it is itself seen as one of the contested issues.

Lest what I am saying be seen as unacceptably conservative, let me grant that there is *always* provision in philosophical inquiry and, therefore, in ethical inquiry, for further questions to be raised. We may ask, for example, what it is that makes the killing of human beings wrong and whether, when we look at the reasons, they really show what they are intended to show. A form of Cartesian skepticism in ethics is not impossible, and transcendental arguments in ethics, as in epistemology, are few and far between. But this is not where we start from or where we are likely to finish in practical ethics, and I think an approach that focused on such possibilities would be like one that treated an inquiry into the principle of non-contradiction as an essential ingredient in a course in the philosophy of science. Even a more general or basic course in epistemology is not likely to see *that* as falling within its brief.

II

It is time to address the issue of "convenient misunderstanding," as Heffernan generously calls it. First, I want to acknowledge that if agency chiefs and others expect courses in criminal justice ethics to have some simple impact on corruption, brutality, and discrimination in criminal justice, and if those of us who teach or advocate courses in it pretend that they will, then naïveté is being shown on one side and bad faith on the other. It is a bit like seeing education as the solution to unemployment. There *is* a connection, but it is not the simplistic connection promised by political rhetoric.[6]

But if there is not a simple connection, it is not because those who teach criminal justice ethics adopt Heffernan's version of the contested issues model and consider corruption, brutality, and discrimination to be morally neutral categories about which students may reasonably display disagreement. As I noted earlier, I doubt whether any but the most extreme advocates of the contested issues approach would consider that those issues were up for moral grabs. The point is not that judgment on these matters is suspended, but that teachers of criminal justice ethics are not, and do not see themselves in the role of, trainers, indoctrinators, or moral clergy. Their task is the much more subtle—and, I think, eminently worthwhile—one of seeking to explore what it is that makes for moral relevance, why it is that corruption, brutality, and discrimination are unacceptable practices, and whether a range of other practices sometimes found in criminal justice contexts—say, the proffering and acceptance of gratuities, the use of chokeholds, and the resort to racial profiles in offender targeting—implicitly suffer from the same kinds of moral failure that is evident in paradigmatic cases of corruption, brutality, and discrimination.

What I am suggesting is very different from limiting course content to "approved professional norms," as Heffernan might fear.[7] Affirmative and industrial action policies, policies concerning high-speed pursuits and the use of handcuffs or firearms, and common practices such as those concerning "professional courtesies," might all be critically examined and views might be advocated (and certainly permitted) that go contrary to existing policies and practices. That may not be possible in a training academy, but it is surely to be expected in a college or university. And it is perfectly consistent with taking an almost axiomatic stand on the things that most trouble agency chiefs—blatant corruption, brutality, and discrimination—moral defections whose unacceptability presently needs no argument.

There is likely to be a genuine process of moral awareness and sensitization involved in this task, not a merely technical inquiry into moral theory or a parade of a range of possible options, and this evolution is likely to occur even if there is no pressure on students to adopt one view rather than another on such practices. The reason for this is simple: coming to understand the diverse factors that inform one's existing moral understandings, the ways in which those factors interact with each other and bear on other situations, and attempting to assemble such factors in some kind of coherent structure of understanding, have the effect, if I may be pardoned the jargon, of "conscientizing" and "empowering" those who engage in such activity. It is much easier to avoid the pull of gut feeling and peer pressure if one has developed a vocabulary and procedure for thinking about and through moral issues.

This is not to be confused with providing students with a "single framework" in terms of which they can resolve "disputed issues."[8] One does not require that one's students adopt some specific moral theory—consequentialist, deontological, or whatever—or that they accept some simple (or complex) moral algorithm or procedure. What one is doing is helping students to find a way of articulating the moral dimensions of their decision making, of seeing what is morally at stake, and of assisting them to work through the situations that confront them in a way that acknowledges their moral dimensions. There is not then a further issue of motivation (left for others to deal with), because the very inquiry in which one is here engaged concerns *reasons for acting* in one way rather than some other.[9]

There is something else, too. If we accept the popular view that large moral failures in the criminal justice arena have probably been preceded by a moral erosion that has involved some of the contested issues on which criminal justice ethics courses commonly focus, then a serious engagement with these contested issues may prepare criminal justice practitioners to deal more effectively with them, and thus serve to diminish the likelihood that shocking and distressing failures will occur down the road.[10]

III

Of course, even if individual practitioners have been sensitized as a result of their course in criminal justice ethics, that is no guarantee of their subsequent conscientiousness.[11] We all know the power of peer pressure, management practices, organizational arrangements, and other circumstances to overpower or stifle the urgings of conscience, and to that extent I am in full agreement with Heffernan's recognition of the important role that courses in public administration can play. Ethical conduct is not a simple function of inner resolve, but is assisted or made more difficult by situational factors, including institutional culture and organizational structure.

However, Heffernan and I may not see this in quite the same way. As I see it, it is an unfortunate feature of courses in criminal justice ethics that they focus narrowly on what might be called interpersonal ethics—the one-to-one interactions of practitioners and clients—for there are just as many significant ethical questions that bear on the structuring of organizations, the ways in which resources and personnel are deployed and decisions are made, and the ways in which appropriate operating conditions are determined. Heffernan is absolutely right to see that criminal justice practitioners do not operate in a vacuum, and that organizational factors are among those that might well determine whether they engage in the kind of egregious behavior that troubles us all. We can examine the extent to which an organization encourages the development of professionalism, the appropriateness and effectiveness of the mechanisms of accountability that it employs, its openness to recuperative change, and so on.

But all of these things are also appropriate subjects for a course in criminal justice ethics; they are not the exclusive preserve of public administration. Of course, the emphases will be somewhat different in each case. But they may complement each other. Just as any course in public administration should acknowledge the moral dimensions of its concerns, so too a course in criminal justice ethics should take into account the institutional dimensions of its concerns.

If we should include in courses in public administration a discussion of strategies for improving the ethical health of criminal justice organizations, this is not because certain social ends are taken as given in courses in public administration and not in criminal justice ethics, but because the practical concerns of courses in public administration are broader than those of courses in criminal justice ethics.

Is there disingenuousness in the promotion of criminal justice ethics? I think that there may sometimes be, though I do not believe that there needs to be. Such disingenuousness as there is, unfortunately is only the tip of the iceberg of disingenuousness that attaches to most institutions that parade the certification they offer as genuine education. What I think teachers of criminal justice ethics can argue without evasion is that what they are doing is directed to an improvement in the quality of moral decision making in and about criminal justice.

NOTES

1. I leave aside the difficulties of making such assessments.

2. William C. Heffernan, "The Aims of Criminal Justice Ethics Education," in this volume, p. 4.

3. H.L.A. Hart, *Law, Liberty, and Morality* (London: Oxford University Press, 1973), esp. pp. 17-24.

4. It is not irrelevant insofar as it is related to the reasons they adduce for it.

5. What may well be contested and be contestable is the designation of someone as a Nazi or racist. And where that is the case, I would be equally uncomfortable about excluding such a person from the teaching of criminal justice ethics.

6. I cannot say that my experience of "agency chiefs and academic administrators" is as uniform as Heffernan's. I *have* met such people; and I have met those

who, believing that criminal justice ethics courses ought to provide some sort of moral motivational training, have no time for what we offer. But I also have met a good number of such people who realize that colleges are not and should not become training institutions, and yet believe there to be moral benefit in courses that claim much less. However, I do not think that our aims are or should be as limited as Heffernan suggests. To do as little as he suggests either reduces such courses to courses *about* philosophy/ethics rather than courses *in* philosophy/ethics, or overlooks the specific focus of such courses—the concern with *reasons for action*. Maybe Heffernan has assisted the confusion by tending to run together courses in ethical theory with courses in professional and practical ethics. Not even I have many hopes for a course in ethical theory. It is far too remote from the action.

7. Heffernan, "The Aims of Criminal Justice Ethics Education," p. 10.

8. Ibid.

9. I think Heffernan is all too skeptical of the Harvard Business School initiative. There is no "convenient misunderstanding" or "misinformation" involved here. A glance at what the ethics teachers in the Harvard Business School are manifestly trying to do makes it clear that their public aim is to improve the ethical character of business. See Thomas R. Piper, Mary C. Gentile, & Sharon Daloz Parks, *Can Ethics Be Taught? Perspectives, Challenges, and Approaches at Harvard Business School* (Boston, MA: Harvard Business School, 1993).

10. It can be thought of as a "broken windows" approach to practical ethics: if we secure the margins, we help to secure the larger territory.

11. Nor do I want to deny that what is done in criminal justice ethics courses is powerless to motivate good conduct. Understanding what it is about certain practices that makes them problematic can provide a bastion against moral compromise that an unexamined practice will lack.

Rejoinders

I. William C. Heffernan

On rereading Professor Kleinig's thoughtful response to my paper,[1] I have concluded that it would not be wise to take the normal route traveled by conference participants—that is, I have decided I should not revise my original remarks to take into account what Professor Kleinig said and so make it seem as I if anticipated his response to me. The fact is I did not anticipate all that he said. Moreover, any attempt to revise my original remarks to take his comments into account would not only give the false impression that I possess extraordinary foresight, it would also distort the structure of my first paper. I thus think it best to let our exchange stand in its original form and to initiate a new one that builds on it.

At first glance, it might seem obvious that an instructor in an ethics course, unlike an instructor in, say, a history or chemistry course, should offer guidance to her students. Ethics is concerned with how individuals should conduct themselves. An ethics instructor, it could thus be argued, should take three steps when teaching her course: first, she should inform students about the proper standards for life; second, she should predispose her students to adopt these standards; and third, she should base grades in part on whether they have actually adopted the standards she is advocating. Ethics courses, it could be argued, are in this sense unique: they impart information only to further the larger aim of providing guidance for life.

To defend this guidance model of ethics instruction, however, one must show that a teacher has authoritative moral insights to impart. There are obvious senses in which teachers can defend their insights as authoritative. For example, a teacher in a professional ethics class can state that the points she is making are based on the pronouncements of a relevant professional body. Grades, the instructor can state, will be based on a student's ability to state authoritative professional norms correctly. Alternatively, an ethics instructor can summarize the norms of the community in which her students live. The aim of the course, the instructor can say, is to socialize students, to acculturate them to norms they do not fully grasp. Given this aim, the instructor could claim, grades should be based on students' knowledge of their community's norms.

But university-based ethics courses—or at least university-based ethics courses that claim to be philosophically oriented—cannot claim to be authoritative in either of these senses. A police academy instructor can point to a positive basis for pronouncements she claims to be authoritative. The police instructor can thus say: "This rule is authoritative because people with authority are prepared to sanction you for disobeying it." A university-based ethics instructor clearly does not want to appeal to authoritativeness in this sense. Such an instructor must reason critically about morality—and so must be prepared to reject even those rules that are authoritative because they are backed by positive law. For the university-based ethics instructor, the authoritativeness of the principles she propounds must hinge on the claim that these principles can withstand the challenges posed by critical reason.

It is because critical reason has been so successful over the last 2500 years in demolishing claims to authoritative moral insight that contemporary university-based ethics courses have (perhaps to the surprise of laypersons) avoided the guidance model and instead adhered to the contested-issues alternative. Occupational ethics courses are perhaps an exception to this trend. In my original essay, I argued that occupational ethics courses are at most an ambiguous exception to the contested-issues model. Instructors in occupational ethics courses, I argued, tend to disavow a guidance aim. I continue to believe that I am right on this point, although I admit that I have no survey data to demonstrate that it is true. But whether I am right or wrong on this empirical point, it is surely a peripheral issue in my exchange with Professor Kleinig. The main issue is whether occupational ethics courses *ought to* follow the guidance model. To say that instructors in these courses should follow the guidance model is to assert that they have insights to impart that can be defended against the challenges of critical reason. Thus, in defending the guidance model for university-based ethics courses, one asserts that instructors in these courses are not dressing up conventional mores in the garb of critical reason. Rather, one is claiming that because instructors possess authoritative moral insights, they can sanction students for disagreeing with what they have to say.

If I understand him correctly, Kleinig offers a three-stage justification for his version of the guidance model. First, he distinguishes between theoretical and practical ethics: the latter, but not the former, Kleinig claims, provides the basis for a course in occupational ethics since its roots are to be found in "the practical concerns of citizens, professionals, and occupants of social roles. . . ."[2] Second, the aim of a practical ethics course, Kleinig claims, is to take students through "a process of moral awareness and sensitization" as they consider issues in their subject.[3] And third, while Kleinig believes that instructors should not give students low grades merely because of the conclusions they reach, he does believe that instructors can properly fault students (and use the coercive mechanism of grading in doing so) for failing to take account of the proper moral considerations when reaching their conclusions.[4]

This stands as a carefully qualified version of the guidance model. Kleinig does not lay claim to *comprehensive* authoritative moral insight; for example, he explicitly rejects the claim that instructors can use the mechanism of a low grade to penalize students for the conclusions they reach.[5] However, Kleinig does claim to possess a number of *fragmentary* authoritative moral insights—thus his statement that instructors can lower grades when students fail to take certain considerations into account in reaching their conclusions.

What is the basis for Professor Kleinig's claim to possess this insight? The question is central to his enterprise. Clearly, he does not want criminal justice ethics courses to be based on the positive norms of an occupation ("No, Mr. Student, you've misunderstand the meaning of Rule 17 of Police Chiefs' Code of Ethics"); nor does he want them to be based on the positive morality of society-at-large ("No, Ms. Student, you simply don't understand the way things are done around here"). Rather, he is making a far more ambitious claim, one that invokes morality *tout court* and so, of course, the pretensions of critical reason. It is in this vein that Professor Kleinig dismisses as "moral 'flat-earther[s]'" those who disagree with him on moral propositions he considers self-evident.[6] Similarly, it is in this vein that he invokes on three separate occasions[7] the word "sensitive" or one of its cognates in suggesting that the aim of an occupational ethics course is to make students "sensitive to" a moral reality he already apprehends. Indeed, Professor Kleinig at one point directly analogizes between the study of what he calls "the moral world" and the study of atomic particles.[8] The reasonable inference to draw from this analogy is that he possesses authoritative moral insight (an insight grounded in a moral sense, perhaps) into at least some features of this moral world and that he is thus entitled to evaluate students' work on the basis of their conformity to his insight.

It is possible, of course, that I have misunderstood the exact nature of Kleinig's claim to possess authoritative moral insight. Even if I have, though, my attempt at reconstruction was hardly in vain, for whether I am right or wrong in my summary of the rationale Kleinig provides for his approach, I have at least succeeded in identifying the central weakness in his version of the guidance model—his casual unconcern for foundational questions about moral validity. On the one hand, Kleinig downplays the need for occuaptional ethics courses to examine foundational questions. On the other hand, though, once one asks what justification he can provide for using the coercive mechanism of grades to deal with students who disagree with him, one finds that he has advanced claims based on a controversial ethical *theory* about why he is right and others are wrong. I suspect Kleinig's unconcern for foundational questions is typical of many courses in occupational ethics. What is distinctive about his approach, however, is his simultaneous lack of concern for foundational issues *and* his insistence that students should suffer penalties for failing to incorporate considerations he considers morally binding on them.

Is it possible to develop a version of the guidance model that addresses foundational issues in ethics? I think it is, but I also think that the more specific an instructor is about ethical theory, the more idiosyncratic the instructor's guidance will become. Think, for example, about Kleinig's approach. In offering a more detailed account of his conception of ethical theory, Kleinig could explain why Cartesian skepticism is unwarranted in ethics and how it is possible to sense the features of a "round" moral world. Building on these foundational points, Kleinig could argue that the moral world is not simply round but that there are "moral continents" of a certain size, "moral plateaus" within those continents, and so on. But, of course, the more specific he is, the greater the likelihood that his readers will reject his claim to authoritative moral insight. On the other hand, if he does not adopt this option—if he offers nothing more than the assertion that moral world is round—then his readers must ask what limits the roundness analogy places on him and on instructors who adopt his position in determining when a student can be sanctioned for moral error. In particular, why should one not conclude, assuming that Professor Kleinig adheres to his theory-lite approach to foundational questions, that the contentless term "moral 'flat-earther'" can be used as an epithet to lower the grades of students who have the temerity to depart from their teachers' pronouncements on morality?

In posing this last question, I am not asking about the philosophical defensibility of Kleinig's approach. As I have already indicated, I believe that his reliance on an analogy between moral and physical perception casts doubt on the theoretical foundations he proposes for his guidance model. The point I am pursuing here has to do with the application of his model—with the license it provides instructors to dress up conventional morality in the robes of critical morality. My concern does not have to do with how *Kleinig* would apply the label "moral 'flat-earther.'" Rather, I am asking how an instructor who reasonably claims to be following Kleinig's approach (but who perhaps differs with him as to what merits the label "moral 'flat-earther'") would apply that label in assessing a student's work. Kleinig, it should be noted, is prepared to allow debate (that is, he is prepared not to apply the sanction of lower grades) to students who take positions about which "reasonable people . . . disagree."[9] What we must ask, then, is how an instructor conscientiously interpreting Professor Kleinig's framework would determine whether a student has taken a "moral 'flat-earth'" position or a position about which reasonable people disagree.

An example will help to illustrate how serious this problem is. Imagine that two (admittedly precocious) students enroll in a police ethics course. One says he wants to consider the possibility of a Nietzschean approach to policing. He disagrees with his instructor's theory about the foundation of ethics, saying that ethics is instead to be understood in terms of a struggle that has been waged throughout history between priestly and aristocratic modes of valuation. Because the student reasons in terms of the latter type of valuation, he condemns informers as "scum." The student states that because he is a superior human being, he can treat inferiors as he wishes once he becomes a police officer.

The other student says she reasons in terms of a Marxist framework. Like the Nietzschean, she denies the possibility of transhistorical moral principles. The Marxist, however, says she is unsure how a police officer following her approach should enforce the law. Perhaps an officer should not enforce anti-theft provisions at all, she says, when proletarians steal from the propertied élite. Or perhaps an officer should enforce the law as strictly as possible so as to contribute, however modestly, to what she believes to be the crisis of late-industrial capitalism.

Are these students advocating "moral 'flat-earth'" positions or are they instead advancing arguments with which reasonable people can disagree? As I have noted, we cannot answer this question by asking how Professor Kleinig would assess them. Rather, we must ask how a teacher claiming to adhere to his framework would evaluate them. And here, of course, we discover the emptiness of his categories—and thus the opportunity they provide instructors to enforce positive morality in the name of critical morality. Nietzsche's and Marx's thought pose particularly severe challenges to the moral foundations of liberal democratic societies. While I disagree with the conclusions of both writers, I take each very seriously. Indeed, I view them as posing some of the most fundamental challenges I have encountered to the principles by which I reason and live. Professor Kleinig may agree with me about the seriousness of the challenges they pose. But that surely is not the point in this context. Rather, the point must be that his version of the guidance model is sufficiently contentless that it authorizes his adherents to lower the grades of each student I have mentioned on the ground that these students are "moral 'flat-earthers.'"

The alternative approach I endorsed in my paper—a contested-issues model of instruction for *all* university-based ethics courses—avoids these difficulties, though it admittedly encounters others of its own. The central value I advocated was that of intellectual autonomy; students, I argued, should be encouraged to think for themselves about the foundations of ethics, the content of general moral principles, and the relationship between those general principles and the specific issues they can expect to encounter while working in criminal justice. Given Kleinig's essay, a subsidiary value merits attention as well. My model emphasizes the connection between theoretical and practical ethics. It takes as one of its points of departure the fact of contest over specific ethical claims and so encourages students, as they try to develop a coherent approach to ethics, to seek "reflective equilibrium" between specific precepts and foundational claims about the validity of ethical propositions. My model would, of course, prohibit instructors from sanctioning students for advocating Nietzschean and Marxist approaches to criminal justice. At the same time, it would not offer such students a free ride: they would have to consider instructor and peer challenges to their thinking.

But what if a student's version of Nietzsche had Nazi overtones, and what if a student's Marxism was tinged with Stalinism? I readily concede that my model prohibits instructors and colleges from sanctioning students for adopting these positions. Kleinig places substantial emphasis on my model's accommodation of such students,[10] but I fail to see why the model should be rejected on this ground. I am simply advocating that one social institution—the university—adhere to a constested-issues approach to ethics instruction. I am not arguing that ethics instruction in a police academy should follow my model. Nor am I suggesting that police departments themselves be stripped of the power to sanction officers for acting on moral principles inimical to the departments' aims. I am simply arguing for open-ended discussion of ethics and its foundations in universities, the social institutions best suited for such discussion.

By contrast with my approach, Kleinig offers just the framework—a dose of derisive comment about moral misperception, a soupçon of "reasonableness"—that colleges and universities can use in presenting conventional morality as if it were defensible from the standpoint of critical morality. The genius of Mark Hopkins's senior course at Williams was that it did not have to be taught under the label "Prescriptive Ethnography of New England Folkways, Supplemented with Idiosyncratic Maxims Provided by the Instructor." Hopkins could claim to reason in terms of authoritative moral knowledge while in fact affirming in broad outline the mores of his tribe and supplementing those mores with prescriptive comments of his own. A similar danger exists for contemporary courses in occupational ethics. I fail to see how Kleinig's version of the guidance model avoids this danger.

II. John Kleinig

(1) The point of my original response to Professor Heffernan was to claim that the relation between the guidance and contested issues models was more complex than he made it out to be. One can recognize the contestability of ethical issues without believing that anything goes; and one can believe in the action-guidedness of ethical inquiry without insisting on the reasonableness of only one particular course of action. My argument (*pace* Heffernan[11]) was not intended to support the guidance model but rather to suggest that the two models were artificial constructs—they do not represent exclusive and counterposed strategies but lie on something of an overlapping continuum. Insofar as I supported any model, it was the contested issues one, but it was tempered by a recognition that there is more to successful reflection on moral issues than a demonstrated familiarity with the relevant philosophical literature, an ability to analyze the moral issues, and competence in making appropriate distinctions. Or, perhaps to put it a little differently, judging something to be part of the relevant philosophical literature, acquiring the ability to analyze moral issues, and gaining competence in making appropriate distinctions are not morally neutral activities. The student who thinks it obvious that blacks and women are naturally inferior, that because sex is pleasurable it is all right to have it with little children or to impose it on unwilling women

(killjoys), or that might is what makes right, is what I called a moral flat-earther.

Heffernan is worried by this presumption on my part—or, if not presumption on *my* part, on the part of others who, presuming the same ability to pick moral flat-earthers, will downgrade Fred Nietzsche and Carla Marx. Unless one accepts a viewpoint-neutral approach or can provide criteria for picking out moral flat-earthers (something that I fail to do), the position I espouse is vulnerable to authoritarian abuses.

I think Heffernan is right to be concerned. Even though my own concern is not with Fred and Carla—disappointingly rare—but with those who espouse the prejudices of talk radio, I did not guard against those teachers who think that Fred and Carla are sure candidates for the flat-earth category, or—maybe even more worrying—those Nietzscheans and Marxists who would downgrade the rest of us. Unfortunately, I know of no foolproof way of ruling out what Heffernan fears. But at the same time, I would claim with equal conviction that I know of no neutral, universal, or uncontested test for determining whether a person shows adequate familiarity with an appropriately wide range of readings, is able to contrast ideas and develop distinctions, and can provide clear analyses of the issues discussed in an ethics course. What we count as having ethical relevance does not escape the influence of our values. The diversity we currently experience does not stop once we shift our focus from guidance to subject mastery, and it is just not possible to separate procedural and substantive issues in the viewpoint-neutral way that I think Heffernan demands.

(2) Heffernan interprets my practical orientation in criminal justice ethics teaching as a "casual unconcern for foundational questions about moral validity." The apparent lack of concern is more pragmatic than doctrinal, and in any case would be overridden were classroom discussion to dictate a move in that direction. I focus my attention where I do because I believe that if we start with foundational questions we will not get around to *police* ethics. Moreover, those who erect their discussion of police ethics on a foundation of general ethical theory generally lapse into algorithmic derivations that distort the structure of moral reasoning.

Nevertheless, behind Heffernan's critique I believe that there lurks a very important and contested issue, and on this he and I may disagree. Does foundational reflection in ethics precede normative commitments on practical questions or does it, rather, constitute some kind of distillation from our everyday practical reflection? Kant, for example, thought the latter: ". . . we cannot do morality a worse service than by seeking to derive it from examples. Every example of it presented to me must first itself be judged by moral principles in order to decide if it is fit to serve as an original example—that is, as a model: it can in no way supply the prime source for the concept of morality."[12] But many others have thought the former. As W. D. Ross expressed it: ". . . What we are apt to describe as 'what we think' about moral questions . . . forms the standard reference to which the truth of any moral theory has to be tested, instead of having itself to be tested by reference to any theory."[13] I happen to be more sympathetic to the latter approach, and this may be interpreted as a lack of concern for foundational questions. It is, however, not so much a "casual unconcern" as a different way of conceiving them.

In the end, Heffernan and I may not be too far apart. Although he is troubled by my judgment that moral flat-earthers have to be graded down, that judgment is intended to do little more than secure the conception of persons that gives moral substance to Heffernan's own position—the individual as an autonomous being.

NOTES

1. John Kleinig, "Response: Moral Neutrality in Criminal Justice Ethics Education,"in this volume, pp. 15-23.
2. Ibid., p. 17.
3. Ibid., p. 18.
4. Ibid., p. 20.
5. Ibid., pp. 17-18.
6. Ibid., p. 16.
7. Ibid., pp. 16, 20, 21.
8. Ibid., p. 17.
9. Ibid., p. 18.
10. Ibid.
11. William C. Heffernan, "Rejoinder," in this volume, p. 27.
12. Immanuel Kant, *The Groundwork of the Metaphysics of Morals,* in H.J. Paton, *The Moral Law* (New York: Barnes & Noble, 1963), p. 76.
13. W.D. Ross, *The Right and the Good* (Oxford: Clarendon, 1930), p. 40.

Chapter 2

I. Teaching Police Ethics: What to Aim at?

Michael Davis

This paper does more than its title promises. It also considers what ethics is, how it can be taught, and by whom. The paper will trespass on topics assigned others. I apologize, but do not repent. Different understandings of ethics yield somewhat different methods; different methods, somewhat different aims. I cannot do justice to my topic, the aims of teaching police ethics, without saying something about these others.

My explicit focus will be not *criminal justice* but *police* ethics. "Criminal justice ethics" has both a wide and narrow sense. In the wide sense, it names a kind of "institutional ethics," that is, a field defined by the moral questions arising within a system of criminal justice (just as business ethics is defined by moral questions arising in business). That is the sense in which the journal *Criminal Justice Ethics* uses it.[1] In the narrow sense, however, "criminal justice ethics" is almost a synonym for police ethics. So, for example, a text like Close and Meier's *Morality in Criminal Justice* has almost nothing to say about criminal justice's many auxiliaries—chemists in forensics, auditors in the district attorney's office, professors of criminology, jail social workers, judges, prison physicians, private security agencies, manufacturers of riot control gear, and so on. *Morality in Criminal Justice* is, in fact, a text in police ethics.[2] So, my focus on "police ethics" rather than "criminal justice ethics" may be more terminological than substantive.

Because I propose to focus on police ethics, I should admit—before it becomes obvious—that I have no experience teaching that subject. Whatever contribution I make to the subject must be an import from foreign climes, the contribution of an intelligent *outsider*.

But what makes this outsider *intelligent*? Here are my chief credentials: I have written a little on police ethics,[3] taught police as part of ethics workshops for government officials, and otherwise brushed the periphery of teaching police ethics. I have taught other practical ethics for more than two decades: legal ethics, business ethics, engineering ethics, medical ethics, and social policy (not only philosophy courses like *Moral and Social Values*, *Political Philosophy*, and *Philosophy of Law*, but also *Foundations of Criminal Justice*). Most important, perhaps, from 1991 through 1995, I held a major grant from the National Science Foundation to help faculty in fields as different as engineering and literature, accounting and sociology, philosophy and veterinary science, integrate ethics into their "technical" courses. Not only have I had to think hard about the problems of integrating ethics into technical courses, I have helped others (about fifty faculty from my own institution and twenty from others) put my conclusions into effect, had them assess the results, and had to compare those results with my hopes.[4] This paper applies that experience to teaching police ethics.

The paper has five parts. The first clarifies key terms, including "ethics." The second explains what teaching ethics (in that sense) *can* achieve. The third identifies ways in which ethics can be taught, recommending the pervasive method. The fourth draws some conclusions concerning what means should be chosen and what aims are reasonable given those means. The fifth argues for an optional philosophy course in police ethics as support for the pervasive method.

I "ETHICS" (AND OTHER TROUBLESOME TERMS)

I begin with an esoteric but important distinction, that between morality and ethics. "Morality," as I shall use the term, refers to those standards of conduct everyone (every rational person) wants every other to follow even if everyone else's following them would mean having to follow them too. Morality (in this sense) is the same for everyone.

Because morality consists of *standards* of conduct, not conduct as such, the fact that a standard is not always observed does not prove that it is not part of morality. Were moral standards always observed, we would have no use for moral terms. "Should" implies "sometimes does not." Yet, if "should" implies "sometimes does not," it also implies "generally does." A moral standard not generally observed is an ideal standard, not an actual one. What we owe an ideal standard is an inclination to change the world so that observing it will become common. But, until the world has changed, we are not bound to observe it. Moral obligation presupposes general compliance with the standard in question, a practice, even if it also presupposes less than universal compliance.

We were all quite young when we learned such basic moral rules as: do not kill; do not lie; keep your promises; do not cheat; and so on. We were still quite young when we learned that these rules have exceptions (for example, "except in self-defense" for "Do not kill"). Now and then, we may change our interpretation of a particular rule or exception—for example, we may come to think that speaking the truth, intending it to be misunderstood, is (or is not) a form of lying. But, since we entered our teens, such changes have been few and relatively minor. Our students are much like us. They arrive in class more or less morally mature. We have little to teach them about ordinary morality.[5] Not so ethics.

People generally use "ethics" in one of two senses, that is, either as a synonym for morality or as the name of a specifically philosophical discipline (the attempt to understand morality as a rational enterprise). The term "police ethics" might then properly be used to name a part of morality, morality in policing, or instead a field concerned to understand that part of morality (by, for example, applying philosophical theories of morality to questions arising in police work).[6]

I shall use "ethics" in a third sense. "Ethics" (in this sense) refers to those special, morally permissible standards of conduct every member of a group wants every other member of that group to follow even if that would mean having to do the same. Ethics applies to members of a group simply because they are members of that group. Research ethics applies to researchers (and no one else); Hopi ethics, to Hopis (and no one else); and police ethics, to police (and no one else). While it is a conceptual truth that rational (human) agents are subject to morality, their subjection to ethics (in this third sense) is a contingent truth. To say that ethical standards are special is to say that they do not apply to everyone. One can be a decent person without ethics (in this third sense of "ethics").

To say that ethics (for example, police ethics) applies only to members of the relevant group (police) is not to say that the standards in question may not resemble those of another group (or even be identical word for word). It is, rather, to identify the origin of the standard, the domain over which it has jurisdiction, and those who have authority to revise, interpret, or repeal it. Even when the ethics of two groups are identical, they need not have been and in time may not be. Something similar is true of the relation of ethics to (ordinary) morality. Police ethics might include standards of ordinary morality, for example, honesty. Police ethics may differ only in demanding a higher standard of honesty than ordinary morality does. To say that police ethics applies only to police is not to deny any similarity between police ethics and (ordinary) morality but to deny that ordinary people are bound by whatever additional obligations police take on.

"Ethics" (in this third sense) is not the plural of "ethic." An ethic, a way of living, may or may not be moral. Ethics (in the third sense) is always moral in at least two senses. First, it is moral because, by definition, ethics is "morally permissible," moral in the weak sense of "not immoral." But ethics is also always moral in a stronger sense, "immoral not to." The ethics of a group is always morally binding on its members (even though not morally binding on ordinary moral agents). The members of the group cannot act unethically without doing something morally wrong.

Ethics-as-special-standard suggests a question neither ethics-as-morality nor ethics-as-study does. How is it possible for a standard to be at once special (that is, not part of ordinary morality) and yet morally binding? The answer is quite simple (though its defense is not): Rational agents do not (except by mistake) set standards for themselves or others without some benefit in view, a benefit they believe they cannot otherwise achieve (or achieve as well). If we call a practice "cooperative" when the benefits that justify each in doing as the practice requires depends (in part at least) on others in the practice doing the same, then violating a rule of a cooperative practice is cheating (that is, taking unfair advantage). All else being equal, cheating is morally wrong; hence, following the rules of such a practice is, all else being equal, morally required.[7] Ethics (in the third sense) defines a cooperative practice. An ethical standard therefore has much the same moral status as a (valid) promise. Though not morally binding on everyone, it is morally binding on those who bind themselves (whether by promising or by participating in a morally permissible cooperative practice).

Ethics resembles law in being a special standard, that is, a standard applying to those it applies to for reasons beyond mere rational agency. Like law, ethics is relative. Ethics differs from law in its closer connection with (ordinary) morality. Law *can* be immoral—or, at least, whether law can be is a question that enduring approaches to law answer differently. Ethics, in contrast, can no more be immoral than counterfeit money can be money. "Thieves' ethics," "Nazi ethics," "torturers' ethics," and the like should always wear scare quotes. Because ethics is closer to morality than law, it can depend on morality ("conscience") for enforcement more than law can.

This third sense of ethics seems to dominate discussions of ethics among members of professions. That is not surprising. A profession is a number of individuals organized so that they can earn a living by serving a certain moral ideal in ways beyond what law, market, and (ordinary) morality require. A group cannot be a profession without setting itself special (morally permissible) standards, that is, without developing its own ethics (in the third sense).

Yet, while ethics is necessary for a group to be a profession, it is not sufficient. Many groups with ethical standards are not professions. For purely conceptual reasons, they belong to another class of entity. Charities, fraternal orders such as the Masons or Elks, and other philanthropic groups cannot be professions because they are not organized to help *their* members earn a living. Labor unions, trade associations, and other organizations of self-interest are, though organized to help members earn a living, not organized to help them earn that living by serving a moral ideal. A business with a code of ethics, though organized in part to serve a moral ideal, is not organized to help *members* earn a living. Those who earn their living from the business, the employees, are not members but agents; those who are more like members, the owners or principals, earn a profit, not a living, from the business (and, indeed, as owners, may be wholly inactive).[8]

To talk of "ethics" in my third sense suggests a question: "How can one benefit from requiring other members of one's occupational group to offer services beyond what law, market, and morality require?" (Or, in other words, "Why would any group want a code of ethics?") The question is neither "Why have morality?" nor "Why be ethical?" Morality is assumed (along with law and market). One decisive reason to be ethical is also assumed: to be unethical is to be immoral. The question is: "Why not make do with morality (along with law and market)?"

The *short* answer to that question, sufficient for our purposes, is that practicing as a member of a profession, rather than as a mere individual, *can* have (morally permissible) advantages more than sufficient to repay the constraints such coordinated practice imposes. Consider, for example, what one's status as a police officer would be if other police officers generally did a better job than what morality, law, and market demand. Would one's status not be better than if they did no more than what morality, law, and market demand? The only hard question is whether such an improvement in status will be enough to repay the constraints necessary to achieve it. The answer to *that* question will depend on many factors, not least of which is what law, market, and morality already demand.[9] Not every occupation should organize as a profession.

Generally, the special standards that constitute a profession's ethics are formulated in a code of ethics, in formal interpretations of that code, and in the less formal practices by which older members pass on the special ways they do things to new members. So, except for those students following a parent into a profession, no one is likely to learn much about a profession's ethics except at a professional school or while practicing the profession. Professional ethics is as much a part of what members of a profession know—and others do not—as their "technical" knowledge. Professional ethics is part of thinking like a member of the profession in question. Teaching professional ethics is part of teaching future members how to practice their profession.

Because this point is easily overlooked, let me restate it in a more provocative way: Professional ethics (in the third sense of "ethics") belongs neither to common sense nor to philosophy but to the profession in question. Knowing police ethics is as much a part of knowing how to do police work, if policing is a profession, as knowing how to subdue a violent drunk or fill out an arrest report. Indeed, insofar as policing is a profession, knowing how to subdue a drunk or fill out a report is in part knowing what the profession allows, forbids, or requires.

Focusing on police ethics, as I propose to do, rather than on criminal justice ethics (in the wide sense), has an advantage now easily appreciated. Because criminal justice ethics (in the wide sense) is necessarily institutional ethics, talking about criminal justice ethics tends to obscure professional ethics. The great number of professions within the criminal justice system discourages explicit discussion of the ethics of any of them. In this respect, criminal justice ethics (in the wide sense) resembles other institutional ethics, for example, business ethics.[10] Because police ethics is potentially professional ethics, a focus on police ethics invites us to consider teaching that subject as professional ethics, that is, not simply as a set of moral problems arising in a certain institution but as a set of moral problems governed (in part) by special standards. Can police ethics in fact be taught as professional ethics? It can be if (a) *special* standards of conduct binding on police as such exist and (b) most police see those standards as ones they want other police to follow so much that they would be willing to do the same if that were necessary to get the others to pitch in. Whether any police code of ethics satisfies both these conditions is, I think, a question any course in police ethics should address.[11]

From now on, I shall use the term "professional ethics" rather than "professional *and* institutional ethics."[12] I shall do this as much for brevity as out of habit. I should nevertheless be understood to include institutional ethics in what I say about teaching—except where context makes clear that I cannot.

II WHAT CAN TEACHING ETHICS ACHIEVE?

Teaching ethics (in my third sense of "ethics") can achieve at least four desirable outcomes: (a) increased ethical sensitivity; (b) increased knowledge of relevant standards of conduct; (c) improved ethical judgment; and (d) improved ethical will-power (that is, a greater ability to act ethically when one wants to).[13] How can teaching ethics achieve all this—indeed, any of this?

Teaching ethics can increase student sensitivity simply by making students aware that they, as members of a certain profession (or otherwise engaged in a certain occupation), will have to resolve certain moral problems. Generally, pointing out a moral problem will mean pointing out the consequences of a seemingly inconsequential act ("a mere technical decision"). Just being exposed to a few examples of a particular problem will make it more likely than otherwise that the students will see a problem of that sort when it arises on the job. So, for example, a student who has seen how using empirically validated criteria for suspicion instead of "common sense" can increase the number of good arrests, reduce the effect of prejudice, and even improve relations with the group that the prejudice injures, is more likely than otherwise to see a moral issue when her first partner justifies a doubtful stop and search as "just common sense" or "street smarts." Why teaching ethics might have this effect is not hard to understand. The mechanism is precisely the same as for teaching students to see technical problems. Knowledge and practice sharpen perception, making it easier both to see a particular decision in context and to imagine what the context might contribute.

How can teaching ethics increase student knowledge of relevant standards? Again, the answer is much the same as for technical standards. For example, a student who has read the "Law Enforcement Code of Ethics" of the International Association of Chiefs of Police is more likely to know what is in it than a student who has not. A student who has had to answer questions about the code is more likely to recall the relevant provisions than one who has not. And so on.

Knowledge of standards includes more than just knowing what the code says. Part of knowing a standard is understanding its rationale (especially the consequences of departing from it). Since all standards require interpretation, another part of knowing a standard is knowing how to interpret it, taking into account not only its rationale but moral, political, and even practical constraints, including the interpretation others are likely to give it. So, for example, part of teaching students to "enforce the laws courteously and appropriately" is to consider what would happen if police enforced all laws all the time, enforced them in a random way, or enforced them in ways contrary to reasonable community expectations. There is no sharp line between raising sensitivity and teaching standards.

How can teaching police ethics improve ethical judgment? Ethical judgment (like other judgment) tends to improve with use (as well, of course, as with relevant knowledge and sensitivity). If an instructor gives a student a chance to make ethical judgments, explain them, and compare them with those other students make, the student is more likely to judge well than if she gets no such experience. The classroom provides a safe place to make mistakes and learn from them—ethical mistakes as well as purely technical ones.

Some of those who argue for teaching ethics through such discussions have argued for the explicit use of moral theory.[14] Their arguments seem to me to rely on a confusion between ethics-as-study and ethics-as-special-standard. My experience is that an instructor can easily lead probing, systematic, and enlightening discussions of ethical questions without mention of any moral theory (and, indeed, without knowing any moral theory). What an instructor needs is not a tool box with one or more theories but a method for guiding discussion, focusing on reasons, and forcing judgments. That is something much less exalted than a moral theory (though such a method can use ideas various theories develop). (For an example of such a method, see the Appendix to this essay.)

But how can teaching police ethics increase a student's ethical will-power? Consider: Is not a police officer who knows that he shares with other officers a commitment to a particular standard of conduct more likely to follow it than one who believes himself alone in that commitment? One benefit of discussing ethics in the classroom is that discussion shows students how much consensus there is—among members of the class and, by extension, their profession—on most of the profession's standards of conduct. There is power in numbers. That is one source of will-power. Another is a sense of a standard's reasonableness. A student who believes he understands what makes a standard reasonable is more likely to try to explain its reasonableness to others—and so, more likely to win their support and to act according to it.

Having stated these aims, I should add two warnings. First, I do not mean to suggest that a college, university, police academy, or any other institution should try to send out graduates who are *perfect* in ethical sensitivity, knowledge, judgment, or will-power. Perfection is not possible. The most we can reasonably aim at, or even hope for, is substantial improvement—improvement relative both to what the graduates were before they entered the institution and to what they would have been had they entered the institution and learned nothing about ethics.

So, second, I think we should take care not to claim too much for what teaching ethics achieves. No matter how much ethics instruction the police have, there will be some police scandals. Teaching ethics seldom turns the evil from their course; it cannot protect the thoughtless from doing what they know they should not or ensure that the well-meaning will not give in to overwhelming pressure. Teaching ethics can, at best, assure that the well-meaning will be substantially less likely than otherwise to do what they should not. And even that is hard to prove.

Improvements in ethical sensitivity, knowledge, and judgment are easy to measure in just the ways we measure improvement in technical sensitivity, knowledge, and judgment. We can give students a case and ask them to identify the ethical issues. The more they identify, the more sensitive they are. We can ask students about codes of ethics, procedures for gaining support for one's position, and so on. The more such questions students can answer, the better their ethical knowledge. We can also ask students what they should do in a particular situation and why. The more ethical issues their choice takes account of, the more ethical knowledge they bring to bear on the choice, the better the ethical judgment they demonstrate.

But we cannot measure improvements in ethical will-power in this way. The test of will-power is action in the appropriate circumstances, a kind of test educational institutions find hard to arrange. Long-term comparative studies of graduates who have had ethics courses and those who have not should yield some measure, provided the effects of will-power can be disentangled from other effects, including those of sensitivity, knowledge, and judgment. For now, we can explain why teaching ethics should improve ethical will-power, but we cannot prove that it does, much less make any estimate of how much it does.

So much for what teaching ethics *can* achieve. We must now consider what we might reasonably aim at given the realities of budget, personnel, and other options.

III FITTING ETHICS IN

There are at least eight ways to teach ethics in an academic environment (in addition to such informal ways as setting a good example).[15] These eight ways are more or less consistent with each other, indeed mutually supportive where necessity does not force a choice.

Two ways are outside the curriculum. One is independent study, for example, giving students the appropriate code of ethics and telling them to read it. The other extra-curricular way is by special event, for example, a public speech on police ethics or a movie like *Serpico* or *The Untouchables* with a discussion afterward of the ethical issues it raises.[16] While these first two ways are not likely to accomplish much alone, or even together, they are better than nothing and can help to set a tone.

One of the eight ways of teaching students police ethics is supra-curricular (operating inside the curriculum as well as outside): hold students to a police code while they are still students. I am not talking about an "honor code." Honor codes are codes of student ethics, not of professional ethics. A student will learn more about police codes living by one than living by an honor code. Of course, "living by a code" means more than having an administrator announce each fall that students will be held to it. Students should have a part in administering it. There should be frequent opportunities to discuss its interpretation, to apply it to particular cases of student conduct, and to evaluate it in light of that experience.[17]

Most police codes are sufficiently like an honor code for this purpose, but sufficiently different to be worth a student's effort to learn the particulars. Deciding, for example, whether "[being] honest in thought and deed" implies giving credit to those who helped one write a paper would provide useful practice in interpreting the code (as well as useful insight into the rationale for crediting others in one's academic work).

The other five methods of teaching students professional ethics are all internal to the curriculum. The easiest, my fourth way, is the guest lecture. (If the guest stays all semester, the course is "team taught.")[18] By itself, the guest lecture makes professional ethics look optional: "If all members of my profession are supposed to know this stuff, why doesn't my prof know enough to teach it?" A similar question arises for the fifth way, the sort of course I routinely teach, a free-standing course in a profession's ethics taught *outside* the department, whether optional or required. ("Why doesn't someone in my department know enough to teach it?") A different question arises for my sixth way, a course in the profession's ethics which, while optional, is taught by a member of the profession: "If this stuff is important, why isn't it required?"

My seventh way, the free-standing *required in-house* course, answers all these questions, but only at the cost of raising another: "How do we fit this into the curriculum?" The last of my eight methods, the pervasive, provides an answer to that question: "You don't have to because you can do something better. You can teach police ethics in a way that brings home how integral it is to police work. You can make police ethics pervade the curriculum."

Criminal justice seems to me to differ in some ways from most fields—such as engineering—in which I have helped to integrate ethics. The great difficulty in criminal justice is not—as in most fields—finding room for ethics but finding room for something more than the obvious.[19] A related difficulty, but one deserving independent mention, is finding something useful to say about the obvious questions. Taking bribes is, for example, unethical (as well as illegal). That is obvious. What is not obvious is: how you refuse a bribe without arousing the hostility of fellow officers who did not refuse; what to do after refusing the bribe; and so on. Such questions of "ethical art," though hard to answer, are not hard philosophically. They are questions to which knowledge of institutions is relevant, questions that people with the right practical or research experience can illuminate, even if they can give no general answer. They are ethical questions that courses in criminal justice should emphasize. But how do you fit such questions into the ordinary course in criminal justice (where "fit" means "comport with" as well as "squeeze in").

The only convincing way to answer that question is to give a few examples of what might be done. These are not alternatives among which one must choose, but options to mix and match (with the understanding that, all else equal, the more the better).[20] They are intended to show that much is possible, not to provide an exhaustive list of possibilities.

One way to integrate ethics into a course is simply to enhance student awareness of ethical issues. For example, during a discussion of crowd psychology, the instructor might describe a situation in which an attempt to arrest in fact set off a riot (without telling students the outcome) and ask how to make the arrest using various theories of crowd behavior. After the students have made their suggestions, the instructor might describe what the officer in question did and what happened, concluding with the question, "Why didn't anyone here suggest not making the arrest? After all, police have discretion to make arrests precisely because there are times when making an arrest would be disastrous." The instructor should do this hoping that at least one student will point out that the class was only asked *how* to arrest, the means, not *whether* to arrest. If a student does point that out, the instructor can reply: "A police officer need not be bound by the form in the which a question is put. If there is a problem with the end, an officer should so indicate. Police are not mere instruments of policy; they are also moral agents." Even a few such comments in the course of a semester can help students get used to looking for the morally significant decisions concealed under a discussion of means.

An easy way to provide information about ethical standards is to pass out a code of ethics at the beginning of the term and refer to it often enough during the term that students get the idea that they should read it. For example, an instructor in the appropriate psychology course might mention, during a discussion of emotions, that the "Law Enforcement Code of Ethics" makes an officer responsible for maintaining "courageous calm in the face of danger, scorn, or ridicule" and ask (without waiting for an answer), "What do the theories we have been discussing tell us about that provision?" If (as I suppose) students of criminal justice are like most college students, they will not have thought about any of the provisions of their profession's code (and, indeed, will probably not have read the code at all). So, passing out the code and referring to it now and then in a way inviting further reflection would be a significant contribution to their ethics education. Asking them questions as homework or on exams that require them to look through the code would, of course, be a further significant contribution.

Teaching the code is, however, not all an instructor can do to add to a student's ethical knowledge. An instructor in police administration, for example, can assign projects requiring students to develop a police ethics case, interview a police officer to find out how he would handle it, and interview a police administrator to find out how he would like it handled. Such a project can help students understand how a police department works, including (along the way) what support there is (or is not) for ethical conduct. The project can also help a student interpret the relevant code provisions.

Students can also be asked (as another step in such a project) to choose their own solution to the problem and explain it as they might in a memo to a supervisor. Students then have an opportunity to exercise police judgment—including ethical judgment (and to practice writing too).

Such a project might have yet another step, though one involving a substantial commitment of class time. Some students might be asked to present their problem, their solution, and their rationale, with the class invited to respond. Such presentations, together with the class response, should not only improve public speaking but should also help students see how much agreement there is among students in their class about what they thought right (and how many good options they may have missed working alone). Such presentations provide an opportunity for students to enhance their ethical will-power (as well as further sharpen their ethical judgment).[21]

These examples are meant to be only that, examples.[22] Integrating ethics into the curriculum is not a matter of a few moments in four years but of many such moments worked together to achieve an overall effect. Ethical discussions should occur often enough to make ethics seem part of police work. There should be a coherent order to these ethical discussions. So, for example, first year courses might emphasize ethical sensitivity. Here are things to look for. The second year might emphasize the knowledge students need to resolve the problems they are now used to identifying, both knowledge of the appropriate code and of its institutional context. The third year might then emphasize getting students to resolve problems and justify their resolutions, using what they learned in the second year. The last year might emphasize classroom discussion of such resolutions. All of this can be done without any change in syllabi and, except for class discussion, without sacrifice of much class time. Integrating ethics is another way of teaching much the same technical material, not a replacement for it.

There are, however, at least three important barriers to adopting the pervasive method. The first barrier is the personnel of the criminal justice program. In some programs, practitioners (or former practitioners) predominate; in others, "mere academics" (generally, sociologists who have no experience in police work except what comes from studying it). Generally, neither practitioners nor mere academics will have had any training in police ethics, indeed, any training in ethics at all (in my third—or second—sense). They will believe themselves unqualified to do what the pervasive method would require of them. The way to get around this first barrier is to re-train faculty, whether informally (for example, by having them observe classes where instructors do integrate ethics) or by formal workshops of the sort I have given over the last five years. The workshops are more effective, although they are also more expensive.

Of course, re-training presupposes a relatively stable faculty, one in whom it makes sense to invest. If many of the staff of a criminal justice program tend to turn over rapidly, either because they are adjuncts, temporaries, and the like, or just because a program has trouble holding faculty, then the investment in re-training will be lost. The pervasive method will be almost impossible to implement until the universities that train criminal justice faculty have integrated ethics into their programs.

The second barrier is related to the first, a seeming misfit between what instructors know and what is being asked of them. Because practitioners have a fund of experience on which to draw, they generally find developing ethics cases easier than do "mere academics." They also generally have a better sense of how the institution in which they work (or worked) actually responds to ethics issues. And they can speak with corresponding authority. For practitioners used to drawing on that authority to teach, the hardest thing is to control the impulse to foreclose discussion by telling students "the right answer" right off. Discussion is an important part of teaching ethics. Here "mere academics" can be helpful, drawing on their knowledge of other institutions to help practitioners see that there might be more than one right answer or that "the right answer" is far more problematic than it seems.

"Mere academics" have the opposite problem. While less likely to tell students "the right answer," they are more likely to glory in teaching that "there are no right answers." They must be helped to see that many ethics questions, the easy ones, do have "right answers," that is, ones no reasonable police officer contests, and that teaching those right answers is important. They must also be helped to see the contribution that their special knowledge can make to solution of the hard ethics questions. Here the practitioners can be helpful, since they are more likely to see the actual relations between academic knowledge and professional practice. Mere academics must also be helped to see that they are allowed to have opinions on the harder questions and to express them in class. They must, however, be prepared, when challenged, to give reasons for their opinions (and admit error when a student catches one). Mere academics must come to see their own opinions as contributions to class discussion, something against which students can define their own position, rather than as a substitute for class discussion they must suppress.

The third barrier to the pervasive method is that few texts in criminal justice are designed to raise ethical issues. Writers of criminal justice texts might here benefit from examining modern management texts, many of which now include good ethics questions at the end of each chapter. But, until texts in criminal justice catch up to those in management (in this respect), the only way around the second barrier is for instructors to develop their own ethics materials. Departments can ease the development of such materials by granting release time for their development and by formal arrangements to allow faculty to share what they have.

The pervasive method requires central planning, but it requires neither that everything be done at once nor that everyone do things the same way. The pervasive method can be implemented over many years. A department might, for example, begin with sensitivity raising, taking as long as necessary to restructure its first year courses before even beginning to work ethical knowledge into the curriculum. Individual instructors can integrate ethics into their courses before their department does. While the effect of the pervasive method probably increases geometrically (up to some limit) as integration increases arithmetically, even one course where ethics is well integrated would probably make an important contribution to a student's education.

IV WHY INTEGRATE ETHICS INTO THE CRIMINAL JUSTICE CURRICULUM?

I have already touched on two reasons why police ethics should be integrated into the criminal justice curriculum. The first is that such integration reenforces what is taught about police ethics elsewhere (for example, in extra-curricular activities); the second, that such integration helps students develop the habit of thinking about ethics whenever thinking about police work. A third reason to integrate police ethics into the criminal justice curriculum is that, as a matter of fact, many students will get no police ethics (before graduation) except as part of the technical curriculum. Required ethics courses are unlikely to become universal any time soon, and other methods tend to miss most students. After graduation, the students are likely to receive no more than a few hours of formal ethics instruction in a lifetime.[23]

There are two more reasons why police ethics should be integrated into criminal justice courses: the fourth you may have guessed from the examples I have given; the fifth may surprise you, though I have substantial empirical evidence from other fields to support what I shall claim.

The reason you may have guessed is that integrating police ethics into technical courses can remind students of what attracted them to police work. So, for example, the social science courses that form the core of the criminal justice curriculum often seem to students to have little connection with what they will actually do as police. Integrating ethics into such a course can enliven the course while helping students see why they need what the course teaches.

My fifth reason for integrating ethics into technical courses, the one you probably did not guess even though I now have lots of empirical evidence for it, is that students will approve. We have required graduates of our workshop to have their students evaluate the ethics component of their program. Class after class, year after year, both at IIT and now at the twenty other schools to which our graduates returned, the great majority of students—often over ninety percent—expressed appreciation for the concern shown ethics, some because they thought ethics important, some because it helped them to understand what they would be doing after graduation. Few wanted less ethics; many wanted more. This last reason seems to me as good as any for doing as much police ethics as possible. Instructors are always looking for ways to make their classes more enjoyable (without pandering). There is, I think, no reason to believe that students planning on a career in policing would differ much in this respect from students of engineering, sociology, law, or the like. Here is one more (respectable) way to make class more enjoyable.

V THE AIM OF A PHILOSOPHY COURSE IN POLICE ETHICS

Five years of teaching faculty to integrate professional ethics into their ordinary courses forced me to reflect on *what* I was doing and why *I*—and two other philosophers—were doing it. If professional ethics is part of a *profession's* art, why were *philosophers* teaching professionals how to teach it? The answer, I think, is that we, as philosophers, made three distinct contributions to teaching ethics pervasively: legitimacy, experience, and insight. Two of these contributions seem to be historical accidents. The third contribution, much less contingent, provides a reason for having a free-standing philosophy course in police ethics even if a curriculum ethics pervades. Let me explain.

Philosophers routinely teach courses with "ethics" in the title. Other departments do not. Hence, for academics worried about "turf battles," philosophers have a clear claim to the word "ethics." Those not in philosophy who want to teach "ethics" have to explain why they are competent (and why the philosophers do not have prior claim). Many disciplines have developed ways to finesse questions about their right to teach ethics. For example, engineers like to talk about "professionalism"; lawyers, about "professional responsibility"; business professors, about "business environment" or "business integrity." But the problem of legitimacy will remain until other fields have established their own recognized tradition of ethics teaching. That day is at least as far off for criminal justice as for most other fields.

Of course, philosophers have their own problem of legitimacy. Most professionals quickly recognize how little a philosopher knows about their field, including the ethical problems that arise, what standards apply, and what responses are appropriate. Philosophers with an expertise in ethics do not, as a matter of fact, generally have an expertise in professional ethics. The fields are largely distinct. Yet, even when philosophers make that clear at every possible opportunity, non-philosophers generally continue to feel illegitimate using the term "ethics"; and, even when they do not, their colleagues think they should.

For this reason alone, those of our non-IIT graduates who have tried to get their colleagues to follow their lead have tried to find a philosopher on campus with whom to work. So far, they have always found one, though some of those found seem initially to have been quite skeptical about a philosopher having any role in teaching practical ethics. The most effective technique for reducing such skepticism has been handing the philosopher something—for example, one of my articles—published in a philosophy journal. The place of publication, as much as the helpful instructions and philosophical content, serves as a credential for practical ethics capable of overcoming a philosopher's professional skepticism. With a philosopher present, our graduates can legitimately talk about "ethics" to other non-philosophers.

The second contribution philosophers can make, even philosophers who have no experience teaching professional ethics, is experience. Philosophers routinely teach through guided discussion. Though philosophers take this method for granted, the standard teaching method for many other disciplines is not guided discussion but lecture. Naturally, members of such disciplines worry about leading a discussion. They will need a few tips (though far fewer than I originally supposed) and a few successful attempts before they feel comfortable guiding discussion. Philosophers can be helpful here, often more helpful than law or business professors who, though they too are used to guiding discussion, tend to guide it in ways less suitable for a discussion of ethics. This difference is, I think, worth a paper of its own.[24]

This second contribution, like the first, is clearly temporary. Non-philosophers can learn in a few hours most of what there is to know about leading discussion. After that, a few months experience is generally enough to bring them even with the philosophers. That, anyway, has been my experience. The third contribution is another matter.

Philosophers seem to bring to professional ethics a systematic approach, and a depth of experience with argument, that non-philosophers do not have and are unlikely to develop (without becoming philosophers). I am not sure why that is. In part, no doubt, it is a matter of self-selection. People become philosophers in part because they differ somewhat from people who become sociologists, physicians, lawyers, or the like. Philosophers take an interest in arguments, distinctions, and definitions with which most people simply become impatient. Philosophers also have a love of abstraction that many disciplines tend to discourage—and a dislike of factual detail that many disciplines find unbelievable.

To whatever self-selection may initially distinguish philosophers from practitioners of other disciplines must be added another cause of distinction, years of exercising certain skills while others exercised others. For better or worse, philosophers devote their lives to arguments, arguments aimed at winning over reason, not just arguments aimed at persuading (as in law or rhetoric). Where a philosopher can use her discipline, she is likely to see questions others do not, to make moves in argument others do not, or at least to do such things with more facility than others do. Philosophy is a distinct discipline (even if it is hard to say exactly what distinguishes it).

If I am right about this, then, philosophers should always have a distinct role in professional ethics, even after every profession has experts of its own. Whether this role will be valuable enough to sustain much participation is another question. My guess is that it will be. Philosophers seem to be useful insofar as change has created puzzling new ethics problems for a profession or made relatively routine responses to traditional ethics problems seem unsatisfactory. Indeed, it seems to me, the reason professional ethics has moved from a marginal field in a few disciplines to an important field both in most professions and in philosophy is precisely that traditional arrangements have broken down. Since the cause of that breakdown, rapid social change, seems to make unlikely the reemergence of a stable tradition any time soon, predicting that philosophers will have a role in professional ethics for a long time seems safe.[25]

But what role? There are two possibilities: first, the central (and practical) role that philosophers now have in, say, medical ethics; or second, the critical but marginal role that philosophers have in science. I believe that the role of philosophers in professional ethics will more and more resemble their role in the philosophy of science. Philosophers will gravitate toward "philosophy of professional ethics" (a subdivision of my second sense of "ethics") rather than (as now) professional ethics (in my third sense). They will leave the practical role to "ethicists" because the practical role requires a knowledge of detail that philosophers generally find uncongenial.

How can police ethics cultivate philosophy's interest in even that marginal role? Police ethics must, first, have problems to interest a philosopher. Police work certainly has those. Second, police ethics must provide philosophers with a reason to take an interest in problems of police ethics rather than other interesting problems. Generally, sustained philosophical interest requires an "economic base," that is, a course in which the philosopher can study relevant texts, try out arguments, and develop a sense of a field's geography. Good work in professional ethics (in my second sense of "ethics") requires familiarity with the profession, not the familiarity of practitioners but much more than the familiarity of an ordinary educated academic. Hence, sustained philosophical interest in police ethics requires a regularly-offered course in police ethics (or some harder to manage equivalent).

The pervasive method may seem to make *any* free-standing course inappropriate, whether or not it is a philosophy course. Professional ethics should pervade the curriculum because that is the way to show students how to integrate ethics into their professional work, because a series of courses in which some ethics is taught is likely to have a larger impact than one course on ethics, and because a free-standing course is too likely to provide most faculty with the excuse they need to do nothing about ethics in their technical courses.

Whether the pervasive method does in fact make a free-standing course in professional ethics inappropriate seems to me a question still open. Many medical and law schools have adopted both the pervasive method and a *required* free-standing course. The free-standing course offers a systematic treatment not possible using the pervasive method. Offered early in the curriculum, such a required course provides a foundation upon which instructors using the pervasive method can build. If every student can be assumed to know the basics of professional ethics, faculty can, for example, refer to the relevant code provision without detailed explanation, leaving more time for examination of ethical issues involving detailed knowledge of the technical material of the course, something not possible in a free-standing course in ethics (especially if that course is offered early in the curriculum).[26]

Such required free-standing courses are, however, now generally taught by members of the profession, not philosophers. There is good reason for that. Though they draw from philosophy both readings for students and background for faculty, these courses are primarily in professional practice. Professions feel better letting their own members teach such a course, in part because members of the profession know their practice better than philosophers do and in part because students are more likely to take the ethics seriously if a member of their would-be profession is teaching it.

A philosophy course in police ethics should, then, be optional. Students should take the course because they want to see what philosophers have to tell them about police ethics. While the aim of the course will be to understand police ethics as a rational undertaking, the primary reason for offering the course regularly will be to assure that the program has an expert in police ethics (in the second sense of "ethics") to call on for help in developing ethics materials, thinking through ethics problems, finding appropriate ethics readings, and otherwise providing support for the pervasive method. Such a philosopher should also support the pervasive method less directly, by contributing to the literature on police ethics. The pervasive method is not an alternative to an optional philosophy course in police ethics.

APPENDIX

A Summary Guide to Ethical Decision Making

1 *State problem* (e.g., "There's something about this decision that makes me uncomfortable" or "Do I have a conflict of interest?")

2 *Check facts* (many problems disappear upon closer examination of the situation, while others change radically).

3 *Identify relevant factors*—e.g., persons involved, laws, professional code, other practical constraints (e.g., under $200).

4 *Develop list of options* (be imaginative, avoid "dilemma"—not "yes" or "no" but who to go to, what to say—at least three).

5 *Test options*, using such tests as the following:

> *Harm test*—does this option do less harm than any alternative?
>
> *Publicity test*—would I want my choice of this option published in the newspaper?
>
> *Defensibility test*—could I defend my choice of this option before a Congressional committee or committee of my peers?
>
> *Reversibility test*—would I still think the choice of this option good if I were one of those adversely affected by it?
>
> *Colleague test*—what do my colleagues say when I describe my problem and suggest this option as my solution?
>
> *Professional test*—what might my profession's governing body or ethics committee say about this option?
>
> *Organization test*—what does the organization's ethics officer or legal counsel say about this?

6 *Make a choice* based on steps 1-5.

7 *Review steps 1-6*:

What could you do to make it less likely that you would have to make such a decision again?

Are there any precautions you can take as an individual (announce your policy on question, change job, etc.)?

Is there any way to have more support next time?

Is there any way to change organization (e.g., suggest policy change at next departmental meeting)?

NOTES

Thanks to John Kleinig for asking me to think about the aims of teaching police ethics, for considerable advice concerning what to read, and for helpful comments on the first draft of this paper.

1. For an example of an important work which so understands the topic, see Lawrence W. Sherman, *Ethics in Criminal Justice Education* (Hastings-on-Hudson, NY: Hastings Center, 1982).

2. Daryl Close and Nicholas Meier, eds., *Morality in Criminal Justice: An Introduction to Ethics* (Belmont, CA: Wadsworth, 1994). This text goes beyond police (strictly speaking) only insofar as it regularly adverts to prison guards and probation officers.

3. See my "Do Cops Need a Code of Ethics?" *Criminal Justice Ethics* 10 (summer/fall 1991), pp. 14-28; "Codes of Ethics," in *The Encyclopedia of Police Science*, ed. William G. Bailey (New York: Garland Publishing Company, 1995), pp. 83-94; "Hands Across the Border: Ethical Guidelines for Transnational Law Enforcement," in *Crime and Law Enforcement in the Global Village*, ed. William F. McDonald (Cincinnati, OH: Anderson, 1997), pp. 187-201; and "Police, Discretion, and the Professions," in *Handled with Discretion: Ethical Issues in Police Decision Making*, ed. John Kleinig (Lanham, MD: Rowman and Littlefield, 1996), pp. 13-35.

4. See, esp., "Who Should Teach Workplace Ethics?" *Teaching Philosophy* 13 (March 1990), pp. 21-36; "Teaching Workplace Ethics," *Thinking* 8 (spring 1990): 33-42; "On Teaching Cloistered Virtue: The Ethics of Teaching Students to Avoid Moral Risk," *Teaching Philosophy* 14 (September 1991), pp. 259-76; "Integrating Ethics into Technical Courses: IIT's Experiment in its Second Year," *Proceedings of the Frontiers in Education Conference* 22 (November 1992), pp. 64-68; "Ethics Across the Curriculum: Teaching Professional Responsibility in Technical Courses," *Teaching Philosophy* 16 (September 1993), pp. 205-35; "Integrating Ethics into an Undergraduate Research Experience" (with Muchund Acharya and Vivian Weil), *Journal of Engineering Education* 84 (April 1995), pp. 129-32; and "Engineering Ethics: Why? What? When? How?" (with Ed Harris, Michael Pritchard, and Michael Rabins), *Journal of Engineering Education* 85 (April 1996), pp. 93-96.

5. Of course, moral judgment does seem to improve in college (and most graduate programs) more than outside. But these improvements, though real, are

relatively small, probably too small to justify even one course with the improvement of general moral judgment as its object. Courses with other objects can, however, make much the same improvement in moral judgment.

6. Among the many good points of the Close and Meier text cited above is its title, in which "morality" has pride of place and "ethics" clearly carries its second sense. There is no fuzziness about whether this is a text on professional ethics.

7. For those with (post-Nozickian) doubts about appeal to the principle of fairness, see my "Nozick's Argument FOR the Legitimacy of the Welfare State," *Ethics* 97 (April 1987), pp. 576-94; and Richard Arneson, "The Principle of Fairness and Free-Rider Problems," *Ethics* 92 (July 1982), pp. 616-33.

8. For more on the distinction between business and professions, see my "Is Engineering Ethics Just Business Ethics?" *International Journal of Applied Philosophy* 8 (Winter/Spring 1994), pp. 1-7.

9. For a more extended defense of this distinction generally (including subtleties ignored here), see my "The Moral Authority of a Professional Code," *NOMOS* 29 (1987), pp. 302-37. For application to policing, see my "Do Cops Need a Code of Ethics?" For application to other professions (or institutions), see my "The Use of Professions," *Business Economics* 22 (October 1987), pp. 5-10; "Vocational Teachers, Confidentiality, and Professional Ethics," *International Journal of Applied Philosophy* 4 (spring 1988), pp. 11-20; "Professionalism Means Putting Your Profession First," *Georgetown Journal of Legal Ethics* (summer 1988), pp. 352-66; "The Special Role of Professionals in Business Ethics," *Business and Professional Ethics Journal* 7 (summer 1988), pp. 51-62; "The Discipline of Science: Law or Profession?" *Accountability in Research* 1 (1990), pp. 137-45; "Thinking Like an Engineer: The Place of a Code of Ethics in the Practice of a Profession," *Philosophy & Public Affairs* 20 (spring 1991), pp.150-67; "Codes of Ethics, Professions, and Conflict of Interest: A Case of an Emerging Profession, Clinical Engineering," *Professional Ethics* 1 (spring/summer 1992): 179-195; "Wild Professors and Sensitive Students: A Preface to Academic Ethics," *Social Theory and Practice* 18 (summer 1992), pp. 117-41; "Treating Patients with Infectious Diseases: An Essay in the Ethics of Dentistry," *Professional Ethics* 2 (spring/summer 1993), pp. 51-65; and "Science: After Such Knowledge, What Responsibility?" *Professional Ethics*, 4 (spring 1995), pp. 49-74.

10. See, for example, Jerry Cederblom and Cassia Spohn, "A Model for Teaching Criminal Justice Ethics," *Journal of Criminal Justice Education* 2 (fall 1991), pp. 201-17. The course described, though easily recognizable as the criminal justice version of a standard business ethics course, does at least mention professional codes now and then (and is, in this respect, superior to most courses in business ethics).

11. For more on this point, see my "Do the Cops Need a Code of Ethics?"

12. An institution, for example, the Chicago Police Department, can have its own special standards. These may or may not constitute a code of ethics (whatever they contain or are called). They will constitute a code of ethics insofar as they are understood as standards "we" should follow because each of us benefits from having the rest follow them and these benefits more than repay any burden we must assume to do our share. The special standards will, however, simply constitute additional regulation if they are understood instead as a legal requirement, something to do to avoid getting in trouble, or something to do because it is personally uplifting.

13. While I think this list of aims identifies the chief ones in a way especially

useful for thinking about teaching ethics, I do not consider it to be either complete or canonical. Compare James Rest, "The Major Components of Morality," in *Morality, Moral Development, and Moral Behavior*, W. Kurtines and J. Gewirtz, eds. (New York: Wiley, 1985). Although John Kleinig, "Teaching and Learning Police Ethics: Competing and Complementary Approaches," *Journal of Criminal Justice* 18 (January 1990), pp. 1-18, identifies only three desirable outcomes—"reinforcement of moral resolve," "moral sensitization," and "imparting moral experience," I do not think we disagree much. His first and second are my fourth and first; his "moral experience" seems to combine my "knowledge" and "judgment." I prefer to separate knowledge from judgment principally because "experience" often gets interpreted as mere knowledge (though no Aristotelian would make such a mistake). Though experience may seem to lend itself to transmission by lecture, judgment clearly requires practice.

14. So, for example, in an otherwise useful article, Joycelyn M. Pollock, "Ethics and the Criminal Justice Curriculum," *Journal of Criminal Justice Education* 4 (fall 1993), pp. 377-90, says "[that] to analyze ethical issues, one should have a grounding in ethical principles" (p. 378). For some idea of the traps awaiting those who try to bring theory in, see the exchange between Sam S. Souryal and Dennis W. Potts, "'What Am I Supposed to Fall Back On?' Cultural Literacy in Criminal Justice Ethics," *Journal of Criminal Justice Education* 4 (spring 1993), pp. 15-41; and Ethan Fishman, "'Falling Back' on Natural Law and Prudence: A Reply to Souryal and Potts," *Journal of Criminal Justice Education* 5 (fall 1994), pp. 189-202.

15. I shall here ignore outreach to practitioners, whether formal extension courses or less formal sensitivity raising (such as having students interview police administrators about how an officer's ethical question would be handled in her department). I ignore outreach not because I consider it unimportant but because I consider it both too important and too large a topic to be crammed into a paper on the curriculum. But I cannot resist pointing out how important outreach is. Nothing we do to teach ethics to pre-professionals will have much effect if, upon graduation, they enter a workplace where no one takes ethics seriously or where, almost as bad, no one knows how to talk about ethics. In such an environment, ethical sensitivity, knowledge, judgment, and will-power (like otherwise unused sensitivity, knowledge, judgment, and will-power) will shrivel like roses in a hard frost. For useful advice on how to organize such an outreach program, see Kenneth Kernaghan and Shirley Mancino, "Approaches to Ethics Education," *Canadian Public Administration* 34 (spring 1991), pp. 184-91.

16 One of my colleagues, Robert Ladenson, has been experimenting with another device, an "ethics bowl." Students form teams of four each to compete, much as on public television's College Bowl. The chief differences between College Bowl and an ethics bowl are: (a) the teams must answer questions asking for a decision in a specific situation; (b) the responses are evaluated by a panel of practitioners (as in a diving contest) with the emphasis on the identification of moral issues, the ingenuity of the proposed solution, and the reasoning offered in its defense, rather than on giving "the right answer"; and (c) the teams have the right to criticize the "official answer" if they believe their own is better (with the panel counting the effectiveness of this criticism in making their final evaluation). After two years of experiment with this format at IIT, the ethics bowl went intercollegiate in spring 1995, DePaul, Loyola, and Western Michigan joining IIT to hold a joint ethics bowl (after each held an internal ethics bowl to choose a team to represent the school). There was a second, and larger, ethics bowl in spring

1996. Students enjoy the competition while appreciating the opportunity the ethics bowl gives them to practice making decisions.

17. For a good critique of the honor system, see the entire issue of *Perspectives on the Professions* 14 (January 1995).

18. Institutionally, a team-taught course is quite different from a mere guest lecture. It requires two salaries rather than one and, if the teachers come from different departments, complex administrative arrangements as well. Team taught courses generally seem to be one way faculty have of learning from one another. After a few semesters, the team generally breaks up, with one member (or both) going on to teach the same course alone. For faculty, a team taught course is like one of my workshops (rather than, as it seems to students, a convenient way of dividing work).

19. This, I think, is one way to read William C. Heffernan, "Two Approaches to Police Ethics,"*Criminal Justice Review* 7 (1982), pp. 28-35. What he calls the "integrity approach" corresponds to what I have called "obvious questions"; his analytic approach, to what I have called "less obvious questions." I prefer my distinction to his because many of the integrity questions are more complicated than his way of putting things suggests. For example, taking bribes is, of course, unethical, but you must understand why bribes are unethical before you can deal with the stoolie's exchange of information for a blind eye, small gifts from merchants, and other favors, which differ from bribes strictly so called but share with them many troubling characteristics. The integrity approach is probably inadequate (though somewhat better than nothing) even in the domain to which Heffernan tries to limit it, the police academy or other professional program.

20. For some non-police examples of integrating ethics, see *Perspectives on the Professions* 13 (February 1994), the entire issue, as well as my "Ethics Across the Curriculum."

21. Because *moral* judgment seems to improve with discussion of hard, morally-significant choices, this method of teaching police ethics should also improve moral judgment (even though that is not its aim).

22. For some other good ideas, see Joycelyn M. Pollock and Ronald F. Becker, "Law Enforcement Ethics: Using Officers' Dilemmas as a Teaching Tool," *Journal of Criminal Justice* 6 (spring 1995), pp. 1-20

23. Compare: Joycelyn M. Pollock-Byrne, "Teaching Criminal Justice Ethics," *The Justice Professional* 3 (September 1993), pp. 283-95; William D. Hyatt, "Teaching Ethics in a Criminal Justice Program," *American Journal of Police* 10 (1991), pp. 77-86; and Dilip K. Das, "Police Training in Ethics: The Need for an Innovative Approach in Mandated Programs," *American Journal of Criminal Justice* 11 (September 1986), pp. 62-80.

24. For some advice likely to be useful to criminal justice instructors (but far too few illustrations), see David Emmons and Larry Nutt, "Values Education and the Criminal Justice Curriculum," *Journal of Criminal Justice Education* 6 (spring 1995), pp. 147-52.

25. For more on this claim, see my "The Ethics Boom: What and Why," *Centennial Review* 34 (spring 1990), pp. 163-86.

26. For one example (Notre Dame Law School), see David T. Link, "The Pervasive Method of Teaching Ethics," *Journal of Legal Education* 39 (December 1989), pp. 485-89.

II. Teaching and Learning in Criminal Justice Ethics

Charles S. Claxton

INTRODUCTION

What should be the aims in teaching criminal justice ethics? To answer that question, we would do well to reflect first upon the overall purpose of education. A comment made by Alfred North Whitehead many years ago is helpful in that regard. He observed, "Your learning is useless to you til you have lost your texts, burnt your lecture notes, and forgotten the minutiae you have learnt by heart for the examination."[1] Whitehead's comment "suggests that the real fruits of education are the thought processes that result from the study of a discipline, not the information accumulated."[2] I would say that the aim of criminal justice ethics education is embedded in that larger purpose of education: the thought processes that result from the study of a discipline. For purposes of this discussion, I suggest that the aim of criminal justice ethics education is *to help learners increase their capacities of thought so they can deal more effectively with ethical issues.*

Taking this purpose seriously invites us to be part of a paradigm shift in higher education described by Barr and Tagg:

> In its briefest form, the paradigm that has governed our colleges is this: A college is an institution that exists *to provide instruction*. Subtly but profoundly we are shifting to a new paradigm: A college is an institution that exists *to produce learning*. This shift changes everything.[3]

A change in consciousness from instruction to learning is already underway in higher education (see Appendix) and is fueled by recent insights about: (a) postmodern perspectives on curriculum development;[4] (b) student learning and development;[5] (c) critical thinking;[6] (d) the bases of knowledge itself;[7] (e) teaching as a scholarly activity;[8] and (f) institutional effectiveness and outcomes assessment.[9]

In an *instructional* paradigm, faculty in criminal justice ethics would typically begin the curriculum development process by focusing on such things as selection of content, identification of texts and materials, and preparation of lectures. These are all important issues, but in a *learning* paradigm faculty would deal with other issues that precede them in consideration. The first is the learners themselves and how their thinking processes change and develop over time.

LEARNERS AND THE CONSTRUCTIVIST, DEVELOPMENTAL VIEW

A stream of research called "constructivism" and "development"[10] helps us grapple with the question that wise teachers have always dealt with: If we are to be effective as *teachers,* how should we be thinking about our *learners*? The *constructivist* view is captured by Aldous Huxley's statement: "Experience is not what happens to you; it's what you *do* with what happens to you."[11] This perspective, according to Kegan, is an invitation to consider "that most human of 'regions' between an event and a reaction to it—the place where the event is privately composed, made sense of, the place where it actually becomes an event for that person." It focuses our attention on the "zone of mediation where meaning is made:"[12]

> [W]hat an organism does, as William Perry says, is organize; and what a human organism organizes is meaning. Thus it is not that a person makes meaning, as much as that the activity of being a person is the activity of meaning-making.[13]

Further, "... we constitute reality, rather than somehow happen upon it.... We literally make sense. Human being is the composing of meaning ..."[14]

The *developmental* perspective builds on the idea of constructivism and argues that, as meaning-making entities, we evolve through predictable and qualitatively different eras (or stages) in our lives. We change the way we construct (or make meaning of) ourselves and the world around us. The mind itself grows, develops, and changes its "shape" as we move through the life cycle. Said another way: as we get older, it is not only that we know more. It is that we *think differently.*

This constructivist-developmental view clarifies the importance and the magnitude of the shift from an instructional paradigm to a learning paradigm. Although the instructional paradigm sees its purpose as "providing or delivering instruction," the constructivist-developmental view, grounded in a learning paradigm, argues that the role of the curriculum is *to support learners' evolution to richer, more expansive ways (or stages) of making meaning.*

STAGES OF DEVELOPMENT

What are the stages of development that college students go through? Parks has conducted research on college students' developmental stages and describes two which seem most relevant to our discussion of criminal justice ethics. She calls the first stage "reflective, *interpersonal* adult thought."[15] Persons typically enter this stage during the teen-age years, and some adults remain here throughout their lives. In this form of thought, persons are able to move beyond thinking in concrete terms of the preceding stage. They can now deal with abstractions, metaphor, and symbols. But persons in this stage are still dependent on authorities outside of the self (for example, parents, teachers, the media). Thus they hold "broad cultural assumptions and beliefs in a tacit, uncritical manner. . . ." They assume "that things just are as they are or that someone else understands and takes care of whatever apparent contradictions or mysteries may appear."[16] The meaning-making system of persons in this stage is based on assumptions that are "tacitly held,"[17] rather than critically reflected upon and consciously chosen. This is true even if these persons hold high positions of responsibility and power in their community, work, or family life.

Persons may move to the next stage as they have new experiences and learn new information which contradicts their way of understanding the world. Parks explains:

> One may begin to wonder more about why things are as they are and if they have to be that way. One may begin to think about one's own thinking—and how it is conditioned by time and place. One may no longer so easily just presume "Authority knows" and may instead begin to take responsibility for knowing for oneself—even at the level of ultimate reality.[18]

Individuals who reconstitute their way of understanding their world move to

> a more critical, self-aware, and *systemic* form of thought. One becomes more inner-dependent (though still taking the views of others into account). One

may continue to value interpersonal reality but simultaneously hold more systemic awareness.[19]

The Parks findings on the stages of interpersonal thought and systemic thought provide a very useful framework for our discussion of criminal justice ethics education. Interpersonal thought is clearly inadequate for professionals in the criminal justice system, which is characterized less by stark categories of right and wrong and more by complexity and ambiguity. This is particularly true in the domain of ethics.

For example, official corruption is a continuing problem in the criminal justice system. As a case in point, the culture of an urban police department may turn a blind eye to indiscriminate use of power and demand that its members do the same. Persons at the interpersonal stage more easily fall prey to "going along." In contrast, persons in systemic thinking have values that have been critically analyzed and embraced, rather than tacitly accepted. They will more likely have the moral and ethical strength to stand aside from that environment and act in ethical ways. Further, interpersonal thought tends to fall into the cultural norm in the United States of compartmentalizing major domains of our lives. Persons at this stage who work in criminal justice may act in ethical ways at home (for example, with their children or spouses) but live out of a different set of values at work ("you gotta do what you gotta do"). The ability to engage in systemic thinking would enable persons working in criminal justice to transcend these limiting (and false) dichotomies.

A large proportion of undergraduates in American colleges and universities are at the interpersonal stage. Thus, we can now refine our statement of purpose for criminal justice ethics education, given earlier, as follows: its role should be *to support students' movement through interpersonal thought and towards (or into) systemic thought so that they may deal more effectively with ethical issues in a criminal justice context.*

CONCEPTUAL FOUNDATIONS FOR EFFECTIVE TEACHING AND LEARNING

But how could we teach ethics so as to facilitate students' movement to higher stages of thinking? A learning paradigm, grounded in the constructivist-developmental view of evolving meaning-making, invites us to respond to this question by revisiting three concepts whose meaning may be more ambiguous than we typically assume: *learning, teaching,* and *knowing.* In a graduate course on Effective College Teaching, a member of my class (a young respiratory therapy instructor at a community college) talked about his early experiences as a faculty member. "I knew what my students were going to be asked on the national examination for my profession. So I told them the kinds of things that were going to be on the test." He paused and then said: "It didn't do any good. " He chuckled and added: "I finally figured out that teaching was more than simply telling them what they needed to know." Most faculty realize that teaching is more than "telling them," but many of the practices in college classrooms, with their emphasis on lecturing to passive students, indicate that much of higher education is about where this instructor was.

David Kolb, a major researcher in adult development, presents a view of *learning* that can help us address this lack of mindfulness.[20] He argues that learning is a two-step process (see Figure 1). In the first step, learners "prehend" information or experience, represented by the vertical axis. (The word prehend means "to take hold of" or "to grasp.") In the second step, represented by the horizontal axis, students "transform" (or "process") the information they have prehended. In the language of constructivism, the learners "make meaning" of the information they have taken in.

This simple (though not simplistic) depiction of learning vividly illustrates the difference between the two paradigms mentioned earlier. Most higher education, caught as it is in an instructional mind set, concerns itself primarily with what happens on the vertical axis; that is, faculty select and "deliver" content to students. In a criminal justice ethics curriculum grounded in a learning paradigm, however, our objective is for students' curricular experiences to be *developmental*. Thus, as much attention is given to the design of learning activities on the horizontal axis (the "meaning-making" line) as is given to what happens on the vertical axis.

Kolb also provides a helpful view of *knowledge*. Drawing on the two axes presented before, Kolb depicts learning as a four-step process (see Figure 2). First, learners have a *Concrete Experience*, where they participate in a direct, "hands-on" experience. Second, the learners engage in *Reflective Observation*, where they reflect upon their Concrete Experience. Third, the professor provides the students with an experience in *Abstract Conceptualization*, where they deal with larger abstractions, or authoritative information from the discipline. This step helps them place their experience in a broader, more objective context. Fourth, the students participate in *Active Experimentation*; that is, they use the authoritative information to guide them in further action as they try out or apply what they have learned in a more complex setting.

Figure 1

Axes of the Experiential Learning Cycle

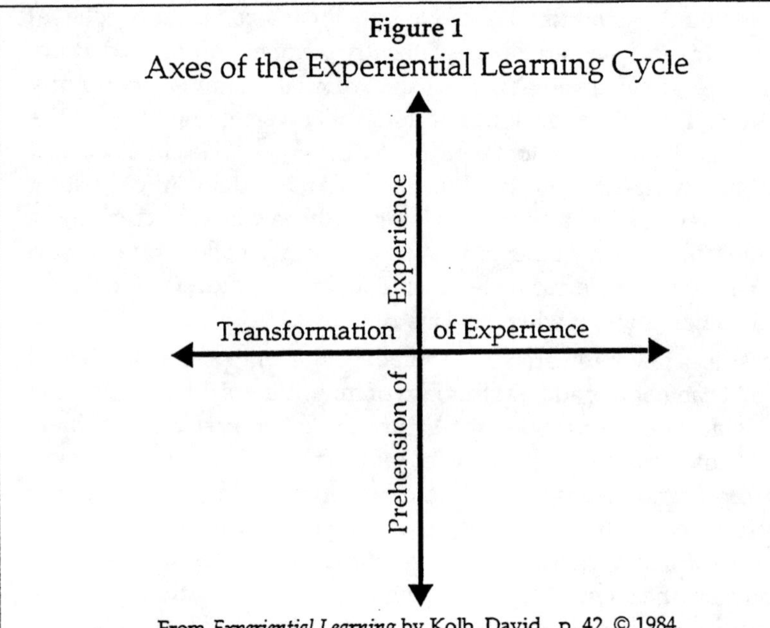

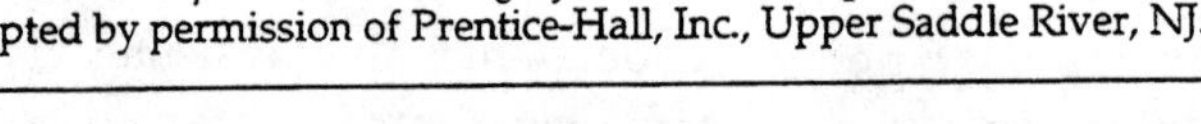

From *Experiential Learning* by Kolb, David, p. 42. © 1984.
Adapted by permission of Prentice-Hall, Inc., Upper Saddle River, NJ.

Figure 2

The Experiential Learning Cycle

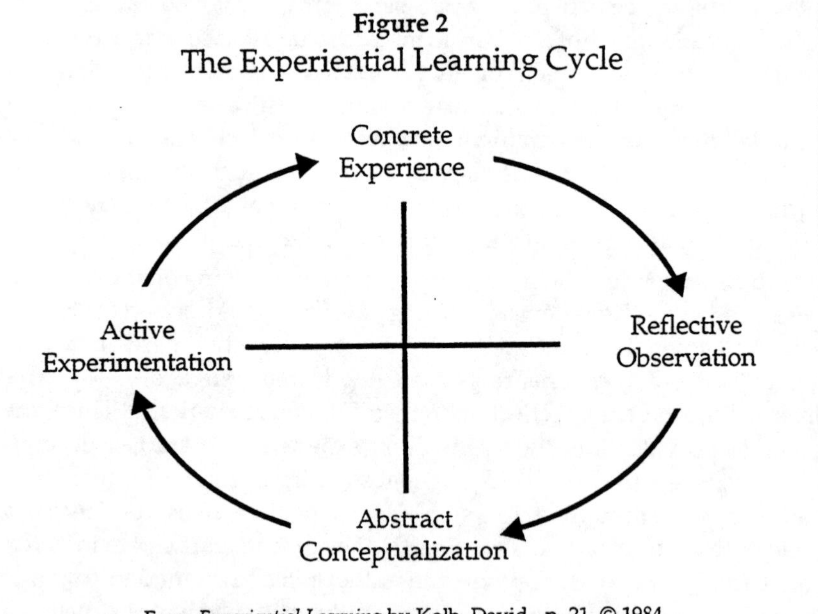

From *Experiential Learning* by Kolb, David, p. 21. © 1984.
Adapted by permission of Prentice-Hall, Inc., Upper Saddle River, NJ.

Kolb uses this reasoning to define learning and knowledge as follows: "Learning is the process whereby knowledge is created through the transformation of experience."[21] Said another way, we create knowledge as we transform (or make meaning of) our experience. Our experience may be direct and subjective (Concrete Experience) or indirect and objective (Abstract Conceptualization). We transform this experience through the more "inner" activity of Reflective Observation and through the more "outer" activity of Active Experimentation. It is clear, therefore, that knowledge is not simply "an independent entity to be acquired (by the learner) or transmitted (by the professor)." Rather, "knowledge is a transformation process, being continuously created . . ." by the learner.[22]

That is the point about teaching, stated in the dense language of social science research, that my graduate student reached on his own: teaching is not "telling"; rather, teaching (particularly teaching that facilitates development) is *the fostering of a creative tension among the professor, the content, and the student to help students construct knowledge for themselves at increasingly complex levels of meaning.*

This line of reasoning about learning and knowledge is congruent with the views expressed by Bruffee.[23] He argues that in post-modern thinking, collaborative learning is conceived not simply as one more "teaching method" but rather a process that is at the heart of learning and knowing. If each of us makes meaning of our experience, then the meaning that is made is unique. Further, what a professor presents in a lecture or an author conveys in a textbook is no more than the meaning he or she has made from the storehouse of practical experience and training in the discipline that each has. Collaborative learning is essential, then, because it enables the professor, the textbook author, and the learners to share the meaning they have made concerning the issue at hand. That is the theoretical reasoning behind the adage frequently heard in education to justify collaborative learning: "none of us is as smart as all of us." In Palmer's phrasing, "knowing and learning are *communal* acts."[24]

In practical terms, of course, the professor and the textbook author generally bring more knowledge and experience to the topic a class is dealing with than the students. Thus, it is appropriate for them to have substantial "air time" in the class through the use of lectures or other approaches. But collaborative learning asks the students to draw on and articulate in class and in assignments their own thinking as well. In the process, they not only learn from each other's experience but understand more fully their own. As such, collaborative learning is powerfully developmental, since one of the marks of development is that the person is increasingly able to reflect upon and be guided by his or her own experience, rather than the dictates of outside authority. The advantage for the professor in collaborative learning is that he or she is able to listen to *the quality of the students' thinking*. Thus collaborative learning provides a very practical way for the professor—drawing on his or her own knowledge and that of the group—to challenge and support the learners' movement to richer ways of making meaning.

PRACTICES IN THE CLASSROOM

Now that we have these definitions of learning, teaching, and knowing in hand, we are ready to deal with practical strategies for teaching in ways that promote development. Parks provides helpful guidance on that issue, and her views warrant an extended presentation here. These come from her research in a five-year project at the Harvard Business School called the Program in Leadership, Ethics, and Corporate Responsibility. Although the student group she studied differed in some respects from students enrolled in criminal justice programs across the country, her conclusions about what is needed in teaching ethics seem fully applicable to the present discussion.

As Parks considers students in the interpersonal stage, she says that substantial attention should be given to the students' orientation to *authority*:

> The conventionally reflective but uncritical young adult . . . will trust authority outside the self in an essentially unexamined, unquestioned fashion. This does not necessarily mean blind obedience to a dictator; more typically it means reflective but uncritical participation in assumed patterns and conventions.[25]

An important aspect of teaching in such instances involves inviting students "to recognize competing authorities and claims, thereby stepping outside of tacit assumptions."[26] Critically important here is "the cultivation of diverse points of view."[27] Parks believes that fostering this diversity of perspective serves two dimensions of what she calls "ethical formation."[28] In the process, "the complexity (and therefore the reality) is heightened. Second, a more empathic imagination is fostered."[29] She explains:

> Studies of those who have exercised moral courage indicate that such people have the capacity to take the perspectives of others, to "walk in another's moccasins" and thereby practice an empathic imagination. A capacity for empathy (as opposed to pity) is the ground of compassion—the ability to suffer with—and the driving energy in the formation of the ethical imagination. By "empathy" we do not mean the sentimental or romantic, or practices

> best consigned to therapists. Rather, we interpret empathy as a strength manifested in the ability to see things from multiple perspectives, be affected by them, and take them into account. The capacity for empathy is a primary element in the formation of effective, ethical . . . behavior.[30]

Parks notes that many of the practices in college classrooms (even in graduate schools) are a form of "infantilization" which "encourage some degree of passivity—a presumed dependence upon the wisdom of the faculty. . . ."[31] In fact, two things are needed:

> First, . . . students need to be given opportunities for active, critical reflection upon the circumstances and opportunities before them. Second, they must be encouraged to become more active agents, most immediately in the present context of their own educational process.[32]

Finally, an effective curriculum in ethics is one that "promotes responsibility, choice, . . . inner dependence, active collaboration, and respectful, meaningful evaluation."[33]

How can we respond to the challenges Parks presents? The Kolb theory of experiential learning can be helpful to us, and I would like to revisit it in a more detailed way than we did before. In so doing, we can illustrate its usefulness as a guide to teaching that supports students' movement through and beyond interpersonal thought. I have adapted an example reported in rich and very helpful detail by Cederblom and Spohn, who teach criminal justice ethics at the University of Nebraska in Omaha.[34]

According to Kolb's experiential learning cycle, students learn most effectively when they deal with the topic or issue in all four modes of the model: Concrete Experience, Reflective Observation, Abstract Conceptualization, and Active Experimentation. In this example, the students are to use two theories (utilitarian and contractarian) to decide what each of them would lead a criminal justice professional to do in particular case situations. Utilitarian theory

> asks (the students) to consider what alternative courses of action are available, to assess the harms and benefits that each alternative probably would produce, and to choose the one that would produce the most benefit or the least harm for everyone affected by the action.[35]

According to the contractarian approach, on the other hand,

> one's obligation is not to make people happy but to be fair. Fairness involves keeping one's agreement (both explicit and implicit), doing one's share in cooperative arrangements, and respecting the autonomy of persons.[36]

In the array of activities for teaching "around the circle of learning," students begin with a Concrete Experience, as they work in small groups to decide how they would resolve the following ethical dilemma:

> You are asked to investigate a domestic disturbance. When you arrive you discover that a woman has been beaten by her husband—she has a black eye and a swollen lip. She begs you not to arrest her husband, and insists that she was to blame for the fight. Will you arrest him?[37]

For Reflective Observation, each small group reports on what it would do and why its members chose that action. This gives the students an opportunity to transform the experience they have just prehended. The class members are able to reflect upon their own experience and hear the conclusions (and the reasoning behind them) of other groups as well.

For Abstract Conceptualization, the students read chapters from the textbook on utilitarian and contractarian theories. At the next class, the professor presents a lecture outlining the highlights of each and the differences between them. In this step, then, the students are prehending experience indirectly through the authoritative information presented by the textbook author and the professor.

At the next class meeting, the students work in small groups on a second case. This time, their task is to decide what the course of action would be if they followed the utilitarian theory and what it would be under the contractarian theory. In this Active Experimentation, the students are transforming through application the information derived from the first case situation, their reflections on it, and the lecture and textbook chapters. As the groups report their decisions, the professor leads the students in further discussion (in effect, another opportunity for Reflective Observation). The class members talk about the thinking that led to their decisions, connections with the earlier lecture and textbook chapters, and any further thoughts they have now on the first case.

In a second round of Active Experimentation, the students are asked to work on another case:

> You are the prosecutor in what appears to you as a cruel case of "gay-bashing." In light of the injuries to the victim and other circumstances, you are considering a felony assault charge. But in a meeting with the defense attorney, she raises the issue of the credibility of the victim/witness. "He comes across as the stereotypical gay," she says. "Look at how he dresses, how he gestures. Listen to how he talks. He was embracing his 'friend' in public when the trouble started with my client. This is as conservative a community as you're going to find. How sympathetic do you think a jury is

going to be? He'll have a tough time on the witness stand—he's so self-conscious. Why don't we just settle on a misdemeanor charge? My client will plead guilty to that."[38]

Earlier, the small groups were asked, what would the utilitarian and the contractarian theories tell you to do? But now students are asked to respond *individually* to two different questions: As the prosecutor, what would you do? And: is your reasoning more contractarian or more utilitarian?

At this point, the learning activity is complete, and we can see that many of Parks' recommendations have been met. First, she suggested that attention be given to the students' orientation to authority by placing them in situations where they recognize competing claims from different sources. In our example, the students wrestled with the dictates of two rival theories, both of which seem logical and reasonable but which in fact lead to very different courses of action. Second, Parks urges that opportunities be provided for students to develop an "empathic imagination."[39] This no doubt occurred when the students were presented with "real-life" situations of domestic abuse and gay-bashing. Under the guidance of a skillful professor, the students would be able to look at the situation from the perspectives of the people involved in the two incidents and to reflect upon how they themselves would feel in those situations.

Third, Parks calls for students to have "opportunities for active, critical reflection" upon ethical dilemmas, "active collaboration," and the experience of being "active agents" in their own learning.[40] All of these have been achieved.

Fourth, Parks suggests that students be able to have "choice,"[41] and I would augment that word by saying students need to be asked to make commitments. The second Active Experimentation exercise is particularly powerful in that regard. Here the professor asked the students not what the *theories* would say they should do about the gay-bashing incident but what *they themselves* would do. Perry says that beyond the stage of systemic thinking is the stage of "Commitment."[42] Here a person has to stand aside from his or her experience, to consider alternatives, and to make a commitment, even in the absence of complete information.

Having the students say what they themselves would do is a form of Commitment (the word is capitalized to distinguish this action as something resulting from reflection and conscious choice, rather than less conscious "commitments"). Of course, for students to participate successfully in that process does not mean that they are now at this advanced stage. Rather, such exercises are *initial forays* towards higher stages. As we provide such opportunities for students, we are supporting them in their evolutionary journey (a Commitment on our part as faculty, by the way), no matter what stage the learners are in.

Beyond Parks' recommendations, some observations about the Kolb cycle itself indicate its usefulness as one example of teaching that supports students' movement through and beyond interpersonal thought. The example demonstrates systematic attention to engaging the students in the dialectical tension between the two ends of the vertical axis. Kolb uses the term "apprehension" to refer to the knowing that comes through Concrete Experience and "comprehension" to refer to the knowing that comes through Abstract Conceptualization. Apprehension occurs in the here-and-now, while comprehension is a "record of the past that seeks to define the future."[43] Apprehension is characterized by *appreciation*, an empathetic, believing stance, while comprehension is characterized by *criticism*, an analytic, detached, and skeptical posture that steps back from the here-and-now experience.

Apprehension is typically not taken seriously in education when compared to comprehension, which is based on a rationalist view of the world and is at the foundation of the scientific method. In response to the over-emphasis on rational knowing, Kolb argues that "knowledge and truth result not from the preeminence of one of these knowing modes over the other but from the intense *coequal* (emphasis added) confrontation of both modes."[44] In other words, education's emphasis on learning through abstractions (primarily through lecture and print) is misplaced. Genuine knowing comes about when learners are encouraged to honor information that is taken in not just through Abstract Conceptualization but through Concrete Experience as well. Thus Kolb has described what he calls a "dual-knowledge theory,"[45] one which places knowing through apprehension and knowing through comprehension on an equal footing.

The example also demonstrates attention to the two ends of the horizontal axis. Reflective Observation is significant, since "reflection on what we have done is a key tool for our own transformation."[46] Active Experimentation is vital also for, as Erikson has said, "Truth is found in action."[47] It is at this moment of action that students are clear as to what they do and do not understand, and thus significant learning can occur.

We should also note that the two rival theories were used by the professor to help the students "think about their thinking," as they reflect upon and apply the two theories. Although Cederblom and Spohn do not use that language, that is clearly what they had in mind when they said they wanted their students to see that if they favor settling on a misdemeanor charge (in the gay-bashing incident) in order to obtain a guilty plea, probably they are adopting a utilitarian strategy—choosing the option that produces the best results. On the other hand, if they view the prosecutor's role as involving an implicit agreement to bring the charge that is indicated by the evidence, and if they use this view as a basis for a felony charge, they should regard their approach as contractarian. Whichever way they are inclined initially, they will understand, on the basis of past discussions, the kinds of criticisms that can be brought against their approach.[48]

Thinking about thinking fuels development, and professors who provide opportunities for their students to do that are making a solid contribution to that end.

These comments about the Kolb cycle and Parks' recommendations are intended to demonstrate the kind of teaching in criminal justice ethics that can support students' development through and beyond interpersonal thought. But there is one other point to be made about the Kolb cycle, and it is presented as an overarching response to the question: What causes development?

Kolb states that development comes about through the "integration of dialectical adaptive modes."[49] He means that as we engage students systematically in the two sets of polar opposites depicted by the experiential learning cycle (Concrete Experience and Abstract Conceptualization on the vertical axis and Reflective Observation and Active Experimentation on the horizontal axis), we are helping them develop skills in integrating opposites that are fundamental to being a mature adult.

A story from press reports a few years ago makes the point. Renaldo Lenares, a 23-year-old house painter, burst into a hospital room in Chicago, held the nurses at bay with a gun, and reached over and pulled the plug on the respirator that was keeping his 11-month-old baby alive. Mr. Lenares was charged with a felony. In testifying in court, he said, "I had to do it. The doctors had told my wife and me our baby would never be well. I could not stand the thought of his living on a respirator. That's why I did what I did." The judge reduced the charge to a misdemeanor and said, "Mr. Lenares, I believe you have suffered enough."

Talking to reporters later, the Cook County Attorney General, Cecil Partee, said, "It was a complex and difficult case. From the point of view of the law, what Mr. Lenares did was wrong. But from the purview and perspective of a parent, it was understandable." In other words, both were right—and yet a decision still had to be made. According to Greek philosopher Heraclitus, "In the tension between the opposites, all things have their being." Kolb's summation is, "The process of learning that actualizes development requires a confrontation of the dialectical conflicts inherent" in the experiential learning cycle.[50]

The experiential learning cycle is not presented here as the single way to teach ethics. There are as many ways to teach as there are individual professors. But it does seem to be a useful lens through which faculty can examine their courses and ask some well-focused questions: Am I providing opportunities for transforming as well as prehending information? Do I truly believe students' direct experience is as important as the expert knowledge presented by the discipline? Do my assignments challenge students to reflect upon their own ethical values, and do I help them face what may be contradictions between what they say and what they do?

More fundamentally, the cycle invites us to examine our own values and attitudes as professors: Do I believe that learning is, at bottom, "an adventure in meaning making"?[51] Am I comfortable with genuine collaborative learning where "the teacher is a leader, but only as an equal member of a community of learners."[52] If criminal justice ethics education focuses clearly on the students' evolutionary journey, what challenge does that present to me about my own?

IMPLICATIONS FOR THE ACADEMIC UNIT

Those questions lead us into an examination of what all this means for the criminal justice faculty, individually and collectively. In reflecting on the criminal justice ethics course she teaches, Pollock-Byrne has said that she does not assume that one ethics class can be "a monumental force in the student's development; obviously, a fifteen week course (or shorter) is not going to be extremely influential on value systems or thinking of 20-30+ year-old individuals"?[53] What is needed if ethics education is to have a genuine impact is, to use Parks' phrase, "an ethically committed curriculum."[54] In such a curriculum, faculty would use their authority to *mentor* students.[55] Mentors are persons who

> possess the grace and strength to convey enormous respect for the emerging competence of the young adult, while simultaneously serving as a beacon that offers a compelling sense of direction in a complex and perilous world.[56]

But "just as a young adult can be mentored into a positive practice of social responsibility, a young adult also can be mentored into the Mafia."[57] What is needed is a *mentoring community*, a group of faculty working together to make available to students "images of interdependence, collaboration, and cooperation,"[58] not only in the courses they teach but in their own work environment.

That presents a daunting paradox, however. To be genuinely effective, criminal justice ethics education needs to be situated in an academic setting that has a sense of community. Yet colleges and universities are invariably characterized by a culture of individuality, rather than collective responsibility. For example, a friend was seeking a consultant for a university retreat designed to help the participants develop stronger skills in collaboration. My friend knew the consultant had done extensive work with other universities on this topic, and she asked if he had any major conclusions based on his experience. He paused a moment and then said: "Faculty don't want to collaborate. And they don't have to."

I think the day when we can say "we don't have to" is fast coming to an end. This is particularly true in criminal justice programs that wish to take seriously Parks' two-pronged challenge of an ethically committed curriculum and a mentoring community.

Community has been defined as "a group of people who have accepted and transcended their differences, so that they can communicate openly and work together effectively toward their common goal."[59] Competition and individualism are so much a part of higher education that we either paper over our differences or simply go our separate ways. We do very little, however, to try to accept our differences and transcend them.

How might a criminal justice faculty build genuine community in settings where it so fragile? Responding fully to that question is beyond the scope of the present paper, but I do have two recommendations, one a broad life stance faculty might consider and the other a specific action strategy.

An analysis by Haughey of the struggles of the former president of Czechoslovakia, Vaclav Havel, when he was in prison as a dissident, reveals an important insight that is relevant to this discussion. Havel had absolutely no power, but he described his spiritual struggle in letters to his wife which were later published as a book.[60] Haughey notes that

> [t]he issue of responsibility looms large in Havel's mature thought. He believes it was the evolving objects of his responsibility that brought him to God gradually over time. Responsibility is the thing that matures a person . . . There is no real identity unless and until one takes responsibility.[61]

Haughey's analysis of the governmental and economic system brought him to the conclusion that in the Czech republic, the problem at its core was a collective *denial of responsibility*. The government knew the system was not working, the industries producing goods knew it, the workers knew it, and so did the consumers. (The cynical joke among the workers was, "We pretend to work; they pretend to pay us.") Havel believed that change would come about only when a critical mass of people accepted responsibility: *for the self, for the other, and for the whole*.[62]

My own experience in higher education is that we as faculty typically take responsibility for ourselves. But we do little with respect to the other two levels. I would argue that there can be no ethically committed curriculum and no mentoring community in criminal justice programs unless faculty assume responsibility along the lines that Havel describes.

The action strategy I wish to present comes from Peter Senge, an expert in helping people build effective collaborative organizations. He has asked the question, "How can a team of committed (leaders) with individual IQs above 120 have a collective IQ of 63?"[63] He is pointing to the lack of skill most of us bring to genuine collaboration, whether it is in academic, business, or other settings. Although we may do good work individually, we often are much less competent when trying to function with others as a team.

He suggests that we can begin to deal with our differences if we understand their origin. In most of our conversations, we are frequently making a subtle effort to convince others to adopt our version of reality. We share our views and our opinions with others, but we do not discuss (often because we cannot remember ourselves) the *assumptions* on which those opinions are based. These assumptions come from our own unique experiences and meanings we have made of them (back to meaning making!). As a result, we spend a lot of our time talking past each other, thus contributing to the win-lose dynamic that characterizes much of our work life. This is particularly the case in colleges and universities on questions about which people feel strongly, for example, curriculum reform and the allocation of resources.

What we need to realize, Senge says, is that what we see as reality is just our version of it, our "mental model" of that particular issue. Mental models are

> the images, assumptions, and stories which we carry in our minds of ourselves, other people, institutions, and every aspect of the world. . . . Like a pane of glass framing and subtly distorting our vision, mental models determine what we see.[64]

Working with mental models can be a beginning point in accepting and transcending our differences. It involves "turning the mirror inward, unearthing our internal pictures of the world, bringing them to the surface, and holding them up for public scrutiny."[65] There are two types of skills we need for this work: "reflection (slowing down our thinking processes to become more aware of how we form our mental models) and inquiry (holding conversations where we openly share views and develop knowledge about each other's assumptions)."[66]

I believe that we can create community and an ethically committed curriculum only if we focus on fundamental questions about criminal justice ethics education and share with each other not only our views but also the assumptions on which they are based. This paper has attempted to make explicit some assumptions about aims, teaching, learning, and knowing. As such, it may be helpful to readers in their own process of surfacing and sharing mental models about criminal justice ethics education. As we support and challenge each other's thinking in this dialogic process, we can come closer to the goal of creating effective educational environments for the students we seek to serve.

APPENDIX

Comparing Educational Paradigms[67]

Instructional Paradigm	**Learning Paradigm**
Mission and Purposes	
1. Provide/deliver instruction.	Facilitate learning.
2. Transfer knowledge from faculty to students.	Elicits student construction of knowledge.
Criteria for Success	
3. Inputs, resources.	Learning outcomes.
4. Quality of faculty/instruction.	Quality of students, learning.
Teaching/Learning Structures	
5. Knowledge is atomistic.	Knowledge is holistic.
6. Independent disciplines.	Cross discipline, collaboration.

Learning Theory

7. Knowledge exists "out there."	Knowledge exists in each person's mind and is shaped by experience.
8. Knowledge comes in "chunks" and "bits" delivered by instructor.	Knowledge is constructed, created.
9. Knowing through abstractions and criticism is seen as the avenue to the truth.	Knowing through direct experience and appreciation, as well as knowing through abstractions and criticism, are honored.
10. The classroom is competitive and individualistic.	Learning environments are collaborative and supportive.

Nature of Roles

11. Faculty are primarily conveyors of learning.	Faculty are primarily facilitators of information.
12. Line governance; independent actors.	Shared governance; teamwork.

NOTES

1. Cited in C. Meyers, *Teaching Students to Think Critically: A Guide for Faculty in All Disciplines* (San Francisco: Jossey-Bass, 1988), p. 2.

2. Ibid.

3. See R. B. Barr and J. Tagg, "From Teaching to Learning: a New Paradigm for Undergraduate Education," *Change: The Magazine of Higher Learning* 27 (November/December 1995), p. 13.

4. See W. E. Doll, *A Post-modern Perspective on Curriculum* (New York: Teachers College Press, 1993).

5. See M. Belenky, B. M. Clinchy, R. Goldberger, and J. M. Tarule, *Women's Ways of Knowing: the Development of Self, Voice, and Mind* (New York: Basic Books, 1986); R. Kegan, *The Evolving Self: Problem and Process in Human Development* Cambridge, MA: Harvard University Press, 1982); idem, *In Over Our Heads: The Mental Demands of Modern Life* (Cambridge, MA: Harvard University Press, 1994); M. B. B. Magolda, *Knowing and Reasoning in College: Gender-related Patterns in Students' Intellectual Development* (San Francisco: Jossey-Bass, 1992).

6. J. G. Kurfiss, *Critical Thinking: Theory, Research, Practice, and Possibilities*, ASHE-ERIC Higher Education Report No. 2 (Washington, DC: ERIC Clearinghouse on Higher Education, 1988); Meyers, *Teaching Students to Think Critically.*

7. K. A. Bruffee, *Collaborative Learning: Higher Education, Interdependence, and the Authority of Knowledge* (Baltimore: The Johns Hopkins University Press, 1993).

8. E. Boyer, *Scholarship Reconsidered: Priorities of the Professoriate* (Princeton:

Carnegie Foundation for the Advancement of Teaching, 1990); K. P. Cross, "Teachers as Scholars," *AAHE Bulletin* 43 (December, 1990), pp. 3-5.

9. P. Hutchings and T. Marchese, "Watching Assessment: Questions, Stories, Prospects," *Change: The Magazine of Higher Learning* 22 (September/October 1990), pp. 12-38; T. W. Banta and Associates, *Making a Difference: Outcomes of a Decade of Assessment in Higher Education* (San Francisco: Jossey-Bass, 1993).

10. Kegan, *The Evolving Self.*

11. Cited in ibid., p. 11.

12. Ibid., p. 2.

13. Ibid., p. 4. The reference is to W. G. Perry, Jr., *Forms of Intellectual and Ethical Development in the College Years: A Scheme* (New York: Holt, Rinehart & Winston, 1970).

14. Kegan, *The Evolving Self,* pp. 9, 11.

15. S. Parks, "Is It Too Late? Young Adults and the Formation of Professional Ethics," in T. R. Piper, M. C. Gentile, and S. D. Parks, *Can Ethics Be Taught? Perspectives, Challenges, and Approaches at Harvard Business School* (Boston, MA: Harvard Business School, 1993), p. 21.

16. Ibid., p. 22.

17. Ibid.

18. Ibid.

19. Ibid.

20. D.A. Kolb, *Experiential Learning: Experience as the Source of Learning and Development* (Englewood Cliffs, NJ: Prentice-Hall, 1984).

21. Ibid., p. 38.

22. Ibid.

23. Bruffee, *Collaborative Learning.*

24. P.J. Palmer, "Community, Conflict, and Ways of Knowing: Ways to Deepen Our Educational Agenda," *Change: The Magazine of Higher Education* 19 (1987), p. 25.

25. Parks, "Is It Too Late?" pp. 49-50.

26. Ibid., p. 52.

27. Ibid., p. 54.

28. Ibid., p. 53.

29. Ibid.

30. Ibid., p. 54.

31. Ibid., p. 58.

32. Ibid.

33. Ibid.

34. J. Cederblom and C. Spohn, "A Model for Teaching Criminal Justice Ethics," *Journal of Criminal Justice Education* 2 (fall 1991), pp. 201-17.

35. Ibid., p. 206.

36. Ibid.

37. Ibid., p. 205.

38. Ibid., pp. 206-07.

39. Parks, "Is It Too Late?" p. 53.

40. Ibid., p. 58.

41. Ibid.

42. W. B. Perry, "Cognitive and Ethical Growth: the Making of Meaning," in A. W. Chickering, ed., *The Modern American College* (San Francisco: Jossey-Bass. 1981), p. 79.

43. Kolb, *Experiential Learning*, p. 102.

44. Ibid., p. 105.

45. Ibid., p. 100.

46. J. Dewey, cited in Doll, *A Post-modern Perspective on Curriculum*, p. 118.

47. E. H. Erikson, *Gandhi's Truth on the Origins of Militant Nonviolence* (New York: Norton, 1969), p. 27.

48. Cederblom and Spohn, "A Model for Teaching Criminal Justice Ethics," p. 207.

49. Kolb, *Experiential Learning*, p. 140.

50. Ibid., p. 134.

51. Doll, *A Post-modern Perspective on Curriculum*, p. xi.

52. Ibid.

53. J. Pollock-Byrne, *Ethics in Crime and Justice: Dilemmas and Decisions* (Belmont, CA: Wadsworth, 1988), p. 294.

54. Parks, "Is It Too Late?" p. 63.

55. Ibid., p. 62.

56. Ibid.

57. Ibid., p. 63.

58. Ibid.

59. The Foundation for Community, Brochure on a Community Building Workshop (Ridgefield, CT. 1996).

60. J. C. Haughey, "A Leader's Conscience: the Integrity and Spirituality of Vaclav Havel," in J. A. Conger and Associates, *Spirit at Work: Discovering the Spirituality in Leadership* (San Francisco: Jossey-Bass, 1994), pp. 41-62.

61. Ibid., p. 57.

62. Ibid., p. 61.

63. P. M. Senge, *The Fifth Discipline: The Art and Practice of the Learning Organization* (New York: Doubleday, 1990), p. 9.

64. P. M. Senge *et al.*, *The Fifth Discipline Fieldbook* (New York: Doubleday, 1994), p. 235.

65. Senge, *The Fifth Discipline*, p. 9.

66. Senge *et al.*, *The Fifth Discipline Fieldbook*, p. 237.

67. Adapted from Barr and Tagg, "From Teaching to Learning," pp. 16-17.

Response to Davis and Claxton: Teaching Police Ethics as Professional Ethics

Dorothy E. Roberts

Like Professor Davis, I too would like to focus on criminal justice ethics in its narrow sense—that is, as police ethics. I have chosen this focus because what intrigued me most about Professor Davis's paper was his treatment of police work as a profession and police ethics as a type of professional ethics.

Also like Professor Davis, I have never taught a class on criminal justice ethics or even attempted to design a course that would make police more ethical. Rather, my primary work relevant to this subject has involved advancing a critique of the way in which the criminal law and the criminal justice system have helped to perpetuate the subordination of blacks in America.[1] Police, of course, have been key players in this history. That role was recently highlighted by the unbridled racism in the L. A. Police Department that was brought to light during the O. J. Simpson trial.[2] Although city officials usually explain such incidents as isolated acts of a few "bad apples," these abuses of power arise from a deeply entrenched racism that pervades every mainstream American institution. Fatal beatings and chokeholds, although sporadic, are related to a far more common stance toward minority communities. In this sense, they are not at all idiosyncratic.

It is with this background as a criminal justice critic that I approach the question of police ethics and how to teach it. Because I believe that it is critical to address the *role* of police in enforcing an unjust social structure, I find Professor Davis's approach to police ethics particularly interesting and useful—although for reasons Davis may not have had in mind.

In "Teaching Police Ethics: What to Aim at?" Davis distinguishes morality from ethics.[3] Unlike morality that applies to everyone, ethics applies only to members of a particular group: ethics, he writes, refers to "those special, morally permissible standards of conduct every member of a group wants every other member of of that group to follow even if that would mean having to do the same."[4] So, *police* ethics applies only to *police*.

Having no formal training in police ethics, I am not sure what official police codes include in police ethics. But what readily comes to mind as a code of conduct that police agree to in the expectation that their fellow officers will comply? One element is the "blue wall" of silence—the rule that no cop should report bribery, drug dealing, physical abuse or other illegal conduct on the part of another officer. Another, at least according to Harvard Law professor Alan Dershowitz, is the understanding that police may fabricate, under oath, facts about arrests and evidence gathering in order to secure the conviction of a defendant they believe is guilty.[5] Yet another is the belief that police may lie to suspects in order to trick them into making a confession.[6] Or that police may take race into account in making a decision whether or not to stop a possible suspect.[7]

Some might argue that this code does not exist, that it is no more than the stuff of television cop shows. At least two of these practices—lying to suspects and taking race into account—are not kept secret at all; indeed, they have been upheld as constitutional by federal courts.[8] At any rate, in designing a course in police ethics one must take into account the probability that some students believe that these are standards that police may and should follow. Certainly many police officers (as well as citizens) believe that police are justified in taking these actions because of the demands of their job. Even Davis suggests that the blue wall of silence is real when he gives the example of taking bribes (which he says are clearly unethical), but then asks students "how you refuse a bribe without arousing the hostility of fellow officers who did not refuse."[9] This example presupposes that (a) some police officers do not refuse bribes, and (b) it is ethical for police officers to remain silent about certain illegal activity by their fellow officers.

These questionable police ethics raise an issue that Davis avoids in his paper: may police abide by ethical standards that are moral to them but would be immoral if followed by the rest of society? Does police ethics allow *exceptions* rather than additions to general morality? I say Davis avoids this question because his definition of police ethics views it as a *supplement* to general morality. Note that he refers to "special, *morally permissible* standards" that police officers share. In addition, Davis writes that to say police ethics applies only to police is to "deny that ordinary people are bound by whatever *additional* obligations police take on."[10] These statements, as well as the gist of his paper, imply that police ethics is in addition to general morality—that is, it must be at least permissible under standards of general morality. But the unwritten codes and Davis's question about bribery suggest that police operate under a set of standards considered morally permissible for police but not morally permissible for the general public.

This, in fact, is perhaps the most troublesome issue that arises from the notion of professional ethics. What is perplexing about professional ethics is not whether a profession may impose on its members ethical standards over and above what is morally permissible, but whether, by virtue of the profession, its members may follow a code that results in conduct that would be *immoral* outside the profession.

In case you think I am picking on police, let me hasten to point out that this question usually comes up in relation to lawyers. People often perceive lawyers as operating under their own ethical code, one that permits them to do things that would be impermissible by general moral standards. The public is not so concerned about rules that require lawyers to be *more* ethical than engineers and philosophers, such as the rule forbidding an attorney from commingling her client's money with her own. The public is concerned about rules that allow lawyers to be *less* ethical. In zealously representing a client, for example, lawyers often fail to reveal critical information to an adversary if the adversary fails to ask for it; or pretend that their client is willing to pay only a $1000 settlement when in fact the client will pay $10,000 if pushed hard enough; or destroy the credibility of a witness the lawyer knows is telling the truth. Lawyers defend these departures from the moral rules against lying and deception by pointing to the demands of their role in the adversary system. To take an example from another occupation, CEOs justify firing hundreds of employees with families to support on the ground that such merciless action is required by their duty to shareholders to maximize company profits.

This way of approaching ethics is sometimes called role morality or role theory. In "Role Obligations," Michael Hardimon explains the importance of the institutional dimension of the moral life—how political, familial, and occupational roles affect moral decision making.[11] He defines role obligation as "a moral requirement, which attaches to an institutional role, whose content is fixed by the function of the role, and whose normative force flows from the role."[12] The norms, in turn, give people who occupy roles reasons for acting: "When people identify with their roles they acquire reasons for carrying out the duties distinct from those deriving from the fact that they have signed on for them."[13] Role morality need not preempt ethical deliberation. What one is required to do as a police officer or lawyer is contested. Neither role morality nor common morality gives individuals definitive anwers to ethical dilemmas. In other words, role morality should not be seen as a way of abdicating responsibility for moral decision making.

The picture gets more complicated when role morality conflicts with common morality. Here, David Luban's critique of legal ethics, *Lawyers and Justice*, is helpful.[14] Luban argues that role morality—justifying action on the ground that "it's my job"—is never enough without examining the justification for the role in the first place. This requires a seven-step process, including identifying the institution, the role, and the role obligation; assessing each in light of the ends it serves; determining whether each is justified; and weighing the justification for the role act against the moral offense at performing it.[15] Needless to say, under such tough scrutiny it is hard to justify acting because of one's role. But it is not impossible.

So, I disagree somewhat with Davis when he says that "ethics . . . can no more be immoral than counterfeit money can be money."[16] People *can* give an ethical defense of their actions based on their role, even though these actions would be immoral if performed outside the role. This view of professional ethics also means that what Charles Claxton calls, in "Teaching and Learning in Criminal Justice Ethics," a false dichotomy between ethics at home and ethics at work may not be entirely artificial.[17]

For example, Davis argues that the phrase "torturers' ethics" should always wear scare quotes, presumably because, since torture violates general morality, the torturer cannot justify his actions using the ethical code of torturers.[18] This conclusion is explored in Arthur Applbaum's article, "Professional Detachment: The Executioner of Paris."[19] Applbaum imagines a dialogue between Charles-Henri Sanson, who tortured and beheaded criminals and enemies of the state both before and after the French Revolution, and one of his critics who contends that Sanson's conduct was immoral. Sanson defends his grisly actions on the ground that they were required by his profession as executioner for the state: "I am much less a hired blade than the surgeon or lawyer," Sanson argues.[20] Did Sanson's personal morality forbid him from killing in cases where his professional role demanded it? Or did his profession render ethical what personal morality disallowed?

To me, what is most important about Sanson's ethical dilemma is that its resolution requires an examination of the executioner's *role*, a role created and supported by French society. The character I found more morally wanting was not Sanson, but his critic, who questioned the executioner's morality while demanding that executions take place. Here lies what I see as the benefit of approaching ethical problems from the perspective of role morality. The value of role morality is not its handy excuse for professionals to be less ethical than the rest of us, but its call for the rest of us to question the role that we expect these professionals to perform. By creating and supporting the role of lawyer, police officer, and executioner, the public is ultimately responsible for the special ethical rules that these professionals espouse. I find this approach more honest than pretending that police officers and other "professionals" abide only by general moral precepts and not by ethical standards, encoded and unwritten, that flow from the nature of their jobs. Bringing professional roles into ethical deliberations can expose sloppy moral reasoning rather than covering it up.

If we are to view police ethics as a form of professional ethics, we must examine the role that police play in society. The role of the police with respect to the black community can be viewed as one of containment rather than one of protection. Feminists have raised similar concerns about police officers' role in perpetuating domestic violence, pointing to the long history of refusal to arrest men who had beaten their wives or girlfriends in their home. Taking these two points together—that professional ethics sometimes justifies departures from general morality based on the profession's role in society and that police have played an oppressive role in American society—gives a different perspective on the aim of teaching criminal justice ethics. These two concerns make it important to include in this education a critical examination of the role of police and how that role relates to police ethics. It would be a terrible mistake to teach a code of ethics that is justified by a repressive role or to pretend that such a code does not exist. I would endorse whichever method—pervasive or free-standing course or some combination of both—that best accomplishes this task.

This critical aim of police ethics education leads me to endorse Professor Claxton's view of learning as a creative, transformational process rather than as the simple transfer of knowledge. The learning paradigm is better suited than the instructional paradigm for looking critically at the role police play. Eliciting student construction of knowledge also has the advantage of allowing greater contributions by students, who are often more likely to be from minority communities than their professors.

I would push Claxton's perspective on learning a step further to incorporate the theories of radical educators, such as Paulo Freire, who advocated a pedagogy of liberation that rejects what he called the banking approach to education.[21] His model replaced the educational method of depositing information with posing problems concerning people in their relations with the world. This liberating pedagogy encourages students both to examine the historical roots of oppressive institutions and to imagine the implementation of new structures. Students are not docile listeners but are jointly responsible with teachers for a process in which they all grow. The crucial piece that Freire brings to the learning paradigm is his aim of getting students to critique oppression. Without this critical aim, the learning process might allow students simply to rationalize their own pre-conceived beliefs about police practices.

Now Freire's purpose was not to educate police officers. His aim was to give oppressed people a critical consciousness that would enable them to understand oppression as a historical reality that could be changed. Freire wanted to change the social order, whereas the role of police is to enforce the social order. What happens when students conclude that some ethical problems arise from the very role that police are called to perform? This conflict seems to support William Heffernan's point in "The Aims of Criminal Justice Education" that ethics courses are incapable of correcting police abuse.[22] Nevertheless, the importance of role morality in professional ethics means that criminal justice ethics professors should try to get students to think critically about the role that society calls police to serve.

NOTES

My thinking on the subjects of police ethics and role morality was greatly influenced by seminar readings and discussions during my fellowship at Harvard University's Program in Ethics and the Professions. I am very grateful to Dennis Thompson, Arthur Applbaum, and the other fellows (Solomon Benatar, Andrew Koppelman, Richard Pitbladdo, Walter Robinson, Marion Smiley, Larry Temkin, and Daniel Wikler) for the opportunity to explore professional ethics in such an illuminating way.

1. See, for example, Dorothy E. Roberts, "Crime, Race, and Reproduction," *Tulane Law Review* 67 (1993), pp. 1945-77; idem, "Punishing Drug Addicts Who Have Babies: Women of Color, Equality, and the Right of Privacy," *Harvard Law Review* 104 (1991), p. 1419.

2. Associated Press, "Mark Fuhrman Takes the Fifth," *Newsday* (April 30 1996), p. A32; Bill Miller, "Officers' Image Tarnished: Simpson Verdict Hightlights Mistrust of Police," *Washington Post* (October 5 1995), p. C1; Richard Price, "Simpson's Majority-Black Jury Hears Tape of Furhman's Slurs," *USA Today* (September 6 1995).

3. Michael Davis, "Teaching Police Ethics: What to Aim at?" in this volume, pp. 36-37.

4. Ibid., p. 37.

5. Anthony Flint, "Bratton Calls 'Testilying' by Police a Real Concern," *Boston*

Globe (November 15 1995), Metro/Region, p. 1. Cf. Dershowitz's "Rules of the Justice Game" in *The Best Defense* (New York: Vintage, 1983), pp. xxi-xxii.

6. Deborah Young, "Unnecessary Evil: Police Lying in Interrogations," *Connecticut Law Review* 28 (1996), pp. 425-26 ("Law enforcement officers lie to suspects, defendants and their attorneys to induce confessions."). See, for example, Illinois v. Perkins, 496 U.S. 292, at 299 (1990) (holding that "an undercover law enforcement officer posing as a fellow inmate need not give Miranda warnings to an incarcerated suspect before asking questions that may elicit an incriminating response"); Lewis v. United States, 74 F.2d 173 (9th Cir. 1934) (upholding confession obtained by police who falsely claimed to have a photograph showing the defendant's thumb print on the decedent's shoe and falsely stated that a witness had seen the defendant at the crime scene).

7. See, for example, United States v. Williams, 714 F.2d 777 (8th Cir. 1983) (upholding police officer's decision to detain two black women during a bank robbery investigation partly because of their presence in a predominantly white neighborhood).

8. See notes 6 and 7 above.

9. Davis, "Teaching Police Ethics," p. 45.

10. Ibid., p. 38 (emphasis added).

11. Michael O. Hardimon, "Role Obligations," *Journal of Philosophy* 91 (July 1994), pp. 333-63.

12. Ibid., p. 334.

13. Ibid., p. 360.

14. David Luban, *Lawyers and Justice: An Ethical Study* (Princeton, NJ: Princeton University Press, 1988).

15. Ibid., pp. 128-47.

16. Davis, "Teaching Police Ethics," p. 38.

17. Charles S. Claxton, "Teaching and Learning in Criminal Justice Ethics," in this volume, p. 62.

18. Davis, "Teaching Police Ethics," p. 38.

19. Arthur Isak Applbaum, "Professional Detachment: The Executioner of Paris," *Harvard Law Review* 109 (1995), p. 458.

20. Ibid., p. 474.

21. See Paulo Freire, *Pedagogy of the Oppressed*, trans. Myra B. Ramos (New York: Herder & Herder, 1970).

22. William C. Heffernan, "The Aims of Criminal Justice Education," in this volume, p. 11.

PART II

Integrating Criminal Justice Ethics into the Curriculum

Chapter 3

I. Teaching Criminal Justice Ethics: Freestanding, Pervasive, and Combined Approaches[1]

Joan C. Callahan

INTRODUCTION

As Deborah Rhode has pointed out, until recently it has been the conventional view among professional school faculty that the teaching of ethics in professional practice is someone else's responsibility.[2] However, a new study conducted by The Institute for Criminal Justice Ethics at John Jay College of Criminal Justice suggests that criminal justice programs at the undergraduate and graduate levels are increasingly including ethics teaching in their curricula.[3] In this paper, I want to address some questions raised by the incorporation of ethics teaching into criminal justice curricula. In particular, I want to ask whether such teaching might be done more effectively using freestanding approaches rather than a purely pervasive approach—that is, by devoting full courses to ethics in criminal justice, as opposed to approaches which do no more than incorporate it into other courses in the curriculum.[4] I will suggest that freestanding approaches are to be preferred, though I will also suggest that an approach which combines freestanding and pervasive methods will be maximally useful for ethics education in criminal justice curricula.

FROM THE "APPLIED" TO THE PRACTICAL

I approach the question of teaching criminal justice ethics as a philosopher whose main area of interest has always been in so-called applied ethics, despite its bad reputation among some of my colleagues in academic philosophy. I have always found their disdain for applied ethics puzzling because many of the canonical figures in moral theory were concerned to address moral questions that were raised by the ideologies and practices of their times. Immanuel Kant, for example, was concerned to secure reliability for moral judgments in a Newtonian world. And Jeremy Bentham and John Stuart Mill were committed to changing a number of the social attitudes and practices of nineteenth-century British society. Even Plato had "applied" worries about the social effects of the teaching of the sophists. And Plato, like all political philosophers since, intended that his political theory have practical application to the construction of public policy. Given the history of moral philosophy, it is odd, at best, that applied ethics is often questioned as a properly philosophical enterprise.

Perhaps the problem is simply a stubborn residuum of moral philosophy's brush with logical positivism. More likely, the cause is some combination of that encounter and the misapprehension that follows from the term "applied ethics" itself, which suggests that doing this kind of ethics merely involves taking general moral theories and applying them to various questions of current societal concern. This model takes "applied ethics" to ask what, for example, Kant's theory or Mill's theory might have to say about the morality of elective abortion, or what Aristotle's theory might have to say about the morality of using certain drugs. Because of this (and despite the fact that linguistic habits die hard), I am going to use the term "practical ethics" for the kind of ethical inquiry that takes as its direct concern the resolution of concrete morally problematic cases and issues of moral urgency in the lived world. Criminal justice ethics falls within the category of what I am now calling practical ethics, and the first suggestion I want to make is that criminal justice ethics teaching should unapologetically adopt a practical focus, using formal moral theory only when this is likely to help with that practical focus. Let me clarify.

Although practical ethics borrows insights from theories of moral axiology (that is, theories of the morally good and evil), theories of moral obligation (that is, theories regarding what is morally permissible, morally required, and morally impermissible) and from metaethics (that is, theories focusing on the meaning of moral terms, the nature of moral discourse, and the justification of moral claims), the task of practical ethics is not simply to work out applications of existing ethical theories. It is, rather, to seek acceptable resolutions for moral problems of present and practical urgency. This involves much more than merely doing some sort of philosophical technology in which high-level theory is simply brought over to practice. When done well, the questions that are addressed in practical ethics continually raise important theoretical and methodological questions for general theories of the morally good and right, and for metaethics. For example, questions pertaining to the securing of adequately informed and voluntary consent to medical or surgical interventions by those in police custody raise a number of significant theoretical questions about what it means for *any* choice to be rational and genuinely voluntary, as well as interesting questions about the relations between the actions of criminal justice professionals and the generation of special duties of care toward those in their custody. Similarly, questions in professional ethics regarding the distribution of certain goods and services (such as legal services) raise deep questions regarding basic human goods and the possibility of maximizing the potential of characteristically human lives in a legally complex society. These questions are continuous with those raised in theoretical ethics. Nevertheless, engaging in and teaching practical ethics differs in some important ways from attempting to construct a full and general moral theory or from teaching moral theory as such. Specifically, there are differences in the content of the questions asked, and in the focus, goals, and methods of practical ethics engagement and teaching.

CONTENT AND FOCUS IN PRACTICAL ETHICS ENGAGEMENT AND TEACHING

Although, historically, moral philosophers generally have been motivated to do their work by a concern with the practical moral questions of their times, the focus of moral theory is on just what the term suggests, moral *theory*. One might teach an excellent course on moral theory, or write an excellent book on moral theory, and yet never discuss any practical moral problems. For example, in a moral theory course, one might concentrate on the nature of different theories of moral obligation, such as Kant's and Mill's, focusing on the relative merits of *a priori* and empirical theories, and ask which type of theory is more likely to yield certainty in morality. In the same course, one might spend considerable time examining Mill's purported "proof" of the principle of utility and/or the purported equivalence of Kant's three formulations of the categorical imperative, and/or the logical differences between W.D. Ross's intuitionism and the intuitionism found in John Rawls's method of reflective equilibrium or in Thomas Nagel's pluralism. Alternatively, one might focus a moral theory course on questions having to do with the very nature of moral discourse or the analysis of moral terms or whether free action is logically or empirically possible. In short, concrete normative issues might never be addressed in a moral theory course, and this, of itself, would have nothing whatever to do with the appropriateness of the course's content or the value of the course.

Matters are different when it comes to engaging in and teaching practical ethics, in which the morally problematic issues of some "form or forms of life" (more or less broadly construed) direct focus and teaching content. In principle, good practical ethics teaching need never concern itself with the finer points of theories from the history of moral philosophy. Indeed, never even mentioning Aristotle, Kant, Mill, Rawls, or any other moral theorist included in the familiar canon of classical and contemporary moral theorists says nothing in itself about the quality of a practical ethics course. In much the same way, moral agents engaging in practical ethics need not appeal to the history of moral theory to accomplish the work proper to practical ethics.[5]

GOALS OF PRACTICAL ETHICS TEACHING

The differences in content and focus in moral theory and practical ethics provide some clues as to how goals in these forms of reflection and in the teaching of these forms of reflection might differ. A legitimate goal in the study of and engagement in moral theory construction might consist in acquainting oneself with one branch of the history of philosophy or one branch of systematic philosophy as a matter of purely intellectual interest, much as an academic approach to religious studies might focus on the understanding of certain religious traditions as a way of deepening one's appreciation of a culture's heritage. That is, a study of moral theory need not concern itself with resolving any real-life moral dilemmas, any more than studying a religious tradition needs to concern itself with resolving theological dilemmas. Genuine engagement in practical ethics, on the other hand, eschews neutrality with regard to the resolution of concrete, morally problematic questions because practical ethics takes such questions as its proximate concern. This concern expresses itself in several projects that need to be pursued in practical ethics reflection and teaching.

1 *The recognition of moral issues.* A first step in practical ethics is the development of skill in recognizing moral issues. Issues having a moral content are characterizable as those that involve the rights and/or welfare

of persons (and/or other sentient beings), the character of the acting agent, the flourishing of relationships and communities, and/or special obligations that attach to special roles. Being able to recognize such issues where they often go unnoticed is crucial. In bio-medical ethics, for example, it is important to see that not all decisions commonly made by health-care providers are medical ones and that providers sometimes inadvertently overstep the bounds of their authority and expertise by making important value judgments for patients. Such decisions might include a physician's electing to treat aggressively a severely damaged infant—a judgment that might be presented to the child's parents as a medical one, but is one that involves a moral judgment which might not be the physician's to make. Similarly, seeing that some rather standard behaviors in the practice of, say, law are manipulative or even coercive is to be aware of morally crucial dimensions of conventional, unreflective action, or practice. Thus, an important first project when engaging in practical ethics is a kind of consciousness raising that enlivens one to the moral complexity of the world. In criminal justice ethics teaching, a large part of the project will be to awaken students to the presence of moral issues where they may not have noticed them.

2 *Development of the moral imagination.* Closely connected to the task of developing skill in the recognition of moral issues is the task of developing the moral imagination. As elementary as it may seem, we are often unaware that our attitudes toward (or indifference to) what is morally acceptable and what is not can be manifested in actions or failures to act that can have serious effects on the rights and well being of other individuals, as well as on the various communities to which we belong.[6] Thus, for example, people who are not enlivened to the fact that certain public or institutional policies or professional practices or common attitudes are oppressive to women, or to members of certain minorities, or to persons generally, may support those policies, practices, and/or attitudes or miss opportunities to oppose them. Such enlivening often requires nurturing the capacity to imagine what it feels like to be a person directly affected by a certain practice, policy, or attitude. Genuine understanding of, say, the position of persons in extremely poor neighborhoods requires that one be able to imagine oneself in the place of people who often are profoundly pessimistic about the opportunities they believe they have for moving out of poverty. To feel disadvantaged from the outset because of one's economic status (which, in the United States, is very often linked to ethnic or racial status) can produce a kind of "innate" discouragement and cynicism that those with different socioeconomic backgrounds will have never

experienced. Thus, being able to imagine, as if they were one's own, the experiences of people affected day in and day out by, say, crushing poverty or racism may be crucial for a police officer's ability to be an effective peacekeeper or otherwise helpful intervener in certain sorts of conflicts.

Similarly, understanding why it is morally problematic to conduct biomedical experiments on prisoners may require that one is able to imagine what life in prison is like and how seductive various benefits of participating in experiments can be—breaks from routine, a little money, some extra attention in the infirmary—and how this raises serious worries about prisoners giving genuinely informed consent to participation in such experiments. Or being able to imagine what it is like to be a member of a hated minority might help a judge to understand why, for example, a law prohibiting homosexual interaction strikes so deeply at the core self of many persons in this society.[7] Developing moral imagination is closely related to the skill of recognizing moral problems, since in using a well-developed moral imagination we often see moral issues (perhaps particularly issues of exclusion or marginalization) where we had not noticed them before.

3 *The sharpening of analytical/critical skills.* At least two other tasks of practical ethics are connected to the issue of moral relativism. Some of us are extremely reluctant to call *any* action or practice or attitude morally wrong. To be sure, calling another person's action or attitude morally wrong does amount to a strong and important claim. And establishing exact criteria for determining moral rightness and wrongness has eluded moral philosophers for centuries. Aware of the hazards of moral evaluation, we often do not want to "pass judgment"—we want to be careful about condemning the actions of other persons, the practices of other societies, and practices in earlier stages of our own society. We want to be "tolerant" of differences, and this is a good thing. But when "tolerance" becomes so extreme that we are left morally resourceless, the virtue of tolerance swells into its excess and anything can become permissible.

One of the goals of thoughtful engagement in practical ethics and practical ethics teaching is to help reveal that even though moral questions are difficult, we can go a long way before we need to say, "Well, we just disagree on our fundamental moral commitments." By honing analytical skills, we can come to see that we share a large common moral ground that can be defended on the basis of reasonable moral principles, and that common ground can provide us with reasons for ruling out certain kinds of actions and practices as morally unacceptable. This is not to suggest, of course, that morally aware, imaginative, and reasonable persons will always agree on how morally problematic cases and issues are to be decided. But it is to suggest that careful reflection on what might initially seem to be an utterly unresolvable case or issue will often reveal that some potential resolutions are not consistent with moral principles to which disputants are committed, or that what was initially thought to be a case or issue requiring some substantive resolution might be given a procedural resolution. For example, in some cases careful reflection might reveal that the question to be resolved is not *what should be done,* but rather *who should decide* what should be done. Thus, sharpening analytical skills can help to rule out certain potential resolutions that initially might seem acceptable, and it can help with the engendering and consideration of potential resolutions that were not initially apparent.

4 *The sorting out of disagreements.* Hard moral questions *are* hard because they tend to leave residues of disagreement among even the most sensitive and astute moral agents. No matter how refined one's analytical skills become, such residua will tend to remain. It is here that tolerance in ethics has its proper place. Among the chief tasks in practical ethics is the two-fold task of learning not only to put *oneself* in the position of others, but learning to put oneself in the position of *others.* That is, part of the task is to realize that there are legitimately differing ways of ordering values and that some differences in value judgment are inevitable and acceptable. This is crucial to remember when decisions will affect people in social locations very different from that of the decision maker; and it is crucial to remember when decisions need to be made collectively.

In such cases, it is important to (a) encourage others to express their moral misgivings about proposed resolutions to morally dilemmatic cases and issues, (b) sort out disagreements that are morally reasonable from those that are not, and (c) work toward acceptable moral closure despite some residual disagreement. Indeed, decisions often will need to be made despite serious and morally responsible disagreements among disputants; and decisions often will have to be made by someone who is ambivalent about the options she or he faces. Helping students to get clear on what obstacles to decisions can be set aside or given a relatively low priority in a particular kind of case is a crucial task in practical ethics teaching.

5 *The influencing of decisions and behavior.* The reluctance of some philosophers to allow the influencing of decision making and behavior as a legitimate goal of reflection in ethics strikes me as odd, at best; it is reminiscent of the unwillingness of moral philosophers earlier in this century to address any normative questions whatever. If practical ethics is

worth doing and worth doing well, it is precisely because doing practical ethics holds out the promise of affecting individual behavior, public policy, the commitments of professions, and so on, in a morally positive way. Indeed, the main difference between studying ethical theory and engaging in practical ethics lies in the latter's goal of contributing directly and immediately to attitudes, behavior, and policy creation in a way that is reflective, well-reasoned, intellectually responsible, and morally sensitive.

IMPLEMENTATION: CLOSURE AND PROCESS

If we accept the goals sketched above as proper to practical ethics, what kinds of problems might be expected in pursuing them, and what strategies might we adopt to avoid these problems?

One problem has already been mentioned—the problem of hasty relativism. Given the pluralism of our society, the desire to be "tolerant," and the very real problems that intrapersonal and intrasocietal disagreements about morality raise, the temptation to retreat into a relativism or subjectivism where everything is permitted, or a simple pragmatism—that is, a view that morality is one thing, getting through life is another—can be pervasive and strong. But such retreats make moral reflection irrelevant because they are really failures to attempt to come to moral closure in the face of moral pluralism and moral complications. A theory of retreat from morality cannot possibly serve as an adequate moral theory. But tolerance and taking pluralism seriously are certainly consistent with responsible moral reflection which works toward moral closure. "Closure" is the *resolution* of a moral dilemma or debate—a resolution that is supported by the best reasons available and recognized by the disputants as a morally responsible solution that takes seriously the positions of those who may still disagree. That is, when there is serious moral disagreement, the task is to search for a decision that everyone involved can "live with," even though not everyone might agree that the solution is ideal. When coming to closure is difficult, the reasons for failure to come to closure can be explored. Is the remaining disagreement one that can be well defended? If not, why not? If so, can anyone offer a solution that avoids the problem(s) that gave rise to the disagreement? If not, given that a decision *must* be made, what can be done or decided to ensure that the least morally-problematic decision is made? Pressing for closure by asking such questions can help disputants to discover the moral ground that they share and can lead to considerable confidence in decisions made after responding to such questions.

In the moral realm, we often labor under conditions of uncertainty. This can be the case whether we are trying to make a hard moral decision alone or with others. Because of the intrinsic uncertainty that commonly attends moral problems, often the best that can be done is to follow a decision procedure that is careful to take into account the morally relevant considerations that support competing resolutions to a case or issue. Although we may never enjoy complete certainty about our decisions in morally hard cases, we can enjoy confidence in the procedures we use to make such decisions. One procedure that I have found helpful in practical ethics teaching is included as an Appendix to this paper.

Given the objectives and the suggested procedures I have outlined above and in the Appendix, it remains to be asked whether these objectives can best be served and whether these procedures can best be employed in freestanding ethics courses, in pure pervasive approaches, or in using some combination of both approaches.

THE BENEFITS OF FREESTANDING APPROACHES

Thinking systematically about ethics is, frankly, new to most college students and more often than not is also new to most graduate students. Because this sort of thinking is often so different from the kinds of thinking students have been asked to do, it is very unlikely that much progress can be made in helping students become adept in practical ethics if they have not had a somewhat protracted exposure to dealing with moral issues in a systematic way. This tells in favor of freestanding courses.

Further, my own experience tells me that it takes students (at both the undergraduate and graduate levels) a while to get through some of their initial skepticism about doing ethics at all, and then a while longer still to begin to make reliable the analytic skills that are called into play in careful thinking about moral issues. This, too, indicates a need for freestanding courses.

What is more, when ethics is relegated to "all" or "most" courses, one or more of at least three things is likely to happen. First, we convey to our students the view that ethics is not really important because we tell them what is important not only by what we include on our required course lists, but equally by what we exclude. This has become a kind of truism, but it cannot be overemphasized. Critical legal theorists, feminists, and critical race theorists (to name only some of the contemporary critics) have helped us to see how systematically we marginalize those who do not match the norms embodied in those of the dominant social groups. In the same way, we marginalize subject matters that have not been taken seriously by those in the dominant groups in our colleges and universities. Failure to establish courses that take morality as their focus continues the marginalization of ethics in all forms of professional education, including the criminal justice professions.

Second, courses often run short of time, and topics not considered crucial to the substantive subject matter are the first to be let go. Leaving the whole of ethics education to the beneficence and competence in time management of already-overburdened faculty puts ethics education on fragile feet. If we are genuinely concerned about ethics education, curriculum administrators need to be sure that there is time in the formal curriculum to focus on it.

Finally, leaving ethics education up to everyone not only runs the risk of its becoming no one's responsibility but also runs the risk of having ethics education done very, very poorly. Even if we assume that our criminal justice faculties always and everywhere comprise morally astute individuals (which, of course, they do not), good ethics teaching, like good teaching in any subject matter, requires certain developed skills. It may well be the case that everyone is capable of contributing something to ethics teaching in the criminal justice curriculum; but to expect faculty with expertise in other areas to assume full responsibility for making themselves sufficiently qualified in ethics teaching to carry the *whole* of that responsibility is, frankly, unfair and (again) it invites poor teaching in the area.

I want to suggest, then, that criminal justice programs should institute freestanding courses devoted to a systematic consideration of ethical issues in the administration of criminal justice. I also want to suggest that these courses be taught by individuals who have ethics as a primary teaching and research focus. Further, I want to suggest that these courses be taught in such a way that they will enroll students from across the criminal justice curriculum. A cross section of students in these courses *greatly* enhances the possibility that students will hear things from their peers that they might not expect to hear—things that will push them to consider as deeply as possible alternative approaches to morally problematic issues and cases in their areas of specialization.

LIMITATIONS OF FREESTANDING APPROACHES: MOVING TO COMBINED CONTINUING APPROACHES

Does all of this mean that pervasive approaches to criminal justice ethics teaching are to be completely avoided? I certainly do not think so. One of the main problems with freestanding approaches is that it is difficult to know when courses devoted to ethics should be taught in the curriculum. If a course is taken too early, students may not have sufficient experience to take full benefit from the course. But if it is not taken early, students may "get the message" early on that ethics is something that can be put off until later—that there is no need to look at the moral dimensions of what they study prior to their ethics course. And, of course, if such a course is taken at the end of a curriculum, that message is all the more forceful. How might such limitations to freestanding approaches be overcome?

I believe that Samuel Gorovitz had the right idea some years ago when he suggested that medical schools should adopt what he called an "intermittent" method for health care ethics teaching.[8] Gorovitz's concern was physician education; but his reasons for "prescribing" a continuing method for doctors in training apply every bit as fully to criminal justice professionals in training. Gorovitz realized that a "single dose" at the beginning of professional education is usually too small and dilute to form the reflectiveness and habits of mind and heart necessary for responsible moral decision making in professional life. At same time, a "single dose" at the end of a professional education curriculum lets pass too many opportunities for needed, careful moral reflection. Gorovitz argued, too, that what I am calling the pure pervasive method is both likely to fail and is unfair to faculty. And so he suggested that

> [s]tudents should be sensitized to the reality and importance of ethical issues as early as possible in their [professional] training. And surely at the end, before they go . . . , there should be another systematic exploration, linked to the . . . experiences they will have [had]. Along the way there should be some thread of continuity—structuring and guiding the reflections that the students bring to bear on ethical matters. Only if the students' exposure to ethical reflection is a continuing presence in their consciousness will this result be achieved.[9]

I agree. The challenges of the combined continuing approach, however, are considerable.

First, it asks for an application of the freestanding approach (minimally) at both the beginning and the end of the professional curriculum. This means making time in curricula that are already perceived by curriculum administrators to be stretched to the limit. Thus, administrators are not likely to be enthusiastic about adding one or two or more courses, even if they are short courses (which I do not think they should be).

Second, the combined continuing approach calls for consistent attention to moral issues as students move through their curricula. I have already mentioned several problems with the pure pervasive approach that re-enter here in the combined continuing approach. How might these two significant problems be addressed?

Regarding extra courses in the curricula: As long as I can remember, the time expectations attached to professional curricula have not changed. Law school is still three years; medical school is still four years, as is college. This strikes me as curious, given the continuing growth of knowledge in every area of study. When professional schools and professional preparation programs are attached to universities, their administrators are notorious for contending that their programs cannot fit in one more college or university-studies requirement. And they certainly know that their curricula cannot accommodate one, let alone two or more courses in ethics. This, however, does not strike me as a problem with ethics courses, but as a problem with the existing time limits on program completion. Why not add a year to our professional programs?[10] With more time, professional school education could be accomplished more humanely. Today, many, and perhaps even most, students in the United States need to work at a paid job while they are in school, and this includes students in graduate programs who have teaching or research assistantships. Given packed curricula, students who need to work extra hours are under tremendous stress. Some relief of that stress could substantially improve the educational experience and, at the same time, help to make students more invested in dealing with hard questions in professional ethics during their school years.

Adding more time to a curriculum also makes it possible to adopt that feature of the pervasive method that is most attractive, namely, the way it keeps the ethical dimensions of professional life in continual focus. Course time for "mainstreaming" ethics teaching could be guaranteed; and with a less compacted curriculum, it would be more reasonable to ask faculty to participate in ethics teaching education themselves, and thereby help to ensure that ethics teaching done throughout courses in criminal justice curricula would be quality teaching. Further assurance that the ethics components of courses would not be dropped out could be secured by helping faculty to *weave* ethics teaching into all or most of the courses in a curriculum, rather than "tagging" it to a section on ethics in other subject courses, a procedure that allows it to be "lopped off" relatively easily.

CONCLUSION

To sum up: Freestanding approaches to ethics teaching in criminal justice curricula are superior to pure pervasive approaches, since freestanding approaches are necessary for the focused, systematic work that needs to be done in quality ethics teaching. On the other hand, there are important benefits to pervasive approaches that freestanding approaches cannot provide, and these should be brought into the teaching of criminal justice ethics. Of particular importance is the keeping of ethical issues consistently before students. Combined continuing approaches capture the best features of both freestanding and pervasive methods, while avoiding the major problems that beset each of these approaches when it is used alone. The primary drawback of combined continuing approaches is that they require more substantial curriculum time than either of the other approaches taken alone. I have suggested that the most promising way to deal with this problem is to add more time than is currently expected for completion of a criminal justice program, whether that be an undergraduate major or a professional school degree. This, of course, is unlikely to be a popular proposal. But nothing follows from that; and it is time that we seriously consider making structural changes in professional education that are long overdue.

APPENDIX: A DECISION PROCEDURE FOR MORALLY HARD CASES[11]

1 *Set out the various possible resolutions of the case.* Be sure to tax your imagination. The case may admit of more alternatives than are initially obvious.

2 *Set out the facts relevant to supporting each resolution you have identified.* Generate as complete a set of lists as possible of the *facts* (known, possible, probable) that might be used to support *each* of the options you have identified as possible resolutions of the case. Relevant facts might include: someone will be or is likely to be harmed (physically, emotionally, financially, in reputation, and so forth) if a particular course is chosen; limited resources expended in one way could be expended in another way, to meet some (other) pressing need; one decision will interfere with the liberty of an individual; a proposed resolution would involve coercion, deception, manipulation, breach of trust, keeping a promise, breaking a promise, exploitation, unequal treatment, and so on.

3 *Set out the moral principles that underpin the selection of the facts on your lists.* That is, each fact you identify as supportive of a possible resolution will be relevant by virtue of some underlying moral principle. Articulate these principles clearly. Relevant principles might include: Prevent harm; Do good; Be fair; Be loyal; Keep your promises; Do not inflict harm on other persons/sentient beings; Maintain integrity; Be candid; Live up to the requirements of your office or role; It is permissible to protect one's

own interests; Respect the liberty/autonomy of persons; Contribute to the flourishing of relationships or this community or that one; and so on. Combining these principles with the relevant facts you have selected will provide moral arguments for the possible resolutions you have identified.

So, for example, an argument from your lists of facts and principles supporting some option (call it "Option A") might look like this:

Premise 1, Principle:	Keep promises
Premise 2, Fact:	Doing X, which will be done if Option A is selected, involves keeping a promise
Conclusion:	Choose Option A

4 *Reflect on the options you have identified and on your lists of facts and principles.* Ask yourself (again) if you have included all potentially acceptable options and if the lists of facts and the principles that led you to select those facts as supportive of the options you have identified include *all* the plausible arguments for each of the alternatives you have identified. Are the lists of facts and principles that support the view you are inclined to take longer than your other lists? If so, *be sure* that you have been as thorough as possible in laying out the facts and principles supportive of the resolutions that differ from the one you are inclined to favor.

5 *Make and articulate your decision.* After careful consideration of the options you have identified and the arguments supporting each of those options that you have identified, select the option you think is the most acceptable.

6 *Justify your decision.* Set out your *positive* reasons for the decision you have made. This will take you back to your lists. Make explicit which considerations on your lists of facts and principles you found the most compelling.

7 *Anticipate and respond to the most serious potential objection to your decision.* Go back to the lists supporting the option(s) other than the one you have chosen. Use these lists to help you clarify what you take to be the strongest potential objection to your position or to the positive argument you made for your decision. What is your reply to that objection? Given your reply, is it reasonable to believe that a proponent of that objection could be brought to appreciate the preferability of the resolution you support?

8 *Clarify the costs or downside of your decision.* Go back to your lists a final time and use them to help you articulate what you take to be the most morally significant cost(s) associated with your decision. (This may be related to what you take to be the strongest potential objection to your decision.)

A procedure incorporating such steps goes a long way toward fulfilling the goals that are suggested in this paper as proper to engagement in practical ethics, which is direct engagement with the hard moral questions that inevitably challenge us all in the lived world of moral responsibility.[12]

NOTES

1. Portions of this paper have been adapted with permission from Joan C. Callahan "'Applied' Ethics," in *The Blackwell Dictionary of Business Ethics*, within *The Blackwell Encyclopedia of Management*, ed. R. Edward Freeman and Patricia H. Werhane (Cambridge, MA: Basil Blackwell, forthcoming); Joan C. Callahan, "From the 'Applied' to the Practical: Teaching Ethics for Use," *American Philosophical Association Newsletter on Teaching Philosophy* 90, 1 (1990), pp. 29-34; and Joan C. Callahan and Patricia Smith, "Liberalism, Communitarianism, and Feminism," in *Liberalism and Community*, ed. Noel Reynolds, Cornelius Murphy, and Robert Moffat (NY: New York University Press, forthcoming).

2. Deborah Rhode, "Professional Ethics and Professional Education," *Professional Ethics: A Multidisciplinary Journal* 1, 1&2 (spring/summer 1992), pp. 31-72, esp. p. 31.

3. Margaret Leland Smith, "The Teaching of Criminal Justice Ethics: A National Survey," in this volume, Appendix I.

4. There is some confusion in the language that is used to discuss the incorporation of ethics teaching in courses with other subject matter. Specifically, "the pervasive method" is sometimes used to refer to ethics teaching that is done exclusively in other subject matter courses, and it is sometimes used to refer to ethics teaching that is done in all courses, *as well as* in one or more freestanding courses. For example, Deborah Rhode moves between these two meanings of the term in "Professional Ethics and Professional Education," and in the Preface to *Professional Responsibility: Ethics by the Pervasive Method* (Boston: Little, Brown and Company, 1994), pp. xxix-xxxi. (See also David T. Link, "The Pervasive Method of Teaching Ethics," 39 *Journal of Legal Education* 4 [1989], pp. 485-89.) In order to avoid confusion, I shall use the term "pure pervasive" method or approach to refer to ethics teaching that does not involve freestanding courses, and the term "combined continuing" method or approach to refer to ethics teaching that combines pervasive and freestanding approaches.

5. Nevertheless, given that the classical moral theorists were often motivated by practical concerns, teachers of practical ethics will quite likely find their works a valuable resource.

6. I leave aside here the question of whether failures to act can count as causes of events or states of affairs, even though this is an intriguing question.

7. See, for example, Lynn Henderson, "Legality and Empathy," *Michigan Law Review* 85 (1987), p. 10. Henderson argues that the legal community is mistaken in conceptually opposing legality to empathy. Contrary to the traditional view that legality or judicial decision making must proceed by means of "cool, detached reason, devoid of emotional appeals," Henderson shows that some legal decisions are best understood and explained as a manifestation or lack of empathetic understanding. Using cases such as *Brown v. Board of Education* (ending segrega-

tion) and *Bowers v. Hardwick* (upholding sodomy laws), Henderson illustrates her contention that not only are appeals to emotion standard fare in legal argumentation, but also that the use of "empathetic narrative" (the telling of a client's story) is an integral part of good legal representation. In discussing *Brown* and *Bowers*, Henderson shows how the ability of a judge or jury to empathize enhances rather than diminishes knowledge regarding the circumstances of a given case. Thus, she points out, it was because the judges in *Brown* were able to empathize with and thus understand the position of black children, that they were able to make a decision in favor of the plaintiff. Just the opposite happened in *Bowers*, however. Here, says Henderson, the inability of the judges to achieve an empathetic understanding of the position of sexual minorities in a highly heterosexualized culture explains the judges' denial of support for their claim to protection.

8. Samuel A. Gorovitz, *Doctors' Dilemmas: Moral Conflict and Medical Care* (New York: Macmillan, 1982; reissued New York: Oxford University Press, 1985).

9. Ibid., p. 204.

10. Another alternative might be to add full summer sessions. However, I would not want to see ethics courses relegated to summer sessions, since this might suggest that they are not as important as academic-year courses. Summer scheduling of courses traditionally central to a curriculum does not raise the same concern about marginalization.

11. Adapted with permission from Joan C. Callahan, "From the 'Applied' to the Practical: Teaching Ethics for Use," and Joan C. Callahan, ed., *Ethical Issues in Professional Life* (New York: Oxford University Press, 1988), Appendix II.

12. Thanks to John Kleinig and Tziporah Kasachkoff for generous and helpful comments.

II. Using Problems and Cases in Teaching Professional Ethics: Theory and Practice

Caroline Whitbeck

In my experience with professional ethics education for young engineers, scientists, and health care providers, I find the use of certain types of cases and problems especially effective. I draw on that experience and on consideration of the moral skills needed for ethical deliberation to discuss methods and case materials suitable for "pervasive" ethics education (that is, methods and materials that are readily incorporated into courses and structured internships throughout the curriculum). Such problems and cases may also be used in freestanding professional ethics courses.

The five sorts of cases and problems I discuss help students to develop deliberation skills, that is, the skills to think through and respond to moral problems. They are: open-ended scenarios presenting problem situations that call for response; complete stories that are cautionary tales from the experience of practitioners of the profession or occupation in question; news stories; stories of exemplary responses; and complete stories or cases on which judgments have been made by authoritative bodies. I discuss in some detail the scenarios that present problems and the cases on which judgments have been issued, because these two are frequently neglected or raise issues that are often misunderstood.

I begin by briefly examining dominant trends in ethics and practical and professional ethics (also called "applied ethics") since the mid 1970s and their effect on the use of cases in teaching and research.

REPRESENTING MORAL PROBLEMS

Biomedical ethics was the first area of practical and professional ethics to develop extensively. In the 1970s, works in practical and professional ethics had titles, such as "Moral Problems in Medicine," that gave reason to believe they would illuminate ways to resolve satisfactorily some ethically significant practical problems that people face. Instead, such works typically focused on *types* of acts, such as euthanasia or abortion, and considered under what *general* circumstances these acts would be justifiable. They did not examine the problem situations of those who typically resort to these acts, much less consider good ways to address those problems. The lack of attention to problem solving was particularly surprising in biomedical ethics, since problems and problem solving was a prominent topic after the "problem-oriented medical record" became the standard of record keeping in hospitals in the 1970s.[1]

As Stuart Hampshire observed in 1949, and again in 1989, the skills needed by an agent—a person embroiled in a moral problem—have been neglected in moral philosophy.[2] The skills of a judge—the skills used to make moral assessments of well-defined actions—receive almost exclusive attention. A judge's skill does help an agent weigh alternatives, once these have been formulated, but are not *all* that an agent needs to deliberate how best to respond to some moral problem.[3] This point is ignored in the work that came to dominate biomedical ethics, *Principles of Biomedical Ethics,* written by Tom Beauchamp and James Childress in 1978.[4] They raise the topic of the agent's deliberation but ignore those aspects of agents' deliberations that go beyond justification and the moral evaluation required for it:

> In this book we examine the reasons that do and should go into moral *deliberation* and into moral *justification* in biomedicine. The reasons that are properly used in justification will also appear in deliberation whenever the agent tries to determine which course of action is right, i.e., morally justified or even obligatory. The reasons present in moral deliberation thus are justifying reasons, because they express the conditions under which a moral action is justified.[5]

The disregard of what is specific to the agent's perspective on moral problems was not, of course, what made this book so influential. Rather it was the work's emphasis on *principles.* When applied ethics, especially bioethics, began to emerge in the 1960s and 1970s, there was a particular interest within philosophical ethics in formulating principles. In his 1957 essay, "Outline of a Decision Procedure for Ethics," John Rawls argued that philosophical ethics ought to provide a decision procedure—a way of settling matters—especially in the case of conflicting values or interests.[6] He sought to do so by formulating principles—in the sense of universal injunctions—and then rank ordering them as to importance.[7]

The concern with the formulation of principles in the philosophical ethics of the 1950s and 1960s was taken by some as a mandate to formulate "principles" that would demarcate what philosophers or ethicists might bring to a discussion in which others, patients and health care providers, had the experience that prepared them to recognize situations for what they were. Beauchamp and Childress exemplify this trend. The interest in formulating abstract principles often led to neglect of the problems experienced by practitioners,[8] and by the 1980s many voices raised independent objections to the emphasis on abstract principles.

In 1981, Stephen Toulmin wrote an influential essay "The Tyranny of Principles: Regaining the Ethics of Discretion."[9] He argued from observation of the actual conduct of moral reasoning, including his own experience as staff to the National Commission for the Protection of Human Subjects of Biomedical and Behavioral Research, that judgment about what is morally acceptable occurs not "top down" from principles but by analogical reasoning from case to case.

In several books and in his essay "Does Applied Ethics Rest on A Mistake?" Alasdair MacIntyre offered a more general criticism of dominant trends in ethics and its influence on applied ethics.[10] In these works, MacIntyre criticized the general view of ethics assumed in the "applied ethics" approach exemplified in Beauchamp and Childress's book. Their view is the twentieth-century outgrowth of the Enlightenment effort to find a foundation for ethics in reason alone.[11] According to the view, ethical demands are made on everyone solely in virtue of their capacity to reason and without regard to their particular attributes or circumstances.[12] Supposedly timeless universal ethical requirements are simply applied in particular circumstances. MacIntyre's objection is to the idea of *timeless* moral rules that can be known *apart from knowing how and to what one is to apply them.* He does not object to the notion of moral rules or principles. He says: a "moral principle or rule is one which remains rationally undefeated through time, surviving a wide range of challenges and objections, perhaps undergoing limited reformations or changes in how it is understood, but retaining its basic identity through the history of its applications. In so surviving and enduring it meets the highest rational standard."[13] Such rules arise *in* social contexts rather than being abstractions, like truths of logic, applied to particular social contexts. MacIntyre places ethical judgment as well as deliberation about action on a new footing, and sees the norms appealed to in ethical judgment as intimately connected with the other practices of a moral tradition.

By making sense of the notion of a moral tradition, MacIntyre's view not only equips ethics teachers better to deal respectfully with diverse moral traditions (rather than discount as irrational those who do not subscribe to rationalist foundationalism or Liberal Theory), but also gives some basis for inquiring into any moral tradition that may exist among practitioners of a given profession or occupation at a particular time and place. Some codes of ethics do reflect such moral traditions, even if, as John Ladd argues,[14] inclusion within a code of ethics does not automatically endow a requirement with moral validity.

HOW MORAL PROBLEMS COME TO BE REPRESENTED AS DECISION PROBLEMS

Since the influence of Beauchamp and Childress in the original edition of *Principles of Biomedical Ethics* directed attention away from those aspects of an agent's deliberation that go beyond moral justification, the agent's deliberation in addressing moral problems came to be misrepresented as merely deciding among pre-determined options. *Moral problems* became in effect *multiple-choice problems*, or "decision problems."

The first step in decision analysis is to "define," or to "identify and bound" the decision problem. This means to identify possible alternative actions, types of relevant information that will be available, possible consequences, and other considerations such as cost and societal impact. One may simply *identify* possible responses rather than devise them only in the special circumstances in which responses are drawn from a known set. Responses may be known because the acceptable responses are defined within a particular occupation. When alternative actions are predetermined in an area of professional responsibility, decisions are largely technical.

When knowledgeable writers on decision analysis identify and bound decision problems to subject them to decision analysis, they are explicit about the decision maker's role in constructing the problem. For example, Milton C. Weinstein and Harvey V. Fineberg, the authors of *Clinical Decision-Making*, describe the task of defining the decision problem as follows: "The first step is to define what specifically is the decision problem at hand and what considerations the decision maker *wants to take into account* in reaching the decision."[15] When faced with a moral problem, part of what is required to act responsibly is a consideration of the morally relevant factors. Representing a moral problem as a decision problem *assumes* that has been done and sheds no light on how to determine the alternative responses or how to decide what considerations are morally relevant.

James Childress is one of those who gives an account of reasoning about moral problems (presented as "cases") that is similar to treating them as decision problems, although he is less explicit than Weinstein and Fineberg about the problem-solver's role in constructing the problem. (Childress is one of the proponents of the applied ethics approach who shows the greatest awareness of its limitations.) Childress describes his method for an "ethical *analysis* of cases," which, he says, is to issue in "an ethically justifiable course of action." His method of case analysis has six steps:

1. Describe *all* the facts in the case.
2. Describe the relevant principles and values of the patients, physicians, house staff and hospital staff, the hospital itself, society, and any other interested parties.
3. Determine the main *clash* of values and principles, e.g., does this case pit physician desire to heal against patient objections?
4. Determine *possible courses of action* that could protect as many of the principles or values in the case as possible.
5. Choose and *defend* one course of action on the basis of the relevant principles and values.
6. In the defense, show that the conditions for overriding prima facie principles and values are met.[16]

Childress is right that his method is one of analysis, but *synthesis* is also required to devise a course of action. His scheme draws attention to some important considerations. For example, his emphasis in step 4 on protecting as many principles or values as possible is a major improvement over earlier applied ethics methods that merely sought to satisfy the top-ranked principle at the expense of others. In what it omits, however, it misrepresents the process of devising a good response to a moral problem, and obscures the elements of an agent's deliberations that go beyond the evaluation of alternatives and so obscures major steps in moral reasoning.

The ordering of steps 5 and 6 suggests that one first chooses and then later develops a justification or a rationalization for one's choice. Let us assume, however, that the justifying reasons enumerated under step 6 of Childress's method also inform the choice of a particular course of action in step 5. Although Childress elucidates how to *defend* or *justify* one's choice, the "determination" of the possible responses remains a mystery.

To *determine* a course of action (rather than to *devise* a course of action) is to select from among possibilities that are established before the agent decides what to do. Indeed, if they were not established for the agent, it is hard to see how this step could be merely analytic. Where the courses of action come from, or how the agent establishes what they are, is not explained. Had Childress offered this method for *trivial* moral problems, one might say that the reasonable responses are obvious. He offers it for cases that are thought to be interesting or difficult, however, since step 3 explicitly assumes that the agent confronts a conflict of values or principles.

Problems in the general sense (as contrasted with difficulties or predicaments) are the stuff of most kinds of work, and moral problems are regularly encountered in (at least) work that bears on human well-being, from engineering to police work to parenting. A common mistake in representing the moral problems that arise in work is the tendency to focus exclusively on problems involving some sort of conflict and to treat that conflict as irreducible. Assuming that some value conflict is irreducible undermines any attempt to find what in dispute resolution is called "an elegant solution," that is, one that satisfies all value considerations or that at least partially satisfies a variety of demands *simultaneously*.

Parents with several children would find it ludicrous to think that they must choose to favor one child's general welfare over the others or each in turn, just because the needs of two or more children often conflict. Most parents try to do a reasonable job of meeting the needs of all family members to some degree, even if the plan is not optimal for any one of them. The same is true of many problems in the workplace. This good sense runs counter to the tendency of some philosophers to view resolution as the task of deciding which interest, right or principle is paramount and acting on it, and sacrificing or infringing others in the process.

Complex moral problems require more than a simple following of moral rules; they require judgment and discretion. Responsibility for some aspect of human well-being typically raises questions of how much: how safe is safe enough, how far to carry an investigation, how vigorously to treat a certain patient—in other words, how can one best achieve certain ends? Arriving at an answer is not an either-or choice. The problem of how to tell a patient about a terminal diagnosis is a prime example of a how-to question that has been widely misrepresented as a question of *whether* to do something—here, to "tell the truth" to the patient. I take this to be another instance of the "lamppost phenomenon."[17] If the illness is terminal, deceiving the patient is not a genuine option. It is now widely recognized, as well as empirically demonstrated, that patients know when they are not being told that they are dying.[18] The question is whether the message will be conveyed in a clear and compassionate way or in an inept, confused and ambiguous way (which undermines the patient's trust). Deficient communication is rationalized as action "for the patient's own good," but the practitioners who withhold a negative diagnosis are almost invariably those who do not know *how* to give it.

CONSTRUCTING PROBLEMS THAT TEACH THE SKILLS OF AN AGENT

Open-ended Scenarios: Learning with Realistic Problems

As I have argued elsewhere, challenging moral problems may be positively understood as design problems.[19] Like interesting design problems, challenging moral problems require synthetic and as well as analytic reasoning. Problems of both sorts usually have more than one solution, if they have any at all. Some answers are better than others, however, and some responses can be so poor as to be considered just wrong.

Education that prepares people to be responsible practitioners should include practice moral problems that develop synthetic as well as analytic skills. To develop such skills, students need practice with problems that reflect the open-ended, multiply-constrained, and ambiguous situations moral agents actually encounter. As I have described elsewhere[20] those problems' statements should simulate problem situations that students will experience in their work by:

- involving agents with skills and experience comparable to that of the students;
- being expressed in the form of open-ended scenarios requiring a response—what can and should you do now, for instance?;
- being stated briefly so it is clear that the discussants clearly see that they must fill in unstated information; and
- allowing for ambiguity in the situation itself—not in the problem statement.

Such open-ended problem statements, along with questions to guide discussion, help students to address actual ethical problems by giving them practice in:

- **thinking through what additional information might be relevant and the difference it would make.**

Questions to ask: What seems to be the problem? If it is not your problem, but creates one for you, what is your problem?

• **envisioning alternative interpretations of the situation**, so as to avoid premature action that could prove disastrous if the situations were other than supposed. (The instructor might invite experienced practitioners to come to the class, or suggest that students interview such people to add their varying interpretations to those of the situations to the students, thereby alerting students to new possibilities.)

Questions to ask: What seems be going on here? How, if at all, might further information resolve the ambiguity of the situation? Are the means for acquiring this information available to you without risk of worsening the situation? How could you go about getting it?

• **brainstorming about possible courses of action to take** and considering their possible consequences. It is a good idea to remind students that brainstorming involves uncritically putting forward a range of ideas about what one might do, so that no one squelches suggestions. *Subsequently*, the class should develop, refine, or discard each proposal in light of its consequences and implications.

Questions to ask: What can or should you do? How can you go about it? (This is a question of both ethics and feasibility.) More specifically: To whom can you take an ambiguous problem? Does your organization have an ombudsman or some other source of unbiased advice about raising an ambiguous problem? Has your organization established ways to raise a problem of the kind this seems to be? How can you find out how to use these ways appropriately?

• **comparing the advantages and disadvantages of various courses of action** by thinking and talking through what to do if each of the proposed responses evoked the most likely or the worst possible responses.

Questions to ask: How can you act so as to be fair to everyone involved, no matter how the ambiguities are ultimately resolved?

Actual cases, based on events in the experience of practitioners, are an excellent source of material for such problem scenarios, but such stories must be screened to make sure that they recount problems that are fairly common. What often stands out in a practitioner's memory is the bizarre or atypical case. To construct good cases the teacher can consult with one or more practitioners, or instruct students to interview them. The approach I call the "project method" is to have each student formulate a problem situation in which he or she is particularly interested, and then to ask practitioners what they would do in that situation. The first few interviewees will usually refine the scenario by telling the student what is unrealistic about the original formulation. With some prompting from the student interviewer, practitioners will usually suggest modifications so that it fits better what the practitioner has seen.[21]

A variant on scenario discussion is conversion of the open-ended story into a script for role play. Role playing also gives useful experience in formulating a response in the midst of a situation, and may additionally stimulate some emotions typical of those circumstances. This may be particularly instructive if the players change roles and experience the situation from several vantage points. It complements but does not substitute for other methods that allow for more reflective consideration since the players' interpretations of their roles also removes some of the ambiguity left by a written description. Role play has some advantages early in a course or with an audience of strangers because playing the parts breaks the ice and makes it easier for the participants to overcome diffidence.

This is an example of a open-end scenario that presents a realistic problem that I use in teaching research ethics to graduate students:

What About Your Contribution?

> For the first year of your graduate studies you worked with Prof. One on the Hot Research project. By the end of the first year you not only became proficient at many of the more routine tasks of the project, but made a small but notable refinement to the approach to the segment assigned to you. At the end of the first year, Prof. One went on leave for a semester and you started working with Prof. Two in the same lab but on a very different project. Prof. One returned for the spring semester and resumed the Hot Research project, among others. It is now autumn and you are beginning your third year. You hear from another student who was working on Hot Research that Prof. One is publishing a paper on some aspects of the project with this student, a paper which presumably contains your refinement.
>
> What, if anything, can and should you do? What should you do as a first step in light of any ambiguities in the situation?

Learning from Cautionary Tales, News Stories, and Stories of Exemplary Behavior

Practitioners readily supply cautionary tales, that is, complete stories in which a mistake or moral lapse led to negative consequences. Cautionary tales help new practitioners learn from the mistakes of others. Students and interns are especially likely to learn from experienced practitioners about interpreting situations and about responses that may seem attractive at first but which prove to be short-sighted. Cautionary tales do not simulate problem situations, however.

This is an example of a cautionary tale I adapted from a longer account by Ernesto Blanco, a teacher of mechanical engineering:

Automotive Lifting Car Seat Project

In the summer of 1989, the son of a friend, Mr. Z, requested that I design an automobile seat capable of rising to help a disable person exit from a car seat.

Because it was a socially worthy venture, and Mr. Z was the son of a friend and short of capital, I did not ask for payment for my services, but for a percentage of his venture. He offered me a minimum of 4% of his venture equity and inclusion as coinventor on any patents resulting from the work.

I then developed the concepts which I discussed with Mr. Z and his partners at several meetings. When I had completed the design sketches and presented them, they were dated and signed by all parties as is the norm in professional practice. He then took the concepts and designs, promising to return them to me after he had made a copy of them. After further work, the design was approved and I recommended a technician friend of mine, Mr. Lichtman, to do the fabrication. Meanwhile, Mr. Z was pressing me to prepare a formal detailed patent disclosure for his lawyer. I gave this to him on January 16, 1990, and he took it to his lawyer and assured me that he would immediately mail me copies of all papers.

Soon after I became involved in teaching for the spring and left the fabrication to my technician friend. (I had no reason to distrust either Mr. Z or his two partners, one of whom was the son of the vice-president of a large corporation that is also my client.) I was later informed by Mr. Lichtman that Mr. Z had applied for a patent and was busy raising capital although he had not informed me. When I tried to contact Mr. Z, he was unavailable. Finally he agreed to show me the system installed in his car. I was becoming suspicious and videotaped the demonstration.

Mr. Z then said that he could not offer me the 4% equity because that would make it too difficult to raise capital. In response to my questions about the patent, he said that the patent was his alone, that I had merely worked for him and my contribution had been minor in filling in his ideas. I was shocked and concluded that he had behaved dishonestly from the start, and that this was why he had failed to return my sketches.

Fortunately, I was not left completely without evidence, since my friend, Mr. Lichtman, had copies of all my work (with dates and signatures), which he had used for his fabrication. He sent these to me and offered to testify on my behalf. I am presently suing Mr. Z.

What precautions might one take in such circumstances that would not be burdensome or insulting to honest clients?

News stories can provide lively and timely teaching material, but because they select the atypical man-bites-dog story, it can take some effort to find stories that draw attention to commonly encountered situations. Some news stories cover events without explaining their origins. Others in which the magnitude of the consequences made them newsworthy may identify condemnable or exemplary responses to common situations. The stories of condemnable responses sometimes function as cautionary tales. The best complete stories are those that include information about the circumstances and resources available to individuals involved in them, or give students and interns some way of discovering that information.

The full story of exemplary behavior usually requires some investigation or, if possible, interviews with the people who behaved in a model way. Some complex full stories of exemplary behavior—such as the story of Roger Boisjoly's attempts to avert the fatal flight of the space shuttle, *Challenger*—may be divided into a series of problem situations that the protagonist handled well. If those problems are carefully explored and are typical of the ones that practitioners commonly face, the stories may augment and refine the hearers' repertoire of good responses. It is best if students have some way of "interrogating the case," that is, of gaining answers to questions about it that they find relevant to ask.[22]

Learning from Judgments

The second sort of case I wish to discuss in some detail is the story of a completed action on which knowledgeable experts have passed ethical judgment.

Some of these cases are situations that official judges have decided. Judges are themselves agents whose actions are judgments made on behalf of groups or organizations. They have the moral responsibility to make fair and impartial judgments. Some judgment cases that are simply intellectual exercises, without ramifications for those whose actions are judged, are useful for practicing the assessment of actions that, as we noted earlier, is included in the skills an agent needs for moral deliberation.

For this purpose, it is useful to examine related Supreme Court decisions. Examination of judgments of authoritative bodies also develops students' ability to recognize subtle moral distinctions and to understand moral traditions in which applicable moral rules have been developed and refined. If available, examination of the judgments of authoritative bodies within a profession can also be extremely valuable. These may highlight pitfalls in a situation that new practitioners will have trouble recognizing.

Students may also have good reasons for disagreeing with those judgments. Such disagreements can generate useful discussions of the perspective and concerns of the body in question, and a consideration of how this perspective and these concerns lead to emphasizing certain considerations at the expense of others.

Especially useful for teaching professional ethics are cases that

1 are typical of situations that commonly arise,
2 ask for reasoning behind judgments of rightness or wrongness of actions, and
3 are given in tandem with some statement of the moral standards that are recognized within the profession or occupation in question.

Cases that call for moral assessment of actions, and do so on the basis of established moral standards, give students exposure to example of questionable actions that they are likely to encounter, opportunities to learn to recognize temptations to which those in their occupation are subject, the temptations that the profession sees it as important to explicitly forbid or at least warn against, and an opportunity to see the moral rules and standards in application.

A model collection of judgment cases—cases that describe typical problem situations, judge whether people in the story acted wrongly, and, if so, what was wrong with what they did, and come with some statement of moral standards recognized within the profession or occupation[23]—is that produced by the National Society of Professional Engineers (NSPE). The NSPE constructs such "sanitized" cases (that is, cases free of identifying information) from complaints that engineers bring against other engineers or from current events. Cases based on the NSPE cases, but adapted for class discussion, may be found on the World Wide Web in the Ethics Center for Engineering & Science[24] and, linked to each discussion case is the original NSPE case and the judgment on the case offered by the NSPE Board of Ethical Review. Each judgment is based on an application of the NSPE Code of Ethics to the case. The Board offers a simple "ethical or unethical" judgment, so their discussions of reasons leading to their judgment are most instructive for the students. On occasions, the Board finds that the provisions of the NSPE Code of Ethics are inadequate to provide a good basis for judgment, and such experiences have led to revisions of the code.

The thirty-two WWW Ethics Center for Engineering & Science discussion cases are more tightly written than the NSPE cases, and focus attention on the problems faced by characters in the story. Such cases are suited for what is widely called "active learning," that is, a learning mode that engages the students as active participants rather than as passive audience in the classroom, and gives the students an opportunity to come to grips with the issues before studying what some authority says about them.

Quoted below is one of the NSPE cases, the discussion and judgment by their Board of Ethical Review. This one has a relatively short case discussion. In this instance, the discussion case was not substantially different from the original but was accompanied by questions as

> How stringent is the obligation to review or comment upon colleague's work?
>
> In general, what are the extent of an engineer's responsibilities for maintaining the profession, professional organizations or professional standards?

(In the WWW version the underlined terms in the questions are links to definitions of the ethical terms.)

Obligation to Write Letter of Recommendation for Other Engineers
Case No. 77-7

Facts

Engineer Smith was being considered for promotion by his employer to a higher level professional position. The employer contacted other engineers who had worked previously with Engineer Smith, for their comments. One of these was Engineer Doe, who was currently employed by another company and who did not have any current direct professional relationship with Smith. Doe replied to the employer that he would not submit a comment on Smith's qualifications or engineering competence because Smith had dropped his membership in the state professional engineering society. Doe stated that in his view it is professionally incumbent on all engineers to support their profession through membership in the professional society, preferably in an active role, or at least by payment of society dues. Smith alleges that Doe acted unethically in submitting that reply to the employer.

Question

Was it ethical for Doe to submit the above reply on Smith's professional qualifications, for the reasons he gave?

References

Code of Ethics—Section 12—"The Engineer will not attempt to injure, maliciously or falsely, directly or indirectly, the professional reputation, prospects, practice, or employment of another engineer, nor will he indiscriminately criticize another engineer's work. If he believes that another engineer is guilty of unethical or illegal practice, he shall present such information to the proper authority for action."

Section 15—"The Engineer will cooperate in extending the effectiveness of the profession by interchanging information and experience with other engineers and students, and will endeavor to provide opportunity for the professional development and advancement of engineers under his supervision."

Discussion

There is nothing in the Code of Ethics which directly or indirectly imposes a duty on an engineer to write a letter or otherwise comment on the qualifications of other engineers. An engineer may ethically decide to ignore a request for personal comment on the attributes or qualities of others.

The novel aspect of this case, however, is whether an engineer may base his refusal to comment on the professional qualifications of other engineers for the reason that the other engineer has chosen not to participate in the professional society. From our vantage point of active membership in a professional society, we are tempted to look with favor on the philosophy of Doe and agree with him that all engineers should support the work of their appropriate professional societies as the only effective means to enhance the role and recognition of their chosen profession.

But the controlling question is whether Doe acted contrary to Section 12's injunction not to injure the prospects of another engineer by the tone and nature of his comment to Smith's employer. Arguably, Smith's employer might read Doe's statement of refusal to comment for the reasons given as a negative comment on Smith's application for a higher position. Although it is a close question, we believe that Doe has done Smith an injustice from an ethical standpoint in submitting negative comments while taking the position that he did not wish to comment on Smith's qualifications. We reach this conclusion with some reluctance in view of our strong agreement with the concept of support of engineering societies by individual engineers, but our bias in that direction is tempered by the equally important principle that individuals are and ought to be free to join or not join voluntary societies or organizations. Contrary to this controlling principle, Doe's approach to the request for comment on Smith was prejudicial without a proper ethical basis.

We have noted Section 15 in the references, but do not feel its relevance needs detailed discussion or analysis because its requirements run only to an interchange of information and experience directly related to the work product of engineering, rather than to the personal attitudes or attributes of individual engineers.

*Conclusion**

It was not ethical for Doe to submit his reply on Smith's professional qualifications for the reasons given by him.

*Note—This opinion is based on data submitted to the Board of Ethical Review and does not necessarily represent all of the pertinent facts when applied to a specific case. This opinion is for educational purposes only and should not be construed as expressing any opinion on the ethics of specific individuals. This opinion may be reprinted without further permission, provided that this statement is included before or after the text of the case.

In my classes, students typically consider the discussion version of a case at one class meeting, focusing on good ways of responding to the situation faced by the characters in the story as well as assessment of the ethical acceptability of what was done. Students then read the NSPE version and the Board of Ethical Review judgment for the next class. They frequently find that some of the factors they considered did not figure in the opinion of NSPE Board of Ethical Review. They also often remark that the Board of Ethical Review's demands on engineers to show consideration to other engineers are excessive. This may lead to a discussion of the character of professional societies. The Board's judgments are not considered sacrosanct; however, the process of considering a case and then considering the Board's judgment helps students better to understand and evaluate their code of ethics and the situations in which it was designed to provide guidance.

In summary, I have discussed the skills necessary to think through and respond to moral problems and five sorts of cases and problems that help students to develop those deliberation skills: open-ended scenarios presenting problem situations that call for response; complete stories that are cautionary tales from the experience of practitioners of the profession or occupation in question; news stories; stories of exemplary behavior; and complete stories or cases on which judgments have been made by authoritative bodies. I have given a brief overview of the recent history of practical and professional ethics and of how the applied ethics approach led to the neglect of some skills necessary for moral deliberation.

NOTES

The research for this paper was supported in part by NSF grant # BBS-8619877.

1. See, for example, J. Willis Hurst, MD and H. Kenneth Walker, MD, *The Problem Oriented System* (Baltimore, MD: The Williams and Wilkins Company, 1972); Arthur S. Elstein, Lee S. Shulman, and Sarah A. Sprafka, *Medical Problem Solving* (Cambridge, MA: Harvard University Press, 1978).

2. Stuart Hampshire, "Fallacies in Moral Philosophy," *Mind* 58 (1949), pp. 466-82, reprinted in *Revisions: Changing Perspectives in Moral Philosophy*, ed. Stanley Hauerwas and Alasdair MacIntyre (1983); and Stuart Hampshire, *Innocence and Experience* (Cambridge, MA: Harvard University Press, 1989).

3. I have argued in "The Trouble With Dilemmas: Rethinking Applied Ethics," *Professional Ethics* 1 (fall 1992), pp. 119-42, against the abstract representation of moral problems, the representation of them as "math problems with human beings" Hence I regard the perspective of the critical spectator who views the

problem abstractly and from "nowhere," as Thomas Nagel puts it (in *The View from Nowhere*), as a useless perspective on actual moral problems. The emphasis upon the perspective of the agent in the present argument complements the perspective of an actual judge, however. The perspective of the actual judge finds discussion in some philosophical treatments. Actual reason in moral evaluation is often not reasoning from principles but reasoning by analogy from one case to another. See the "casuistic" approach of Albert Jonsen and Stephen Toulmin described in their book, *The Abuse of Casuistry: a History of Moral Reasoning* (Berkeley, CA: University of California Press, 1988). The perspective of a judge who reasons analogically from cases acknowledges its historical and cultural perspective in the tradition of cases that it uses. This is in contrast to the dominant approach of reasoning abstactly from principles.

4. Tom Beauchamp and James Childress, eds., *Principles of Biomedical Ethics* (New York: Oxford University Press, 1979), now in its fourth edition.

5. Ibid., p. 4.

6. John Rawls, "Outline of Decision Procedure for Ethics," *Philosophical Review* 66 (1957), pp. 177-197.

7. "Ethical principles," with which Rawls proposed to construct a decision procedure, are rather different from what many non-philosophers mean by the term, namely basic ethical considerations. Basic considerations—for instance that people are of value in their own right—should be taken into account in solving moral problems, but they do not yield specific prescriptions for action, nor do they lend themselves to ordering independent of context. In "The Trouble With Dilemmas: Rethinking Applied Ethics," I have argued that the tendency to seek principle in Rawls's sense is related to the widespread tendency in "applied ethics" to force moral problems into the form of dilemmas.

8. An insightful account of the limitations and self-deception of the abstract approach that until recently dominated philosophical ethics but which, unlike the present essay, is addressed primarily to philosophers and theologians, is given in Stanley Hauerwas and David Burrell, "From System to Story: An Alternative Pattern for Rationality in Ethics," first published in Stanley Hauerwas, *Truthfulness and Tragedy* (Notre Dame: University of Notre Dame Press, 1977), pp. 15-39, and reprinted in *Why Narrative?* Stanley Hauerwas and Gregory Jones, eds. (Grand Rapids, MI: William B. Eerdmans, 1989).

9. Stephen Toulmin, "The Tyranny of Principles: Regaining the Ethics of Discretion,"*The Hastings Center Report* 11(December 1981), pp. 31-39.

10. Alasdair MacIntyre, "Does Applied Ethics Rest on a Mistake?" *The Monist* 67(1984), pp. 498-512; *After Virtue: A Study in Moral Theory* (Notre Dame, IN: University of Notre Dame Press, 1985); and *Three Rival Versions of Moral Inquiry: Encyclopedia, Geneologist and Traditions* (Notre Dame: University of Notre Dame Press, 1985). See also his *Whose Justice? Which Rationality?* (Notre Dame, IN: University of Notre Dame Press, 1988).

11. Not all of the well-known philosophers of the Enlightenment subscribed to this foundationalist program. Baier argues that Hume's ethics prominently included consideration of factors other than reason and that Hume takes moral subjects to be very much as we know people to be. See Annette C. Baier, "Extending the Limits of Moral Theory," *Journal of Philosophy* 83 (October 1986), pp. 538-44, and "A Naturalist View of Persons,"Presidential Address delivered before the Eighty-Seventh Annual Eastern Division Meeting of the American Philosophical Association in Boston, MA, December 29, 1990, *APA Proceedings*, 65 (November, 1991), 5-17.

12. MacIntyre, "Does Applied Ethics Rest on a Mistake?" p. 499.

13. Ibid., pp. 508-09.

14. John Ladd, "The Quest for a Code of Professional Ethics: An Intellectual and Moral Conflict," reprinted in *Ethical Issues in Engineering* ed. Deborah Johnson (Englewood Cliffs, NJ: Prentice-Hall, Inc. 1980), pp. 130-36.

15. Milton C. Weinstein and Harvey V. Fineberg, *Clinical Decision Analysis* (W.B. Saunders Company, 1980), p. 4 (emphasis added).

16. To this Childress adds five conditions. Among them are these two: "the agent must seek to minimize the negative effects of the infringement" and "the competing principle or rule is *stronger* in the situation." The modifier "in this situation" shows an appreciation of the importance of context in ordering principles. The six-step procedure is slightly abbreviated from "Guidelines for the Ethical Analysis of Cases," handed out by Childress at the AAAS Minority Scholars Workshop on Values and Ethical Issues in Science & Technology, July/August 1991, and quoted by permission. He states that the method is adapted with major modifications from Loyola University Stritch School of Medicine, Medical Humanities.

17. The tendency to distort problems to make them fit one's tools is called "the lamppost phenomenon," from the story about the drunk looking for his lost wallet under the lamppost, rather than where he lost it, "because the light is better."

Elsewhere I have argued that the large amount of attention given to such issues as whether to tell the truth to patients or to lie for what one believes to be the patient's own good is an artifact of those issues being representable as conflicts of moral rights or moral principles. See "Why the Attention to Paternalism in Medical Ethics?" *Policy and Law* 10 (1985), pp. 181-87, and "Ethical Issues Raised by New Medical Technologies," in *The New Reproductive Technologies*, ed. Judith Rodin and Aila Collins (Hillsdale, NJ: Lawrence Erlbaum Publishers, 1991), pp. 49-64.

18. See, for example, Barney Glaser and Anselm Strauss, *Awareness of Dying: A Study of Social Interaction* (Chicago: Aldine, 1965).

19. "Ethics as Design: Doing Justice to Moral Problems," *Hastings Center Report* 26 (May-June 1996), pp. 9-16. This is the first chapter of *Ethics in the Works: Understanding Ethical Problems in Engineering Practice and Research*, due to be published in 1997 by Cambridge University Press.

20. "Teaching Ethics to Scientists and Engineers: Moral Agents and Moral Problems," *Science and Engineering Ethics* 1 (1995), pp. 299-308.

21. Examples of such projects may be found in the "Problems" section of the WWW Ethics Center for Engineering & Science at http://web.mit.edu/ethics/www/. A published example is Tyson R. Browning, "Reaching for the 'Low Hanging Fruit': The Pressure for Results in Scientific Research—A Graduate Student's Perspective," *Science and Engineering Ethics* 1 (October 1995), p. 417.

22. Stories of such exemplary action, including Rachel Carson's campaign to restrict pesticides and Roger Boisjoly's attempts to avert the Challenger disaster, may be found in the "Moral Leaders" section of WWW Ethics Center for Engineering & Science.

23. Judgment cases might have other forms, of course, such as adjudication between claimants.

24. A sample of thirty-two of these cases may be found on the WWW in the section on "Engineering Ethics Cases" of the WWW Ethics Center for Engineering & Science at http://web.mit.edu/ethics/www/engcase.html.

Response to Callahan and Whitbeck: Practical Ethics, Moral Theories, and Deliberation

Frances M. Kamm

In these comments on Joan Callahan and Caroline Whitbeck, I will first describe and discuss their views on ethical theory and practical ethics, considering each author separately. Then I will have a concluding look at three different procedures for solving ethical problems that are discussed in their papers. I found their papers interesting and stimulating, and appreciate the opportunity to reflect on them.

JOAN CALLAHAN

Callahan argues for a combination of freestanding and pervasive ethics instruction. I am quite in agreement with this conclusion. I also agree that practical ethics is not merely the application of historically important principles to practical problems, and that practical ethics, unlike moral theory, is more significantly concerned with solving practical problems. However, I believe, probably more than she does, that a philosopher who is interested in practical ethics should be able to think carefully about practical problems without feeling compelled to reach a bottom line. If one is thinking about the bottom line, there may be a tendency to oversimplify and to suppress subtleties that would eventually yield a better, more correct answer. This should be transmitted to students as well; one should not discourage students from becoming more subtle and interested in parts, for fear that they will never resolve the whole.

My major questions concern her view of ethical theory. She seems to equate doing ethical theory with considering principles put forth by historically well-known philosophers or schools of philosophy.[1] And she also appears to think that doing ethical theory merely consists in studying these principles, "much as an academic approach to religious studies might focus on understanding . . . as a way of deepening one's appreciation of a culture's heritage."[2] But a study of moral theory need refer to neither historical schools nor figures, and it is done with the aim of finding the true theory rather than mere acquaintance with a cultural heritage. For this reason, even if doing theory does not necessarily involve finding solutions to moral problems, it bears on finding some solutions. For if we had a true and complete theory, for example, about what factors were morally relevant and what principles were correct, it is unlikely that this theory would be irrelevant to solutions of real problems. Of course, the problem may be that we lack such a true and complete theory.

Callahan says that one "need not appeal to the history of moral theory" to do practical ethics.[3] This is true, but the history of theory is not theory itself. She believes in freestanding ethics courses because she thinks that people with expertise in ethics, in particular, should have a role in teaching professional and practical ethics. If these are people who are acquainted with and are capable of thinking about ethical theory, the question arises whether their acquaintance with theory helps to make them better than other people at doing practical ethics. If it does, then why would students not become better at doing practical ethics as a result of some acquaintance with theory? Right now, many text books in practical ethics have sections dealing with theories. I would be reluctant to eliminate these sections, though reference to them might well come after an exposure to problem types and specific cases.

Callahan says the goals of practical ethics instruction are: (a) enabling people to recognize moral issues and problems, (2) development of their moral imagination, (3) sharpening of their analytic and critical skills so that they see that relativism is not, in general, true, because some positions can be argued for more successfully than others, and (4) development of their ability to find practical solutions to problems even in the presence of remaining disagreements which are reasonable because analytic/critical skills cannot resolve them. My concern is with (4). I am unsure whether Callahan thinks that (a) each of us should understand that, after critical and analytical skills run out, the disagreements between us are really of no importance because different positions are equally morally acceptable, or whether (b) each of us may appropriately continue to believe that his or her position is the correct one—even though it is not unreasonable for others to disagree. If her position is the former (as it seems to be), then we each should believe that, to decide what to do after a certain point, we might as well toss a coin. If the latter is her position, then the problem is more serious since we will have to decide what to do when some solution is really better than others, but we do not have knockdown arguments to convince every reasonable person of this. It is important to realize that in trying to find a solution to this latter problem of action-when-there-is-disagreement we are really discussing a different question from the one with which we began, namely, what is the right answer to the moral problem? That is, each may believe she knows the right answer, and she or some may be right, but a second problem has appeared, namely, what to do when we cannot convince every reasonable person of that correct answer. Liberal political theory is a typical attempt to deal with this second problem—how we may have to behave as though no answer were correct, even though one is, when there is disagreement.[4]

CAROLINE WHITBECK

Whitbeck begins by emphasizing three broad points of disagreement with the way in which practical ethics and ethical theory are done: (1) *Types* of problems, for example, the problems of abortion, assisted suicide, and so forth, are dealt with rather than particular cases in which choices arise for people. (2) No attention is given to how people come to *devise* solutions to ethical problems. Rather, the emphasis is on giving justifications for choosing one course rather than another, as if these possible courses were already available as on a multiple choice test. This is a mistake, she says. (3) Ethical principles are thought of (a) as necessary to make ethical decisions, (b) as universal and true as a function of pure reason, and (c) as arrangeable in a hierarchical and systematic way, so that if there is a clash between principles there is a preference for ranking one over the other. These are all mistakes, she claims. She refers approvingly to Toulmin's claim that we decide problematic cases by reference to analogous cases rather than by reference to principles, and also to MacIntyre's view that principles are not universal but developed within a tradition. In addition, she claims that rather than ranking principles one should try to satisfy each to some extent (like children in a family, she says).

Her first broad point is well taken; in a practical ethics course there should be some attention to real life cases, especially if this course is taught in a professional school. But the analyses yielded by consideration of *types* of problems is bound to be relevant to decisions in the particular case. Further, *types* of problems may include many specifics. For example, a type of problem is how the permissibility of abortion differs if a woman has voluntarily created the fetus rather than if she had sex voluntarily without intending to create it. Still, a particular case may involve multiple types of factors overlapping in a unique way, and learning to disentangle and appreciate the interaction of factors is important. It is important in part so that people not point to the potentially infinite number of particular cases just in order to say that philosophical analysis is useless in any but simplified cases.

Her second broad point is especially directed at the method of deliberation and justification that she attributes to James Childress. She thinks he is wrong to link deliberation and justification too closely since the latter does not explain how we reach the options we then try to justify. But, in defense of Childress, we might argue that ideally the awareness of the reasons (facts and values or principles) that justify an option should be just what leads one to recognize the option. If one is a rational being, then the awareness of the facts and values that justify a course of action should also motivate one's action and lead one to formulate the course of action. It would be odd to believe that one thinks up a course of action for reasons completely independent of those which justify it; for example, one thought of it because it reminded one of what one's mother did, but the reasons which make it justified have nothing to do with it being what one's mother did. If one did think of options independently of the reasons which justify them, this would be a sort of creativity that might be prompted by discussion or by taking a walk or by anything stimulating or relaxing. Is this the method of devising options that Whitbeck thinks is most important? If so, she is discussing the *causes* of the generation of options, rather giving us a *reason* to devise one option rather than another. Presumably, when people get together to discuss options—perhaps because they find that this causes them to have more ideas—they focus together on the facts and values, and these give them reasons for devising options.

The steps she recommends to students in dealing with a problem are to get all the facts, to figure out what the problem is (considering various interpretations of this), and then to "brainstorm" about options.[5] What exactly is "brainstorming," and how does describing it in this way tell us any more about *how* to devise options than what Childress says when he tells us to consider all the facts and values in the situation and then to determine options? He says "determine" and Whitbeck says "devise" but, other than her suggesting that we go to people who have been involved in real life cases for ideas about what to do, rather than thinking up options for ourselves, and her emphasis on discussion, she gives us no more insight than he does into how we think up options. Perhaps empirical research can help with this empirical, rather than philosophical, question.

Let us consider her third general point. Using analogous cases and pointing to morally relevant factors that are present in a situation can be very useful. But if one is thinking hard, presumbly one will begin to think about what makes the cases analogous, and will then consider whether this general property one picks out should be refined a bit more because other cases of which it is true should not be settled in the same way. This is the way in which one begins to formulate principles that go beyond mere factors, and explain when factors are determinative and when they are not. (This is what happens when one starts by saying that not harming is more important than aiding, and then notices cases where we may harm in order to aid. One tries to distinguish the cases by refining the initial claim about what is more important. Then one is on one's way to a principle.)

Possibly such principles originate in traditions, but when traditions conflict one would like to be able to compare them for validity. *Contra* MacIntyre, this presumably requires an appeal to "purer" reason that is not merely confined to working out a tradition. Finally, sometimes it may be possible to satisfy various principles or claims that seem to be in conflict, as Whitbeck wishes us to do. But Childress, whom she accuses of emphasizing clashes of principles, also asks us (in his step 4) to try and find solutions that take account of as many morally relevant considerations as possible. Presumably this is to be done consistent with giving more weight to more important ones or giving lexical priority where this is demanded by morality. Whitbeck asks us to find solutions that are "fair to everyone involved,"[6] but doing this is not the same as "satisfying" or "being fair" to various moral considerations. For example, sometimes fairness to people requires that we simply ignore the moral consideration of utility.

PROCEDURES

In conclusion, how do the procedures offered by Callahan, Childress, and Whitbeck compare? Here are their essential steps.

Callahan:
1. Set out possible solutions
2. Get the facts supporting them
3. Get the principles supporting the facts
4. Be sure you considered all solutions
5. Select the one you prefer
6. Justify it by reference to 2 and 3
7. Anticipate objections (by checking 2 and 3 for opposing options)
8. Consider the cost of your decision

Childress:
1. Describe all facts
2. Describe all principles relevant to the facts
3. Consider the clash of principles
4. Determine possible courses that deal with as many of the principles as possible
5. Pick one solution and defend it
6. Consider minimizing negative effects and whether overriding them is possible

Whitbeck:
1. Get all the facts
2. Determine what is the problem
3. Consider alternative interpretations
4. Brainstorm for possible solutions
5. Consider the advantages and disadvantages of various solutions

In my discussion of Whitbeck, I have already compared her views with those of Childress. Let me add only that I am not clear where in the determination of the problem or of alternative interpretations identification of the particular moral elements comes in. Now let me consider Callahan. What I find most striking about her method is that she wants us to think up various possible solutions to a problem at the beginning of our deliberations, then to find facts and values or principles to support the solutions. These steps (1 to 3) are the reverse of the order of justification, which, she says, goes from (3 to 1), and practically the reverse of what Childress recommends. His step 1 is close to Callahan's 2, presumably because he thinks one cannot think up options unless one has first had exposure to the facts in some way. His step 2 is her step 3, his step 4 is her step 1. (Presumably, his step 4 also incorporates her steps 2 and 3. If so, her method *starts* at what Childress thinks is step 4. My chief concern is that Callahan's step 1 is forced and "unnatural": I think that to begin one's consideration of a problem by having to think up all the solutions, rather than by developing further the one which seems most plausible to one, is too artificial. If one looks at facts and moral characteristics and thinks up a possible solution, one should later consider alternatives as objections to one's preferred course. (It also seems to me that her step 8 is redundant in view of step 7, because the costs of one's decisons are likely to be part of what an alternative position objects to.)

NOTES

1. Joan C. Callahan, "Teaching Criminal Justice Ethics: Freestanding, Pervasive, and Combined Approaches," in this volume, pp. 91-92
2. Ibid., p. 92.
3. Ibid.
4. See, especially, John Rawls, *Political Liberalism* (New York: Columbia University Press, 1993).
5. Caroline Whitbeck, "Using Problems and Cases in Teaching Professional Ethics: Theory and Practice," in this volume, p. 112. See the last section of my response (*supra*, p. 127) for a summary of her recommended procedure as well as those of Callahan and Childress.
6. Ibid., p. 112.

PART III

Strategies in Teaching Criminal Justice Ethics

Chapter 4

Psychology's Contribution to Effective Models of Ethics Education in Criminal Justice

Elizabeth Reynolds Welfel

Forty years ago psychologists were resistant to the inclusion of ethics education in the curriculum. One national survey of psychology educators showed that most faculty believed it to be unnecessary, ineffective, or unimportant.[1] The prevailing attitude was that ethics could not be taught because moral values had long since been formed and were not likely to change in college or graduate school. In this view, a student's morals or ethics were determined by early socialization experiences and the inculcation of values from parents and adult role models. Psychology educators equated ethical professional practice with moral character and assumed that moral character was essentially fixed and unchangeable. They postulated that if admissions committees did their job properly, and screened out self-serving applicants lacking in moral character, then no further attention to ethics was needed.

Psychology educators also believed that professional ethics were obvious and straightforward, a set of standards easily comprehended and followed by any well-intentioned practitioner. Moreover, they viewed ethics violations as anomalous occurrences, rarities that affected so few practitioners that they did not deserve more than brief mention in the curriculum. Faculty questioned the merits of devoting class time to so infrequent a problem when there was hardly enough space in the curriculum to teach the content students really needed to know to become competent psychologists. Similar sentiments have probably been expressed by colleagues in criminal justice who are skeptical of the need or value of ethics education.

In contrast, current research shows that virtually all psychology educators identify ethics education as an essential part of the professional curriculum, strongly endorsing their personal responsibility to foster responsible ethical decision making in their students.[2] In fact, many graduate programs now mandate an entire course on ethics in the curriculum and include ethics discussion in other courses and internships as well. What caused this remarkable change? A number of factors played some role, but primary among them are the following:

- the evidence from social science that morality is not a matter of inculcation or imitation of others, but rather a developmental process that is influenced by biological, cognitive, and social factors;
- the knowledge that moral and intellectual development are life-span processes, not completed in adolescence, but continuing well into adulthood, especially when people are involved in intellectually and morally stimulating environments;
- documentation that psychologists violate ethical standards more frequently than had been assumed and that clients can be irreparably harmed by unscrupulous professionals. (One of my colleagues, Karen Kitchener, referred to her service on the Ethics Committee of the American Psychological Association as "the discovery of sin."); and
- the recognition that ethical decision making is often inherently difficult, both intellectually and emotionally, and that ethical standards are not as easily applied to complex situations as was first thought. Thus, even well-intentioned, well-trained professionals can make improper choices that harm them and those they serve. Not only is knowing what is right harder than was first imagined, but doing that which one thinks should be done is also more demanding than anticipated.

Here I will elaborate upon the theory and research that has guided psychology's transformation from skeptic to advocate for ethics education. Although I cannot claim universal agreement among psychologists with the concepts described herein, there is broad consensus about the "basic truth" of the information included. I hope that the developmental path taken by my profession will make the journey toward effective ethics education smoother and more successful for criminal justice educators. Specifically, I discuss the interplay between psychological characteristics of the individual and the environment that psychologists have come to recognize as crucial to the development of ethical professionals. It begins with the contributions of the more "basic scientists" of moral development and proceeds from there to the contributions of applied psychologists who have examined the practical aspects of designing ethics curricula for higher education.

As a final introductory note, it is important to clarify two things—developmental psychologists focus primarily on moral development and give less attention to professional or applied ethics. However, because applied ethics is a subdivision of the construct of morality, the work of developmental psychologists can be transferred to this domain with few modifications. In addition, researchers in professional psychology have produced a substantial body of literature on the ethical decision making of students and practitioners that serves as another important guide to designing effective ethics education. Obviously, these models will require modification to meet the unique demands of criminal justice education.

THEORIES OF MORAL DEVELOPMENT

Psychology's recent interest in morality was sparked by Jean Piaget, the Swiss psychologist whose theory of intellectual development during childhood radically changed the profession's conceptions of child development and Western societies' models of elementary and secondary education. After Piaget identified predictable and universal stages of intellectual development between birth and adolescence, he turned his attention to the way children approach moral issues. In fact, it was children's deep interest in moral issues that faced them that caused him to explore the topic. He observed the concerns of children with issues of fairness and cooperation when they played. In fact, they seemed to spend as much time devising, debating, and revising the rules for their games as they did playing the games. Piaget's theory of moral reasoning was really an outline, and sketched the broad strokes of a developmental process with less specificity than his model of cognitive development. Although the particulars of his theory have since been supplanted by more comprehensive and better supported models of moral development, his work still forms the cornerstone of psychology's conception of morality.[3] Piaget's foundational contributions are:

- the view that the development of morality is not simply the result of an indoctrination of values from those in the child's environment. Morality is not learned by imitation, nor is it a matter of conformity with existing social values. It is worked out in an orderly developmental pattern that is affected as much by intrapsychic as by external factors.

- the belief that moral development parallels intellectual development insofar as it proceeds in predictable developmental stages that are progressively more complex. Each stage builds on the one before it and development moves forward stage-by-stage as each stage builds upon its predecessor;
- the understanding that the rate of moral development is a function of biological, social, and educational factors. The rate of development can be quickened somewhat by the right combination of social and educational factors, but the pace of development is ordinarily not rapid and is not easily altered by short-term efforts to change it. In fact, Piaget was bewildered with what he termed "the American obsession" with accelerating the process of moral and intellectual development through education;
- the connection between intellectual development and moral development was clarified. Because the resolution of moral questions is at least partly an intellectual process, one's capacity for mature moral reasoning is strongly influenced by one's stage of intellectual development; and
- a model for understanding how the process of stage change takes place. In Piaget's view, people attempting to resolve moral questions tend to try to assimilate new information into their existing frame of reference. When their existing stage cannot satisfactorily accommodate the new information, they move forward to the next stage of development. Just as biological processes prefer homeostasis over change, so too do psychological operations favor the retention of existing approaches to resolving moral and intellectual questions. Change to alternative frames of reference occurs only when the inadequacy of the current system is abundantly clear to the individual. (This point serves to remind those of us involved in ethics education for professionals to expect our students to resist change when approaching ethical issues.)

REST'S FOUR COMPONENT MODEL OF MORALITY

Non-psychologists are most familiar with the work of Piaget, Kohlberg, and Gilligan, who have centered their research on how people evaluate moral issues, how they reason about them, and the criteria they use to decide which action is most moral. However, morality is much more than moral reasoning, and other psychologists have attended to its broader definition. The work of James Rest of the University of Minnesota is particularly valuable, even though his name is not as widely known. Rest has spent his career developing an objective, easy-to-administer measure of Kohlberg's stages of moral reasoning, conducting research on moral reasoning and placing moral reasoning in the broader context of morality and moral behavior. Rest's work not only clarifies the other important components of moral behavior beyond moral reasoning, but also acts as an important template for organizing effective ethics education in the professions.[4]

Rest begins with a definition of morality. He defines a moral action as any action that has significant implications for the welfare of others. The welfare of others is a general expression that does not imply that there must be a specific victim for an act to be immoral, although acts with identifiable victims would certainly fit under this rubric. Embezzling money from one's employer is immoral because it negatively affects the future of the company and the long-term employment of other employees. Passively watching a crime take place when one could easily call the police without risking harm to oneself is immoral because the welfare of another person is at stake. (Obviously, committing the crime is immoral for the same reason). Teaching a course without knowledge or competence is immoral because the welfare of one's students is negatively affected by the instructor's incompetence. Ethicists believe that immoral acts negatively affect the welfare of the person who commits the acts, either because they diminish moral character or because they form a "slippery slope" that leads to even worse actions.

Rest details four components that are essential to moral behavior. His account is grounded in the question, "What must we suppose happens psychologically in order for moral behavior to take place?"[5] These four components act in concert to determine the choice an individual will make. Conversely, an immoral act can be accounted for as a deficiency in one or more of these components. One caution is in order as we begin a description of each component—Rest warns readers not to view these components as linear or exclusively cognitive. The process is often highly emotional and usually not completed in a step-by-step manner. Moral action is seldom the result of a deliberate, well-thought out plan of action. Usually it is more intuitive and those who act morally tend not to be able to describe the process that preceded their decision to act responsibly. Only upon careful reflection does the process get clarified and the rationale become conscious.

Component One: Interpreting the situation as a moral one

This component deals with the process of recognizing the moral dimensions of a situation. *Moral sensitivity*, the most common name for this component, involves a process of identifying the implications of one's actions on the well-being of others. The capacity to imagine alternative scenarios, take on the roles of others, and have empathy for others are all parts of this process. Consider the following illustration: I am sitting safely in the living room of my condo when I observe a burglar who is attempting to break into my neighbor's home. The burglar is an adolescent, armed only with a crowbar and a drive to steal. Many things may go through my mind at this moment. I can spend the next few minutes feeling grateful that this criminal chose the neighbor's home or feeling pity for this poor neighbor who just lost his job. In an alternative scenario, I could have focused my attention on the technical aspects of the unfolding crime—the adolescent's expertise with the crowbar or his failure to wear gloves to conceal fingerprints. If the teenager is experienced in breaking and entering, I might even have admired his speed and confidence at the procedure. None of these responses shows what Rest calls moral sensitivity because I have failed to interpret the situation as a moral one. It never occurred to me that anything moral was at stake. I showed little empathy for my neighbor and could not put myself in his place or imagine what I might have wanted him to do had he observed my condo being burglarized. I missed completely the idea that something inherently wrong was taking place. Therefore, without moral sensitivity I could not act morally, except, of course, by chance. It is only when I recognize that I have some responsibility to help my neighbor that I have the potential to act morally. Of course, morality does not require me to wrestle the burglar to the ground or to endanger myself, but it does require me to call the police or take some action that may prevent the completion of this burglary.

There are other situations which a person may identify as having a moral dimension, but for which there is no compelling personal responsibility to act. For example, one may read about or see in the media a situation that one identifies as having moral dimensions, but for which the person sees no personal moral responsibility to act. I may read in a newspaper about an accountant who acted as an informant for the Internal Revenue Service, providing confidential data to the IRS. I may recognize that this accountant acted unethically, but see no personal obligation to act in any way. In other words, the duty to evaluate personal moral responsibility is not automatically a component of moral sensitivity. Only in situations in which a person has the opportunity to affect the welfare of others does this aspect of the construct come into play.

People who are morally insensitive need not have malicious intent. In fact, the literature on ethical violations by professionals from many occupations suggests that moral insensitivity often results from ignorance and distraction by other elements of the situation.[6] Research shows, for example, that mental health professionals often fail to see the ethical dimensions of their work because they are concentrating on the technical or clinical aspects of cases.[7] For example, when mental health professionals are focused on working out a complex diagnosis or engaging a client who is resistant to counseling, they are vulnerable to missing the ethical issues before them. What is particularly disturbing about this finding is that exclusive attention to clinical or technical issues can blind professionals to even the most obvious and well publicized ethical issues in their fields. Mental health professionals who end up facing ethics committees or disciplinary hearings by state licensing boards frequently indicate that they never saw the ethical implications of the situation that confronted them. Had they been alert to the ethical dimensions they would have acted differently.

How does one acquire moral sensitivity? A host of factors is probably at work, including one's personal history, socialization, prior experience with similar moral issues, and stage of moral reasoning. Research has suggested that sensitivity to the ethical dimensions of professional life can be heightened by formal training in ethics, with special emphasis on practice with hypothetical dilemmas similar to those that professionals experience in practice.[8] Other psychologists suggest that experiences in role taking build moral sensitivity,[9] as can training experiences that promote the development of empathy with those who are served by the profession.

Component Two: Moral reasoning

The recognition that a situation has ethical dimensions is not to be identified with ethical action. Moral sensitivity represents the foundation upon which a moral action rests, but it is not the whole structure. *Moral reasoning* is the process of identifying potential responses to the situation and weighing their merit as ethical choices.

Consider another scenario: A shopper in the supermarket sees another shopper at the check-out line drop a twenty-dollar bill on the floor. No one else observes the event or spies the bill on the floor. Assuming the person is conscious of the moral dimension to this event, he or she must decide what should be done. Two primary choices emerge: give the money back to the other shopper or pocket it oneself. (I suppose that if one is overwhelmed by the problem, one could pretend the money is not there and just walk by.) The person then evaluates the moral alternatives and comes to a conclusion about the right thing to do. In this simple scenario, there is little doubt about what a person should do, but in more complicated circumstances the deliberations can be less conclusive. Several options may appear moral, or every option may have negative as well as positive dimensions. The criteria by which we evaluate morality are not universal either. There are variations based partly on culture, religious background, personal values, and the rules and norms of society.

Psychologists have identified another important source of variation in the criteria for resolving moral issues—developmental differences in the complexity of moral reasoning of which people are capable. Lawrence Kohlberg completed the seminal research in this area and the last thirty years have seen a burgeoning body of research to support and amend his model.[10] An alternative way of examining this subject was subsequently proposed by Carol Gilligan.[11] Gilligan's aim was to create a construct more attentive to the forms of moral reasoning she saw as especially common in girls and women. Both of these models identify stages in moral development between early childhood to adulthood that are tied into a person's biological, cognitive, and social development. Because the largest body of research has used Kohlberg's model, it will provide the base for my discussion of moral reasoning.

Specifically, Kohlberg postulates three qualitatively different levels of moral reasoning. Each level is further divided into two stages. Rest and Narváez captured the essence of Kohlberg's stages well when they wrote, ". . . the best short description of the six stages is to view them in terms of six conceptions of how to organize cooperation."[12] The first level is the preconventional level in which the criterion for morality is self-interest. All moral development begins at this level which is exemplified by children who define right and wrong according to the association with detection and punishment or the potential for advancing self-interest. They see the best ways to foster cooperation with others as being obedient to their wishes (Stage 1) or exchanging favors with them to achieve short-term goals (Stage 2). A young person whose predominant stage of moral reasoning was preconventional would approach the shopper's dilemma above with two primary questions: Would I be caught? (because an act is wrong if I get punished for it) or, What do I gain or lose by each course of action? (if an act advances my interest, it is inherently moral and I expect all people to act to enhance their own interests).

Most children, through biological maturation, education, family relationships, and other socialization experiences, develop past this level to what Kohlberg calls conventional moral reasoning. At this level, the criteria for determining what is right or wrong refer to social norms and rules or laws. The older child defines morality by reference to the family or group norms (Stage 3) and the adolescent or young adult uses societal rules and laws to determine what is right (Stage 4). Between Stage 2 and Stage 3 people learn that there is more to human cooperation than favors exchanged, and they expand their notion of morality to account for continuing relationships with those who are close to them. Courses of action that promote the continuance of those close relationships are characterized as good. So, the shopper's moral dilemma for a Stage 3 thinker would be framed as a question about what behavior would be accepted by the family or group. At Stage 4 a person develops a way for achieving cooperation between larger groups in society by recognizing that morality must include cooperation with strangers and even enemies if anyone's well-being is to be protected. The law becomes the criterion for defining what is moral because it is the law that keeps smaller groups in society from dissolving into anarchy. At Stage 4, if an action violates a law, then, it is inherently wrong. At this level, the notion of an immoral law is an oxymoron. Thus, a Stage 4 shopper's criterion for deciding what is moral is the law; if the law prohibits keeping others' lost money or mandates returning it to the owner, then one would be acting immorally if one did not conform one's activities to it. If, however, the law is mute on the subject, the person is free to take whatever action seems appropriate without concern about moral implications. Of course, the laws referred to in Stage 4 thinking need not be civil or criminal laws. One might refer to religious law in the same way. (From this frame of reference it is interesting to think about the claim of the Freemen in Montana. From what I read in the news reports, the Freemen seem to have claimed that they did not need to honor civil or criminal law because the only law that mattered is their religious law).

The most mature moral reasoning occurs at the postconventional level and encompasses Stages 5 and 6. At this level (achieved by some but not all adults), the criteria for deciding what is moral derive from universal moral principles rather than from any specific law or norm. In other words, the person views laws as fallible, with the potential to serve either moral or immoral aims depending on who enacted them, and relies on guidelines believed to be more fundamental than particular laws or rules. This is not to suggest that laws may be ignored or are necessarily immoral, but rather that the existence of a law or rule is not in itself sufficient to guide moral behavior. In essence a person at Stage 5 or 6 looks to principles as visions to guide cooperation in an ideal society. Thus, a postconventional shopper who spies a twenty on the floor would frame the dilemma in terms of the action that would best advance the good of the whole society or the action that would be most consistent with universal moral principles (such as the inherent worth and dignity of all people). In the supermarket scenario, these concerns would lead one to approach the other shopper and inform her that she dropped money on the floor: that course of action is more consistent with universal moral principles than any other action. However, in many other, more complex situations, there may be no correspondence between the choice made and the level of moral reasoning. For example, a student may reveal to me in therapy that another faculty member at the university is coercing him into a sexual relationship and threatening to fail him if he does not comply. The student may also ask that I hold that information in complete confidence because of his shame and reluctance to risk public knowledge of his humiliation. His request for confidentiality may prevent me from acting to stop the faculty member's sexual harassment. Should I honor the confidence or violate it to save this student and possibly other students from such criminal behavior? In this scenario, there is no single answer associated with higher stage moral reasoning. One can use postconventional reasoning to support several potentially ethical resolutions.

Forty years of research has shown that the preconventional stages occur in childhood and that the postconventional stages generally do not occur until adulthood, if they occur at all. Most adults mature to the conventional level, but some remain at Stage 2. Those who progress to the postconventional stages do so as the result of a combination of personal and environmental factors. Specifically, advancement to higher stages of moral reasoning has been strongly associated with the attainment of higher levels of education. Those with four-year college degrees score higher than those with two-year degrees, and they, in turn, score higher than high school graduates. Persons with graduate and professional training outscore those with bachelor's degrees and, as might be expected, those with advanced degrees in moral philosophy achieve the highest level of moral reasoning of any group tested.[13] The extensive research exploring the factors that spur moral development is an important resource for ethics educators. In spite of early claims to the contrary, there are no significant gender differences in moral reasoning, but females tend to score slightly higher than males on measures of Kohlberg's stages. Cross-cultural research has found the same age/education-related patterns of development as those identified in Western countries. In short, though some questions remain about the particular stages or whether Kohlberg's work encompasses all aspects of moral reasoning, there is substantial evidence of its validity as a model of the course of maturation in moral reasoning. Certainly, research shows its usefulness as a guide for designing the moral reasoning dimension of ethics education in the professions.

This model of moral reasoning makes the variability in our students' responses to ethical dilemmas more comprehensible. In large measure, the divergent views they express about ethical issues reflect different criteria for determining what is moral. When these criteria are understood as reflections of their stage of moral development, we can impose order on what formerly appeared chaotic, and we can gain insight into the steps we need to take as ethics educators to foster more mature ethical reasoning. (Later in the article I will address the practical implications of these findings for ethics education in the professions.)

Component Three: Deciding to carry out the moral alternative

The third component in moral action is *moral decision making,* coming to a personal determination to perform the action that a person has evaluated as the most moral. In practical terms this component provides answers to the question, "Will I do that which I have decided I ought to do?" Needless to say, knowing what is right and doing what is right are not identical. People often engage in activities they know to be wrong. Psychologists who study moral motivation have termed the considerations that may interfere with moral decision making as *competing values.* Other values compete in two ways. They may overcome a professional's better judgment about what they will do in a situation, or they may be given lower priority than other values. Obviously, moral values are not the only values humans have, and sometimes other values take precedence. For example, I may learn that my coworker is using drugs on the job. I may see this as a moral dilemma for me because I have seen its negative effects on the clients we are pledged to serve and on the reputation of my agency and profession in the community (moral sensitivity). I may conclude after some thought that I should confront my colleague and insist that she get help and stop endangering clients in the meantime (moral reasoning). I also know that if that personal conversation fails to gain results, I should probably take further action. However, other values guide my behavior in addition to my ethical values. I may value a cordial, cooperative working relationship with all my colleagues and fear the tension and anger that my intervention may cause. If cordiality is more important to me than ethics, I will not choose to act ethically. Similarly, if I worry that I may lose my job for causing trouble, I may elect to remain silent out of self-interest. Interestingly, ethicists suggest that when making decisions about moral issues people often exaggerate the difficulty of carrying out the moral action and minimize the problems with the less moral alternatives.[14] It is important to note that values such as cordiality with colleagues are not immoral in themselves. They indeed carry some moral weight. Cordiality, loyalty and concern for the welfare of one's family are good things to value. However, when professionals elect to weigh cordiality more heavily in their decision making than client welfare, they are choosing an action that, according to professional ethical standards, is less moral than protecting a client from an impaired practitioner.

When professionals who like to see themselves as ethical people get caught between competing values, they get very uncomfortable. They dislike their impulse to avoid the ethical action because it conflicts with their self-image. When faced with such cognitive dissonance, professionals sometimes redefine the problem so that they can still view themselves positively. In the above situation, I may hypothesize that my coworker is taking medication for an illness and that the medication is responsible for the unprofessional behavior. If I convince myself that this is true, then I am enabled to believe that I do not have a moral responsibility to act or to inform a superior because the medication use is probably temporary and is not the result of any addiction. Of course, this explanation may be correct, but when a professional is attempting to resolve competing values, the facts of the case are not ascertained and speculation substitutes for truth.

Research from psychology shows that a disturbing number of mental health practitioners admit that they would do less in a situation than they know they should do.[15] In this research, practitioners and students had little trouble identifying the ethical choices in hypothetical dilemmas presented to them. However, up to one-half of those sampled stated they would carry out a less than ethical action. Were similar studies to be carried out with other professionals, I imagine the results would be quite similar. There is no reason to believe that competing values operate differently for mental health professionals than for others. This points to the compelling power of other values, even in hypothetical situations, and to the need for professional ethics education to attend not only to the development of moral sensitivity and mature moral reasoning, but also to the influence of competing values in moral decision making.

Frequently, students have little sense of how much may be at stake if they fail to act ethically. They fail to recognize the harm that can come to the other parties and to themselves, and they do not take a long-term view of the issue. Some decisions not to act ethically come from values that are generally good, such as loyalty to colleagues or concern for one's family's future. I may decide not to intervene when a colleague misbehaves because I believe that this colleague is my friend and that his needs and privacy should be respected. Loyalty to colleagues is a desirable characteristic, especially in dangerous professions like law enforcement. However, other values can take priority over loyalty especially when the violation is serious and threatens clients, other colleagues, and the reputation of the profession. Students can be taught how to weigh loyalty against other values and to examine the implications of decisions to give priority to loyalty.

These findings also help educators to appreciate the scope of the task before them and to push them to keep focused on the distinction between moral reasoning and moral action. They are especially important for academics to keep in mind. As people who place such high value on reasoning processes and analytical operations, these results remind us that right thinking is only one aspect of responsible behavior.

Component Four: Implementing the moral decision

Even when the moral values prevail over other values, an ethical action is not guaranteed. A person must actually implement that which has been decided upon. As we all know, there are difficulties in this process. Rest refers to old-fashioned features such as character, integrity, courage, and perseverance as central to translating a moral commitment into a completed act. Other psychologists have labeled these characteristics professional virtues and have argued for their centrality in ethical practice.[16]

When implementing moral actions, people often feel isolated from others and worried about the costs that their moral behavior may impose. All too often, these feelings are justified because coworkers will ostracize them for making trouble, and superiors will make their work life more difficult or will even rid the workplace of the "troublemaker." We have all read and heard media reports of the devastating effects of whistleblowing on military and government employees. Careers have been ruined by attempting to do that which is right. Unfortunately, thus far, little empirical study of component four has been conducted. Nevertheless, there are still important ways in which understanding this component can assist in the design of an effective ethics education.

First, we know that professions that have well-constructed, comprehensive codes of ethics give individuals more support in this process, somewhat reducing moral isolation with the recognition that the action is endorsed by the profession even if scorned or misunderstood by coworkers and superiors. This may be a small comfort, but it is a comfort nonetheless. A stronger source of support comes from leaders in the workplace who have communicated their commitment to ethical values and who have encouraged employees to take an ethical stance on difficult issues. Business calls such leadership "creating an ethical culture," and I believe future research will demonstrate that professionals employed by institutions in which an ethical culture has been fostered are more likely to make moral decisions and are more empowered to carry them to conclusion in spite of the personal costs encountered. Other scholars have also cited the importance of informing students about the moral strength sometimes needed to carry out ethical decisions.[17] Such knowledge arms them for the emotional pain they will encounter and encourages them to build up defenses against any negative consequences that may unfold. Psychology has taught us that an expected event is usually easier to cope with than an unexpected event.

On a personal note, since I have been teaching professional ethics for more than a decade to psychologists and counselors, I have often been used as a support by practitioners trying to persevere with the ethical course of action in the face of resistance. For these practitioners, at least, the warnings I made when they were students about the obstacles to ethical action equipped them to seek out appropriate help to reduce their isolation and to reinforce their commitment. I doubt that my experience is unique.

IMPLICATIONS OF MORALITY RESEARCH ON THE DESIGN OF ETHICS CURRICULA

American psychologists and educators have spent the better part of the last three decades exploring the conditions under which moral development ideally occurs and whether it can be accelerated. Most studies have centered on changes in moral reasoning and have neglected changes in other components, but a few studies of ethics education in professional training seem to suggest that what holds for ethics education also holds for ethical sensitivity.[18] The moral reasoning research has focused on a variety of populations, from young children to high school students, to college students and those in professional school. The research has concluded that moral development can be fostered under certain conditions. However, the findings do not imply that one cannot simply teach advanced stages of moral reasoning to students. People seem unable to understand levels of moral reasoning significantly more advanced than their own.[19] In fact, they cannot even correctly identify higher levels when they see them.

Consequently, efforts to teach students at Stage 3 on Kohlberg's model to think like people at Stage 5 or 6 are doomed to failure. Interventions designed to expose people to stages of moral reasoning slightly more advanced than their own have shown more success. This is a challenge that students seem more able to meet, provided the moral education activity is carefully structured and relatively long lasting.

The moral education research directs us to other guidelines for promoting development as well. The length of the intervention has been shown to be particularly important. Short-term interventions accomplish little, regardless of structure. So, compressing ethics education into six-week, intensive ethics courses is not supported by the psychology literature. Instead, the moral education research identifies a need for interventions that last several months. Obviously, the content and structure of the educational interventions are just as important as their length. Well designed courses frequently discuss hypothetical cases that are complex and controversial so that students get practice analyzing issues for which no single right answer exists. Ideally, these cases should be true ethical *dilemmas*, that is, situations about which a professional can see some good and evil resulting from virtually every alternative. Cases involving issues that are answered by direct reference to a section of one's code of professional ethics should be reserved for preliminary discussions, to accustom students to the case-analysis process and to ensure that they understand the directives in the code of ethics. Active peer and instructor interaction during case analysis deepens and quickens the learning experience. In contrast, instructor lectures about cases seem to have significantly less power to foster student growth. Students who hear a variety of perspectives and criteria for resolving moral dilemmas are more likely to mature in moral reasoning. Hypothetical dilemmas make abstract moral issues more concrete and humanize moral principles. The instructor's role in guiding discussion is to help students become aware of the underlying rationale for their moral choices and to understand how other students' criteria for making moral choices may differ. Finally, when discussing hypothetical situations, students should be encouraged to examine the issues from the perspectives of all the parties involved, taking on the roles of each party, and thereby gaining both understanding and empathy for each participant's situation. In my classes I encourage students to role play how the next session or interaction might play itself out between the parties. For example, if the hypothetical case dealt with a client who has asked that sexual harassment be kept confidential, I would have my students take the roles of the client and the counselor and simulate various responses to the dilemma. Such role plays provide them with enhanced emotional empathy as well as cognitive understanding of what is at stake for each party in the situation.

Other developmental psychologists have addressed the need for an emotionally supportive environment in moral education classes. This support functions to overcome the resistance to change that Piaget first identified. Intellectual and moral challenges to existing frames of reference are easier to absorb when they are presented in an accepting and warm environment. Resistance to change often expresses itself as a low tolerance for ambiguity or as irritability with information that does not fit an existing frame of reference for resolving moral issues. Students who feel valued and respected by professors and classmates tolerate such feelings better and keep engaged in the intellectual aspects of the issue longer.

For professions that have written codes of ethics, psychologists recommend not only fostering comprehension of the contents of the code, but also examination of the ethical principles underlying that code.[20] Students should be taught that codes do not appear out of thin air, but are based on principles that are deeper and broader than any statement in the code. Understanding these principles is essential for several reasons. First, no code of ethics can be a blueprint for all professional behavior. Codes do not address new and emerging issues of practice, nor do they direct professionals to specific actions in complex situations. Moreover, codes fail to be specific on a number of topics, giving only broad aspirational statements in many areas. Finally, codes are written in a political and organizational climate which does not always value ethics above all other considerations and which has a self-protective function as well as that of safeguarding the public welfare. Taken together, these limitations mean that professionals need a base for ethical decision making when the code is inadequate to a dilemma they face. Becoming familiar with the underlying ethical principles gives students another way to sort out the complex ethical considerations in any given situation.

For example, in psychology and the mental health professions, five ethical principles have been identified as the bedrock upon which the codes are built.[21] These principles are respect for autonomy, beneficence (the obligation to do good), nonmaleficence (the obligation to avoid harm), justice, and fidelity (loyalty to promises made). So discussions of hypothetical dilemmas in professions with a code of ethics would include discussion of how the code applies to the case and the ethical principles embedded in the code's statements on the subject. Obviously, the ethical principles underlying responsible criminal justice practice may differ, but the notion that codes are really understood and absorbed only when their underlying rationale is clear to the practitioner is a universal one.

When an ethics code exists, students need to be taught its contents and its limitations. Because no code answers every ethical question in practice, students need a framework for ethical decision making that can guide them through the issues unaddressed by the code. For students of psychology and mental health counseling, I have offered the following flowchart for sorting through the complex ethical decision-making process:[22]

Step 1 : Develop ethical sensitivity

Step 2: Define dilemma and options

Step 3: Refer to professional standards

Step 4: Search out ethics scholarship

Step 5: Apply ethical principles to situation

Step 6: Consult with supervisor and respected colleagues

Step 7: Deliberate and decide

Step 8: Inform supervisor; implement and document actions

Step 9: Reflect on the experience

I believe that the potential value of this model is its capacity to help students keep their thinking clear and orderly, and their emotional stress at a manageable level. This model can have utility for criminal justice education insofar as it provides a systematic approach to resolving ethics questions that attends to written codes, scholarship, and the need for individual deliberation about complex ethics problems.

Finally, research from psychology and the health care professions points to a final issue for other professionals teaching ethics to be alert to. Human service professions carry with them a heavy emotional burden. Practitioners are vulnerable to burnout, substance abuse, emotional problems, and secondary post-traumatic stress.[23] When any of these dysfunctions occur, the practitioner's work is compromised, and his or her competence to perform the work is radically diminished. Such impairment is an ethical problem because it results in inadequate service to the client, risks to colleagues, and damage to the reputation of the profession. Ethics education should, therefore, attend to these potential problems and frankly discuss their relationship to unethical and irresponsible practice. Once alerted to these issues, students can be informed about strategies recommended by psychologists and counselors to prevent further deterioration and can get assistance to recover.[24]

My final recommendation for ethics education in the professions deals with what I term "the fallibility factor." It is unrealistic to think that we can design an ethics education curriculum so ideal that it can prevent all future ethical misconduct. If the truth be known, there is scant evidence about the impact of ethics education on reducing ethical violations in practice.[25] Even after we have gathered more extensive empirical evidence that ethics education programs actually change professionals' behavior, no study will show perfect compliance with all ethical standards for every person throughout his or her career. Given that reality, effective ethics education must address the issue of a professional's responsibility once an ethical violation has been committed. Truly ethical professionals will not be perfect persons, but they should be equipped to take responsibility for their mistakes. Frank discussions of how students might go about such a recovery process are in order in all professional ethics classes. Obviously, acting to minimize damage to clients and colleagues is at the core of such a recovery. Without such content in the ethics curriculum, we are adding to our students' moral isolation when grappling with tough issues and are suggesting that ethics violations are too awful to admit and so despicable that they cannot be recovered from. In such an environment, professionals are at greater risk of denying or running away from their problems. Obviously, that is not an outcome anyone desires.

SPECIFIC APPLICATION TO CRIMINAL JUSTICE ETHICS EDUCATION

Although there are no empirical studies of the application of this approach to ethics education in this discipline, several recommendations seem logically consistent with the model.

Criminal justice educators need to explore the kinds of competing values that are most likely to influence the ethical decision-making of those in the field. Criminal justice is an occupation in which many different good values may be at odds with each other. For example, loyalty to colleagues is a value that is sometimes inconsistent with devotion to justice or public service. Loyalty to coworkers is, of course, a morally desirable quality for those whose work involves danger. Should it take precedence over other moral values? Under what circumstances should loyalty be sacrificed for a greater good? These are critical questions for criminal justice educators to examine themselves and address in their ethics teaching.

Criminal justice is an occupation in which workers often do not have the luxury of time to reflect and deliberate about ethical dilemmas; choices must be made quickly in most cases. Thus, the use of hypothetical dilemmas in classes to sensitize students to the common ethical dilemmas in their chosen profession is especially valuable. With hypothetical cases, students do have the opportunity to reflect, discuss, and analyze the ethical implications of their actions. In such interactions, students benefit from exposure to a variety of views on an issue and learn from each other as well as the instructor. Review of hypothetical dilemmas helps to develop their capacity for critical thinking and probably affects their intuitive response to the immediate crisis.

Burnout, emotional problems, substance abuse problems, and other personal issues that distract criminal justice professionals from their work are ethical issues insofar as they compromise competent performance. Criminal justice professions are so demanding and stressful that virtually all workers are at risk for them. Educators in this discipline would serve the profession well to include discussion of such matters in ethics classes, demonstrating the impact of such problems on a person's capacity to act responsibly, and offering practical guidelines for preventing their occurrence. Such activities, no doubt, occur elsewhere in the curriculum, but they ought to be reinforced in this course as well.

Ethics discussion ought not be limited to the course with this title. The entire curriculum ought to be infused with discussions of the ethical dimensions of each subject. Only such a comprehensive approach will communicate to students the centrality of ethics knowledge to effective criminal justice work.

Finally, ethics educators must be willing to grapple with the thorniest ethical dilemmas in the field, the issues about which there is little consensus and in which no truly right or wrong answers exist. In these dilemmas ethics educators model problem solving and coping with the emotional stress of attempting to resolve such issues. Thus, when students experience such dilemmas in their work, they will have resources upon which to draw.

SUMMARY

In short, psychology's contribution to ethics education is its insight into the developmental aspects of morality, especially its conceptions of the stages of moral reasoning that are so influential in professional ethical decision making and its explication of the four components of moral behavior. Moreover, psychologists' work in designing and testing various structures for moral education has direct bearing on the structure of curricula in the professions. These findings suggest that effective ethics education should present students with opportunities to analyze complex hypothetical dilemmas that encourage them to focus on the rationale for their interpretations of the dilemmas, making more explicit the criteria they use to judge moral issues. The goals of such education should be realistic because students are unlikely to make radical changes in their stage of moral reasoning during the length of one course, but growth is clearly possible. Opportunities for role taking and empathy building are also central to the success of this instructional methodology. In addition, the researchers recommend that the emotional atmosphere of the classroom be conducive to the free and open expression of ideas because in such an atmosphere students are better able to cope with information at odds with their current style of moral reasoning. Next, students should be given some kind of model for the process of ethical decision making to help them keep their analysis of the issues clearheaded and to reduce the stress inherent in any ethical issue. Finally, students should come away from ethics education with realistic expectations about ethical practice and with awareness that, if they violate ethical standards, they are not ethical monsters, though they do have a responsibility to remediate the difficulties they have caused and to take steps to prevent their recurrence.

The central message from psychology to criminal justice is that a carefully planned ethics curriculum that attends to the students' current levels of ethical sensitivity and moral reasoning and that includes discussion of the emotional and social difficulties of implementing ethical decisions represents a powerful strategy for graduating students who are well-informed about the ethical dimensions of their work and capable of translating that knowledge into responsible practice.

NOTES

1. N. DePalma and R. Drake, "Professional Ethics for Graduate Students in Psychology," *American Psychologist* 11 (1956), pp. 554-57.

2. C. A. Vanek, "Survey of Ethics Education in Clinical and Counseling Psychology," *Dissertation Abstracts International* 52 (1990), 5797B (University Microfilms No. 91-14, 449); E. R. Welfel, "Psychologist as Ethics Educator: Successes, Failures and Unanswered Questions," *Professional Psychology* 23 (1992), pp. 182-89.

3. J. Piaget, "Piaget's Theory," in P.H. Mussen (ed.), *Carmichael's Manual of Child Psychology* (New York: Wiley, 1970), vol. 1, pp. 703-32.

4. J. R. Rest, "Morality," in P. Mussen (ed.), *Manual of Child Psychology*, in J. Flavell and E. Markman (eds.), *Cognitive Development* (New York: Wiley, 1983), vol. 3, pp. 556-629; idem, *Moral Development: Advances in Research and Theory* (New York: Praeger, 1986); idem, "Why Does College Promote Development in Moral Judgment?" *Journal of Moral Education* 17 (1988), pp. 183-94; J. R. Rest and D. Narváez, *Moral Development in the Professions: Psychology and Applied Ethics* (Hillsdale, NJ: Lawrence Erlbaum, 1994).

5. Rest and Narváez, *Moral Development in the Professions*, p. 23.

6. Ibid.

7. R. T. Lindsey, "Moral Sensitivity: The Relationship Between Training and Experience," Paper presented at the Annual Meeting of the American Psychological Association, Los Angeles (August 1985); J. M. Volker, "Counseling Experience, Moral Judgment, Awareness of Consequences and Moral Sensitivity in Counseling Practice," Paper presented at the Annual Meeting of the American Psychological Association, Toronto (August 1983).

8. Rest and Narváez, *Moral Development in the Professions*; Welfel, "Psychologist as Ethics Educator."

9. N. A. Sprinthall, "Counseling and Social Role Taking: Promoting Moral and Ego Development," in Rest and Narváez, *Moral Development in the Professions*, pp. 85-100.

10. L. Kohlberg, *The Philosophy of Moral Development* (San Francisco: Harper & Row, 1981), vol. 1; L. Kohlberg, *The Psychology of Moral Development* (San Francisco: Harper & Row, 1984), vol. 2.

11. C. Gilligan, *In a Different Voice* (Cambridge, MA: Harvard University Press, 1982).

12. Rest and Narváez, *Moral Development in the Professions*, p. 5.

13. Rest, *Moral Development: Advances in Research and Theory*; idem, "Why Does College Promote Development in Moral Judgment?"

14. M. Josephson, "Teaching Ethical Decision-making and Principled Reasoning," *Ethics: Easier Said than Done* 1 (1988), pp. 27-33.

15. J. L. Bernard and C. S. Jara, "The Failure of Clinical Psychology Graduate

Students to Apply Understood Ethical Principles," *Professional Psychology: Research and Practice* 17 (1986), pp. 313-15; J. L. Bernard, M. Murphy, and M. Little, "The Failure of Clinical Psychologists to Apply Understood Ethical Principles," *Professional Psychology: Research and Practice* 18 (1987), pp. 489-91.

16. N. M. Meara, L. D. Schmidt, and J. D. Day, "Principles and Virtues: a Foundation for Ethical Decisions, Policies and Character," *The Counseling Psychologist* 24 (1996), pp. 4-77.

17. K. S. Kitchener, "Psychologist as Teacher and Mentor: Affirming Ethical Values Throughout the Curriculum," *Professional Psychology: Research and Practice* 23 (1992), pp. 190-95.

18. E. R. Welfel, *Ethics in Counseling and Psychotherapy* (Pacific Grove, CA: Brooks/Cole, in press).

19. Rest, *Moral Development: Advances in Research and Theory*.

20. K. S. Kitchener, "Intuition, Critical Evaluation and Ethical Principles: The Foundation for Ethical Decisions in Counseling Psychology," *The Counseling Psychologist* 12 (1984), pp. 43-55.

21. Ibid.

22. Welfel, *Ethics in Counseling and Psychotherapy*.

23. Ibid.

24. A. Pines and E. Aronson, *Career Burnout: Causes and Cures* (New York: Free Press, 1988).

25. Welfel, "Psychologist as Ethics Educator."

Response to Welfel: The Influence of Metacognition and Epistemology on Moral Reasoning

Robin Flaton

Welfel's article explores the ways in which psychology contributes to the field of applied ethics.[1] She begins by highlighting the contributions of several developmental psychologists—Piaget,[2] Kohlberg,[3] and Rest[4]—to our current understanding of moral reasoning. She maintains that Rest's four component theory of moral development[5] offers the most insightful framework for exploring the psychological processes involved in the production of moral action. This conclusion is based on the fact that the theory not only includes the construct of moral reasoning,[6] but also considers the psychological components of moral sensitivity, moral motivation, and moral character.

Although Rest's theory may be a practical place to start when designing an ethics curriculum, there exists research, not addressed by this theory, which might provide additional clarity to our understanding of the mechanisms that promote ethical development. The aim of this paper will be to consider what is known about reasoning generally and how this might impact upon moral reasoning specifically. There are two features of cognitive development which significantly impact on critical thinking skills and, therefore, may also impact and perhaps even moderate moral development. Those skills are a person's metacognitive competence and epistemological position on the nature of knowledge. My research has focused on critical thinking skills in the social realm, specifically reasoning competence on a juror task.

METACOGNITIVE COMPETENCE

It has been suggested that reasoning at its most fundamental level involves the cognitive coordination of theory and evidence. If individuals are to perform well, they must be able to: (1) consider the theory and evidence as separate constructs, and (2) take their own thoughts about each construct as objects of analysis.[7] The first aspect of this reasoning process is to recognize the separate nature of theory and evidence, thus allowing the individual to evaluate separately a theory held at arms length against the evidence presented. Evidence that supports a theory may be easily integrated, but what happens when the evidence contradicts the theory held by the individual? Is the theory revised or does the individual dismiss or rationalize evidence by distorting its meaning or only selectively attending to its supportive features?[8]

The second requirement is the conscious reflection on one's own thoughts —metacognition.[9] Metacognitive competence involves what Piaget called formal operations or operations on operations.[10] Evidence demonstrates that, when learning, people do not simply accumulate knowledge until they have enough to answer a question or resolve a problem.[11] Adults and children approach new tasks using existing theories.[12] The challenge of metacognitive competence is not to think with a theory, but to think about the theory. (The term theory is used broadly to encompass preconceived ideas about a problem's solution.)

EPISTEMOLOGY

As cognitive development progresses from birth through adulthood, each individual conceptualizes the notion of "knowledge" itself. A theory is developed with respect to what is knowable, how it is known, and how certain one can be about what one knows. There are numerous frameworks that conceptualize the possible epistemological positions an individual can hold on the nature of knowledge.[13]

Perry's work on intellectual and ethical development has contributed significantly to a characterization of epistemological positions.[14] He found a progression of nine developmental positions on the nature, origins, and value of knowledge. Further analysis of these positions has led to the integration of several into three basic positions: absolutist, relativist, and evaluativist.[15]

The first position is an absolutist epistemology in which an individual maintains a belief that knowledge is certain and absolute. Thus, when an answer is ascertained or a theory is subscribed to, it becomes the truth and any challenge is futile. Absolutists maintain extremely high levels of certainty regarding their own theories. They may acknowledge that other opinions exist, but their firm belief in their own correctness relieves them from having to give more than cursory consideration to opposing viewpoints.

The second position is held by the relativist (a.k.a. multiplist) who avows that nothing can be known with certainty. These individuals do not speak of factual truth, as do absolutists, but of ideas and emotions which can be neither proven nor denied. With a strong personal attachment to their ideas, relativists claim that even were their theories proven incorrect, they would not abandon them. At the core of this epistemological position is the notion that everyone has the right to her or his own opinion and that conflicting viewpoints can coexist without any need for reconciliation. In fact, conflicting viewpoints must coexist since there is no way to ascertain if any one is more valid than any other.

Lastly, an evaluativist position exists where an individual demonstrates a high degree of certainty about a theory but makes no claim of absolute certainty. The evaluativist believes that divergent viewpoints can be reconciled through careful analysis of evidence and all possible theories. And through the evaluation of costs and benefits of each theory, the best theory can be selected, yielding an even greater measure of certainty. Although an agreeable resolution is not always reached, the process of reasoned debate is believed to be the best path to a solution.

EPISTEMOLOGY AND MORAL REASONING

We begin by asking whether a person's epistemological position could be related to the development of her or his moral reasoning? Research on informal everyday problem solving in the social realm could help to answer this question. Kuhn found that the reasoning process that manifests itself in social problems is constituted by a system of argument in which an individual attempts to structure her or his response by weighing all evidence which bolsters or weakens a theory, discounts alternative claims, considers any counterarguments that may be produced, and rebuts any such counterarguments.[16] The construction of a reasoned argument is pivotal to everyday thinking and captures the internal dialogue that people engage in when they reason about any dilemma, social or moral. Kuhn, Weinstock and Flaton found a relationship between competent use of the skills of argumentation and the subject's epistemological position.[17] Subjects who were most competent in the skills of argument (understood as the ability to support the theory held, to discount alternative theories, to counterargue, and to rebut) reflected an evaluativist approach; whereas those least competent in the skills of argument reflected an absolutist position.

This indicates that absolutists, once they have found their answer/ theory, dismiss or ignore contradictory evidence, and then do not practice or develop the skills of argument because once the answer is found, further consideration is deemed fruitless. Although there were no clear findings on relativists,[18] we can theorize that since their position is one that claims all answers/theories to be equally correct, there is little impetus for a relativist to practice or develop the skills of argument. Only evaluativists recognize that the path of reasoned debate leads to the best of the alternative solutions and thus see the value of cultivating the skills of argument.

As Kuhn, Weinstock, and Flaton state: "If knowledge is entirely objective, certain and simply accumulates, as the absolutist believes, or if knowledge is entirely subjective, subject only to the tastes and wishes of the knower, as a multiplist believes, critical thinking and judgment are superfluous."[19] So if a person's epistemological position impacts on his or her ability and desire to reason, so that argument is not believed to be valuable, then, when approaching a moral dilemma, an absolutist or relativist after selecting his or her answer/theory will not attempt further consideration of the facts or evidence. This may explain in part why some students may benefit less from ethics courses.

In moral reasoning, there exists a dichotomy of content and strategy. Welfel's example of a student who is sexually harassed by a faculty member and who asks his therapist to keep this matter confidential can be used to illustrate the dichotomy.[20] At each of Kohlberg's six levels of moral reasoning you can choose several solutions. But, regardless of the content choice (to keep or not keep the matter confidential) what is important is the reasoning style that underlies the solution, and, as we have seen, the reasoning style may depend on the person's epistemological orientation.[21] At each level of reasoning there are qualitatively different types of arguments to be made for any solution chosen. So, two therapists may choose the same answer, but their process of reasoning might be quite different. No single answer is associated with good reasoning.

PROMOTING AN EVALUATIVIST POSITION

If a person's epistemological position impacts on the development of good moral and ethical reasoning, then we must ask, "how can we foster the development of higher epistemological positions, particularly an evaluativist perspective?" Research on moral reasoning provides a partial answer by establishing education, not age, as the most powerful predictor of development in moral judgment.[22] The development of moral reasoning is highly correlated with years of formal education, especially if a person continues his or her education beyond high school.[23] Furthermore, evidence exists of differences in the epistemological positions of high school students (of the same age) who identified themselves as college-bound and those who stated they would not attend college.[24] College-bound high school students were more likely to be relativists or evaluativists while non-college-bound students were more likely to be absolutists.

Rest suggests several possible explanations for the impact of formal education: (1) collegiate socialization; (2) a particular skill or piece of knowledge taught; (3) formal education indirectly promotes a general world view; (4) a college environment is intellectually stimulating and promotes reflection; and (5) individuals seeking higher education are cognitively different, predisposed to reflection.[25] Most institutions of higher education hold philosophies that recognize and advance the value of and need for reasoned debate. The structure of these institutions provides opportunities in class and among peers for students to engage in and practice their skills of argument. What Rest identifies as collegiate socialization, general world view, and stimulating environment, are subsumed under and explained by the evaluativist pedagogical approach to learning taken by these institutions. They challenge students to improve their skills of argument by analyzing and evaluating their theories. So, students who enter college with absolutist or relativist positions often advance towards a recognition and acceptance of an evaluativist position during the course of their education.[26]

Programs that attempt to advance moral reasoning have had a greater impact on adults (over 24) than on younger people. Rest explains this as the result of adults volunteering to participate and of their having more life experience.[27] An alternative or more specific explanation might be that adults have better metacognitive skills, more practice with the skills of argument, and are thus more likely than younger subjects to have an evaluativist epistemological position. Therefore, adults are able to benefit more from these programs.

Welfel and others suggest that courses in ethics education should focus on the evaluation of potential moral dilemmas.[28] Research supports the view that the best way to develop moral reasoning is through the use of moral dilemmas.[29] Whether the educator uses the case study method,[30] role playing,[31] or a combination of pedagogical techniques to present the moral dilemmas, three objectives can be met. Analysis of moral dilemmas demonstrates the value of reasoned debate, including the consideration of all available evidence and alternatives, and the belief that once carefully considered one course of action may be the best of all the possible alternatives. Second, the use of dilemmas makes evident an educator's commitment to reasoned debate. And finally, the student's engagement in the task of analyzing the moral dilemma allows him or her to practice the skills of argument.

Perry maintained that the course of epistemological development may be intimately related to moral development because in order for a person to move from a lower stage to a higher stage, the person must have the courage to challenge his or her existing assumptions and expectations and the psychic strength to redefine and extend his or her thinking.[32]

CONCLUSION

In moral reasoning, people may not attain the level of ability they demonstrate in cognitive development (formal logical operations),[33] but there may nevertheless be ways to foster moral development. Since an epistemological position has an impact on the ability to use the skills of argument, then, if the skills of argument are practiced and if the value of reasoned debate is promoted, a person's epistemological level may increase. Metacognitive awareness and control will also increase with the practice of the skills of argument. Improvements in epistemological position and metacognitive competence may, therefore, lead to greater competence in moral reasoning. If good skills of argument are used in the course of moral reasoning, then what Rest calls moral motivation and moral character should be considered part of any good moral reasoning process.

NOTES

1. Elizabeth Reynolds Welfel, "Psychology's Contribution to Effective Models of Ethics Education in Criminal Justice," in this volume, pp. 131-52.

2. Jean Piaget, *The Psychology of Intelligence* (London: Routledge & Kegan Paul, 1950); idem, *The Origins of Intelligence* (New York: International Universities Press, 1952).

3. Lawrence Kohlberg, *The Philosophy of Moral Development* (San Francisco: Harper & Row, 1981, 1984), 2 vols.

4. James R. Rest and Darcia Narváez (eds.), *Moral Development in the Professions: Psychology and Applied Ethics* (Hillsdale, NJ: Lawrence Erlbaum, 1994); James R. Rest, *Moral Development: Advances in Research and Theory* (New York: Praeger Press, 1986).

5. See Rest, *Moral Development: Advances in Research and Theory*, p. 3.

6. Kohlberg, *The Philosophy of Moral Development*; Piaget, *Moral Judgment of the Child* (New York: The Free Press, 1965).

7. D. Kuhn, E. Amsel, and M. O'Loughlin, *The Development of Scientific Thinking Skills* (New York: Academic Press, 1988).

8. D. Kuhn, "Children and Adults as Intuitive Scientists," *Psychological Review,* 96 (1989), pp. 674-80.

9. D. Kuhn, " On the Dual Executive and its Significance in the Development of Developmental Psychology," in D. Kuhn and J. Meacham (eds.), *On the Development of Developmental Psychology* (Contributions to Human Development, vol. 8) (Basel: Karger, 1983), p. 98; L. S. Vygotsky, *Thought and Language* (Cambridge, MA: MIT Press, 1962).

10. Piaget, *The Origins of Intelligence.*

11. Kuhn, "On the Dual Executive and its Significance in the Development of Developmental Psychology."

12. D. Kuhn, M. Garcia-Mila, A. Zohar, and C. Andersen, "Strategies of Knowledge Acquisition," *Monographs of the Society for Research in Child Development,* 60 (1995).

13. J. Broughton, "Not Beyond Formal Operations But Beyond Piaget," in M. Commons, F. Richards, and C. Armon (eds.), *Beyond Formal Operations: Late Adolescent and Adult Cognitive Development* (New York: Praeger, 1983), pp. 395-411; K. S. Kitchener, "Cognition, Metacognition, and Epistemic Cognition: A Three Level Model of Cognitive Processing," *Human Development,* 26 (1983), pp. 222-32; D. A. Kramer, and D. S. Woodruff, "Relativistic and Dialectical Thought in Three Adult Age Groups," *Human Development,* 29 (1986), pp. 280-90; W. G. Perry, *Forms of Intellectual and Ethical Development in the College Years* (New York: Holt, 1970). For a survey of epistemological frameworks, see B. Leadbeater, "The Resolution of Relativism in Adult Thinking: Subjective, Objective, or Conceptual?" *Human Development,* 29 (1986), pp. 291-300.

14. Perry, *Forms of Intellectual and Ethical Development in the College Years.*

15. B. Leadbeater and D. Kuhn, "Interpreting Discrepant Narratives: Hermeneutics and Adult Cognition," in J. Sinnott (ed.), *Everyday Problem-Solving: Theory and Application* (New York: Praeger, 1989), pp. 175-90.

16. D. Kuhn, *The Skills of Argument* (New York: Cambridge University Press, 1991).

17. D. Kuhn, M. Weinstock, and R. Flaton, "How Well do Jurors Reason? Competence Dimensions of Individual Variation in a Juror Reasoning Task," *Psychological Science,* 5 (1994), pp. 289-296.

18. Ibid.

19. D. Kuhn, M. Weinstock, and R. Flaton, "Historical Reasoning as Theory-Evidence Coordination," in M. Carretero and J.F. Voos (eds.), *Cognitive and Instructional Processes in History and the Social Sciences* (Hillsdale, NJ: Lawrence Erlbaum Associates, 1994), p. 384.

20. Welfel, "Psychology's Contribution to Effective Models of Ethics Education in Criminal Justice," p.

21. Kuhn, Weinstock, and Flaton, "How Well do Jurors Reason?" p. 293.

22. Rest and Narváez, *Moral Development in the Professions: Psychology and Applied Ethics.*

23. Rest, *Moral Development,* p. 34.

24. Kuhn, *The Skills of Argument,* pp. 192-93.

25. Rest, *Moral Development*,_ p. 34

26. Perry, *Forms of Intellectual and Ethical Development in the College Years*, pp. 207-15.

27. Rest, *Moral Development*, p. 85

28. Welfel, "Psychology's Contribution to Effective Models of Ethics Education in Criminal Justice," p. 139; K. Winston, "Teaching with Cases," in this volume, pp. 161-81.

29. Rest, *Moral Development*, p. 79.

30. K. Winston, "Teaching with Cases," pp. 161-64.

31. Kohlberg, *The Philosophy of Moral Development*, vol. 2, p. 292.

32. Perry, *Forms of Intellectual and Ethical Development in the College Years*, p. 215.

33. D. Kuhn, J. Langer, L. Kohlberg, and N. Haan, "The Development of Formal Operations in Logical and Moral Judgment," *Genetic Psychology Monographs*, 95, (1977), pp. 97-188.

Chapter 5

Teaching with Cases

Kenneth I. Winston

My assignment is to talk about teaching practical ethics by the case method. I shall do so by focusing on one area of criminal justice ethics, namely, police ethics. Within police ethics, I shall narrow my attention to one issue: the use of deadly force. And regarding this issue I shall discuss at length only one instance of deadly force: an incident that occurred on March 7, 1990, when for the first time in the history of the Houston Police Department a policewoman shot (and killed) a suspect. I take this approach not because of any special expertise (either in police ethics or the use of deadly force), but because by chance I spent considerable time developing a narrative case that features the shooting in Houston. I have taught this case more than half a dozen times and find that it is an effective vehicle for raising certain ethical issues. By concentrating on this one case, I can illustrate both the strengths and weaknesses of the case method of teaching ethics.

WHY NARRATIVE CASES?

To begin, I want to say a few words about what I mean by an ethics case, and what its advantages are over other teaching materials called cases.[1]

In general, a case is an extended narrative, usually between ten and twenty pages, chronicling an actual situation in which the protagonist of the story faced a pressing ethical conflict and had to decide how to resolve it. The narrative offers a detailed account of the circumstances that generated the conflict, including the institutional context of decision making, the relation of the protagonist to other agents, and so on. It also offers at least some of the considerations that could figure into reasoning one's way to a resolution of the conflict. Typically, the account ends at the point when a decision is required (it is a "decision-forcing" story), thus posing for students the question of how to proceed. In a variation on this format, the narrative could reveal the decision actually made by the protagonist in the situation described. Then the task, pedagogically, is retrospective assessment of the appropriateness of the decision and the reasoning process that led to it. In either version, the essence of good case discussion, as Dorothy Robyn has written, is controversy; the case engages students and forces them to think through the factors relevant to resolution of a serious ethical problem in the face of critical scrutiny by classmates with different views.[2]

What are the advantages of narrative cases? Since the type of protagonist I am interested in is a public official operating in a complex institutional setting, the context of ethical conflict is a crucial part of the story. Only narrative cases include an extended account of the institutional context and thus force students to reflect as much on the environment of decision making as on the logic of argument. As a result, narrative cases train students in moral perception as well as analysis. The resources available for resolving a conflict, or the obstacles that may prevent it, need attention. A public agent asks: Whom should I consult? Whom can I persuade? On what grounds? But also: How should I proceed when time is limited, information incomplete, and my colleagues are in disagreement? Which contextual factors will make an optimal choice less likely? Are they intractable? Why? To teach practical ethics, I want to suggest, is to focus as much on the latter set of questions as on the former.

Moreover, only the details of a real case situate ethical conflict in such a way as to encourage the exercise of moral imagination in the search for innovative solutions. Without knowledge of the constraints and opportunities present in the environment, reasoning is either sterile (having no real application) or artificial (producing solutions all too easily).[3] In many instances, the principal effort may be to figure out what the problem is. Even then, the proper goal of the agent could be not to devise an answer to a specified problem but to chart a course of further deliberation: seeking more information, identifying the grievances of relevant parties, eliciting support for the agent's concerns, and so on. (Sometimes the most compelling lesson of a case lies in what the agent should have done differently to defuse the ethical problem before it got to its current stage.) In general, it is important to disabuse students of the idea of a determinate decision procedure in practical ethics, but also important to teach that one can be methodical in handling a conflict.

Even though an effective case generates controversy, a class could very well progress to an unexpected consensus, perhaps by reframing issues, challenging assumptions, and engaging in collective self-education. Narrative cases facilitate this process by lending themselves to the simulation of problematic situations through role playing, constraining students to adopt the perspective of agents attempting to make a decision and thus immersing them in ethical conflict as it is lived. Role playing also highlights the collaborative nature of public decision making. Even when an agent has to act single-handedly or assume ultimate responsibility for an outcome, decisions by public agents are not made in isolation. They are members of a team (even if complex and hierarchically organized) and have a responsibility to think about effects their acts may have on the integrity of their agency and its ability to continue its mission. Indeed, decision making by individuals occurs in a context of continuous deliberation among team members about their agency's agenda and its governing norms. By focusing on the quality of deliberation, a good case discussion makes evident the limited capacities of individuals regarding ethical matters; people do not have privileged access to moral truths. A particular agent may have an opinion—a plausible, even well-considered opinion—about what morality requires or what course of action would serve the public good. But it is only one opinion among others, and it could be flawed, even idiosyncratic. Role playing makes evident how deliberation with others provides checks on—and thereby assists—each agent's perceptions and reasoning.

Because of the possibility of consensus, it is unwise to assume that there is never a right answer in an ethics case. Even when a class session ends in disagreement, the conversation that spills into the hallways and lunchrooms may take unanticipated twists and move toward convergence. In fact, there is a pedagogical benefit to having at least a few cases scattered through a semester's syllabus which do have right answers, in the sense that, after animated exchanges of view and extended argumentation (within the compass of a class period), students realize that a certain judgment of the situation is the only sensible one. In this way, they have occasions to reaffirm settled moral points and appreciate that not everything is up for grabs in moral thinking.

Another advantage of adopting an agent's perspective is that one can better learn the pitfalls of decision making when stakes are high and demands are conflicting. Observing a situation from the inside, with its mix of commitments and constraints, opportunities and dangers, helps one appreciate the forces that produce insincere or hypocritical reasoning, self-serving posturing, and other pathologies of moral decision making under pressure. There is nothing quite like the case that illuminates for students the large repertoire of excuses—"no harm will be done," "these are just the rules of the game," "besides, everyone else is acting badly"—used by public agents to warrant ethically questionable behavior. In this way, students are sensitized to—and, one hopes, armed against—the possibility of their own corruption.

OTHER TYPES OF CASES

Although I have devoted some attention to the advantages of narrative cases, I am aware of the ongoing debate about whether practical ethics is best taught by the use of such cases. Some ethics teachers prefer what might be called legal cases, that is, the type of fact situation that appears in appellate court opinions. Although they also describe real events, legal cases are highly abbreviated and typically constructed with an eye to the applicable laws to be invoked for arriving at a decision. Because of this ulterior purpose, fact-descriptions offered by a judge in the written opinion of a legal case are not necessarily reliable. Even the very best judges, like Benjamin Cardozo, may be inclined to manipulate fact-descriptions in light of intended outcomes, and be so removed from the event under review as to lose sight of its ethically salient features.[4]

Nonetheless, philosophers especially may be inclined to prefer this type of case because the function of cases, in their view, is to serve as tests for selecting among alternative principles or theories. In other words, what drives the preference for legal—or even completely hypothetical—cases, for some teachers, is the aim to construct an abstract and comprehensive moral system. For myself, I can say only that I have no such ambition. Practical ethics, as I conceive it, is a form of reflective problem solving, and it needs to stay close to the ground to be useful. Of course, the pedagogy of practical ethics, so conceived, does not preclude the use of hypotheticals, in the sense of imagined variations on an actual case. But such hypotheticals remain rooted in the experiential reality depicted in the case and employ it as a touchstone for any novel formulations of principle.[5] This approach reflects my concern that "unrealistic" hypotheticals decontextualize ethical conflict and lose touch with the practical considerations that often determine which judgment—or which rule of conduct—is the most reasonable in the circumstances.

Even teachers who do not aspire to theory construction may prefer legal cases if they conceive of their pedagogical task as introducing students to a code of ethics, that is, learning a set of rules regulating their professional conduct. Condensed or hypothetical cases appear to be effective in helping students to grasp the meaning of rules by applying them to simplified, prototypical fact-situations. However, I do not believe that an orientation to rules trains students in the most important skills they need for ethical decision making. It is true that people who enter a field with a highly articulated code of professional conduct—such as law, health care, engineering, policework, and so on—should have a thorough grounding in their code, if for no other reason than because we want to be able to hold them accountable in certain predictably-recurring circumstances. But some professions, such as public management, do not have a highly specified code. The code that exists for public managers is brief and vague—and does not begin to address the central ethical conflicts that public managers confront.

Moreover, even where elaborate rules exist, they are of limited utility. Let me identify quickly, without fully defending, my reasons for this claim. We know from the study of Anglo-American common law that decisions in specific cases do not determine (unique) rules. By the same token, rules do not decide cases.[6] The gap is bridged only by judgment. One reason for the gap is that the materials relevant to moral deliberation are more extensive than any available set of rules. They include principles, values, ideals, and so on, not all of which can be formulated as rules. (These resources are especially important when two rules in a code conflict.) Even when a rule serves as a rough guide, the social or institutional context of application is essential to understanding its purpose and scope. Often enough, in fact, there is a mismatch, where following the rule would contravene its purpose. The upshot is that, for sound ethical decision making, individuals need other capacities than the ability to follow a rule. These are second-order competences (or virtues) which enable individuals to recognize occasions when rule following becomes problematic. In a world of uncertainty and fortuitous happenstance, the competences of reflectiveness, sympathy, and prudence, among others, are crucial to one's being an effective moral agent. Teaching practical ethics, in my view, includes training in these skills.

Of course, circumstances arise in which we may want individuals to stick to specified rules and not concern themselves with problems in their application. A code may be designed to preclude all-things-considered deliberation, perhaps to minimize mistakes in reasoning, to control the corrupting influence of self-serving judgment, to coordinate the activities of many agents, and so on. However, in such circumstances, we do not fool ourselves into thinking that rule following is especially virtuous. We have policy reasons and institutional reasons for intentionally limiting people's moral vision in such instances.

A NARRATIVE CASE ON POLICE ETHICS

Now that I have offered some general remarks on case teaching, let me turn to the specific case in police ethics that I wish to discuss. The case developed fortuitously when a student at the Kennedy School of Government took a reading course with me on gender and public policy. She was a member of the Houston Police Department (HPD) and had access to the department's arrest records. She discovered that no woman on the force had ever shot a suspect, yet the rates of arrest for policewomen were at least as good as the rates for their male counterparts. This led her to wonder about gender differences regarding the use of deadly force—and more generally.

Midway through the semester, the first use of deadly force by a Houston policewoman occurred, and that incident gave me the idea of writing a case. To give the case focus, we decided it should include two main components: first, an account of my student's experience in the HPD (she is disguised in the case as "Alice Appleby"), then the shooting incident. Since Appleby was a friend of the policewoman involved, she was able to verify the details of the story. (Extensive news accounts were another primary source.) Later, the policewoman, Tinsley Guinn-Shaver, herself visited the Kennedy School and was interviewed by my research assistant, Jillian Dickert, who prepared the case. During this visit, Guinn-Shaver revealed that she had written her own account of the shooting, and we decided to incorporate it into the case.[7]

The story is dramatic. Without the gory details, it is, in brief, this. Guinn-Shaver was on night patrol duty on Houston's West Side when she stopped a car with an expired out-of-state license plate. The driver, it turned out, was wanted in two states for parole and probation violations. She had a felony arrest to make, but she had to do it alone because the backup units which ordinarily would be summoned in such situations were involved in an extended stolen auto chase. When she attempted to handcuff the suspect, he struggled violently, ramming his head into her face, and fled. She pursued and caught up with him within a block. They struggled again and once again he eluded her grasp. She pursued again, and this time, as they fought on the ground, the suspect's attack became extremely vicious; he hit Guinn-Shaver in the face with her radio and then her flashlight. He fled again, and although dizzy and disoriented she pursued him again. This time, as they struggled again, she felt herself sinking beneath his blows and thought she might pass out. "Out of desperation," as she put it, she pulled out her gun and struck the suspect several times with it. Despite her pleas to desist, he kept fighting, so she pointed the gun and pulled the trigger. The suspect fell helplessly to the ground. At that point, a backup unit arrived, eight minutes and thirty-five seconds after the initial contact. An officer said, "Are you all right?" She replied, "No . . . I shot him."

TYPES OF ETHICAL CONFLICT

What issues are raised by Guinn-Shaver's story? It is helpful to distinguish two types of ethical conflict which arise for agents in public roles. In both instances, ethical duties derived from the role itself clash with duties derived from an external source which also has authority for the agent. Guinn-Shaver's story illustrates both types. In the first category, the external standard is the agent's morally- or religiously-informed conscience. Thus, a case could recount the story of an agent struggling to follow a duly-enacted law or to obey the legitimate order of a superior, where the law or order requires conduct that the agent abhors as a matter of sincere conviction. Such a case focuses on the clash between personal beliefs and public duties. On one side, failure to adhere to a conscientious conviction poses a serious challenge to the agent's moral integrity; on the other side, the agent's belief—no matter how sincere—may have no moral standing with other agents involved in the action and may be incompatible with the duties of the role. At first glance, Tinsley Guinn-Shaver's conduct may not appear to illustrate this type of conflict, but a little reflection leads to a different conclusion. If we accept the hypothesis that a person's moral consciousness is deeply informed by gender, and that one of the key points of distinction is women's disposition to non-violence, a potential conflict between personal standards and public duties becomes apparent. I shall return to it in a moment.

The second type of conflict between internal and external standards turns not on personally-held views but on established precepts of common morality, which are binding on everyone regardless of role. Conflicts of this type raise the question whether public agents are entitled to the benefits of a "special ethic" exempting them from the moral constraints that apply to ordinary citizens. Here, a first glance may suggest that the idea of a special ethic fits Guinn-Shaver's case since authority to use deadly force is a distinguishing feature of a police officer. However, we need to be careful. True, police officers have authority to do what ordinary citizens are not permitted to do. It does not follow that police authority necessarily excludes considerations of common morality. Thus, recent efforts to specify the conditions under which police use of deadly force is justified may be understood as clarifying how the police role incorporates, rather than excludes, such moral constraints. Of course, in practice not all police behavior reflects this limitation. The Houston Police Department in particular had a reputation as trigger-happy. Guinn-Shaver was deeply concerned to change this reputation, and so was struggling to integrate a principle of respect for life (or minimal use of deadly force) into a reformed understanding of police work. That struggle identifies a second ethical conflict raised by the case; again, I shall return to it in a moment.

TEACHING THE CASE

So far I have only hinted at two themes raised by Guinn-Shaver's story. I want now to elaborate these themes by talking about the teaching of the case. My aim is not so much to offer a "class plan" as to sketch a set of connected questions which I use to guide class discussion. (Most of the background information about the HPD is taken from the case itself.)

Typically, students enter the class charged up and ready to express their reactions to the main incident in the case, Guinn-Shaver's confrontation with the suspect. I try to disarm them a bit and impose some discipline on their thinking by beginning with a general question about the function of police in society. The likelihood is that they have not thought about this question directly, but they will have things to say once the question is posed. (It does not take much prodding for them to generate standard conceptions of policing.) My aim here ultimately is to ask why police carry guns. Students are vaguely aware that gun use is not part of police work in every society. They are ready to concoct explanations for why it is so in the United States, having to do with the history and pervasiveness of violence in this country. Pedagogically, the point of this exercise is to make explicit the premises needed for any argument justifying the use of deadly force in a particular circumstance.

The case itself guides students toward a focus on deadly force by opening with sociologist Egon Bittner's characterization of the police role as that of addressing human problems "when and insofar as the problems' solutions may require the use of force at the point of their occurrence."[8] The use (or threat) of force is authorized in order to prevent situations of conflict from getting worse. Thus, police officers have a latitude in the choice of solutions not available legally to other citizens.

However, after placing the use of force at the center of policing, the case immediately makes this feature morally problematic by pointing to some pathologies of police practice, such as unjustified shootings of citizens. In particular, the case sketches the troubled history of the Houston Police Department, which was known for its aggressive, confrontational style of policing. As researchers have noted, the Houston department "long prided itself on taking names and kicking ass."[9] Policing was not easily distinguished, at times, from harassment, especially of the city's minority populations. Even in cases of genuine criminality, officers' reactions were often disproportionate to the needs of the situation. According to department lore, for example, "in the good old days a burglar caught in a house was likely to die there."[10] In 1989, a lawsuit filed by the family of a black woman who was shot to death by an off-duty police officer claimed that the city tolerated the use of excessive force "to such an extent that it [had] become custom and habit."[11]

In 1982, Mayor Kathy Whitmire attempted to extirpate this culture of violence by appointing Lee Brown, an African-American and an outsider, to head the department. The hope was that Brown's innovations as director of public safety in Atlanta could be introduced in Houston to improve police operations. And indeed Brown's tenure as chief in Houston was marked by pioneering reforms—in many respects, a model of managerial success.[12] He redefined the fundamental mission of the department, shifting it away from the cowboy "spirit of adventure" in favor of a community-oriented "spirit of service," and introduced various operational innovations that changed the way Houston police officers did their work. Among reforms addressing the use of deadly force, Brown established a firearms policy stipulating that officers could not *draw* their weapons unless their lives, or someone else's, were in danger. Despite Brown's many successes, however, the pattern of excessive police violence continued. In 1989, forty civilians were shot by police, resulting in twelve fatalities. That was the highest number of shootings since 1982—itself a record year—when fourteen civilians were fatally shot and thirty-five wounded.[13]

In January, 1990, Chief Brown left Houston to become police commissioner in New York City. (He later served as President Clinton's "drug czar.") Mayor Whitmire replaced him with Elizabeth Watson, who had directed Houston's West Side Command Station—the site of Brown's initial experiments in neighborhood-oriented policing. Watson, a Brown protégé, became the first woman police chief in the history of the Houston department and only the second in charge of a major police force in the U.S. (The first was in Portland, Oregon.) Watson's appointment provides a bridge to the second large theme of the case: gender difference. So once the issue of the use of deadly force is squarely in front of the class, I turn the discussion to several sections of the case that address women's experience in the Houston department. (This is the component based on Alice Appleby's research and personal report.) It is well known that women's entry into policework, which began in significant numbers in the middle 1970s, has not been easy. Male resistance is typified by the reaction of some Houston officers to the announcement of Watson's appointment. They went up to female members of the force and curtsied and asked whether curtsying would be the policy rather than saluting.

Regarding the use of force, some observers have suggested that patrolwomen, when confronted with danger or violence, are more likely to use their guns than male officers, to compensate for their vulnerability. Yet none of various studies that have been done on policewomen reveals any indication that they either fire or unholster their weapons more frequently than male officers.[14] When Alice Appleby reviewed police shootings in Houston over the fifteen years since women began patrol duty, from 1975 to 1990, she discovered that female officers never discharged their weapons to kill, injure, or apprehend a suspect. This aroused her curiosity, so she interviewed them and asked why they had never used deadly force. They spoke mainly about the availability of a larger repertoire of skills for defusing confrontational situations, including patience, finesse, the ability to read interpersonal signals like body language, the absence of a need to prove their invincibility, and less likelihood to assume that most people have malevolent intentions.

These comments support the hypothesis of gender difference. In teaching the case, I often supplement it with a selection from Carol Gilligan's *In A Different Voice*, which helps to place the policewomen's remarks into a larger framework about differences in moral consciousness.[15] (Another possible reading is Sara Ruddick's discussion of "maternal thinking."[16]) In introducing Gilligan, I do not mean to suggest that the hypothesis of gender difference is necessarily sound. There are many obstacles—conceptual, empirical, and normative—to its acceptance. My own view is that the range of variation in traits is greater within one sex than between the sexes. Further, what differences exist are often contingent or situational; that is, so-called female or male traits may have more to do with different activities, opportunities, and obstacles encountered than with constitutional differences.

Still, just because the hypothesis has widespread currency, there are sufficient (what one might call) political reasons for focusing attention on it in the way that the policewoman case does. Police departments, like many other public agencies, are in the middle of a cultural, as well as institutional, adjustment of major proportions in attempting to make a place for women in policework. Male officers may be inclined to resist this development by exploiting the gender hypothesis, magnifying difference in order to enhance their own claim of dominance. Thus, they regard qualities associated with women as less functional for the work that needs to be done. Interestingly, one response to this claim could be for women to emphasize similarities, rather than differences, in order to ease their entry into policework. Alternatively, women could exploit the hypothesis of difference as well, to establish the one-sidedness of the present arrangement and support the legitimacy of their entry in order to achieve an appropriate balance.

The sections in the case on Alice Appleby's experience as a cadet in the police training academy and then as an officer on patrol provide anecdotal support for both gender strategies. Appleby was the only one of ten women in her entering class who managed to graduate from the training academy four months later. She was convinced that the hostile treatment of women, not the rigor of the training, explained the thinning of the ranks. The male cadets felt that women could be police officers only because the law demanded it, not because women might be just as good at the job. Appleby proved otherwise. For example, twice in her defensive tactics class, she was viciously attacked by two different male cadets who were determined to prove that no woman could arrest a man if he did not permit it. Both times she ended up with bruises and busted lips—and a handcuffed, prone, and embarrassed male cadet. More generally, Appleby scored better than any of her male peers in marksmanship, high-performance driving, and physical endurance. As a result, her success could be attributed to gender similarity.

On patrol, however, gender difference came into play. Since Appleby had earned the rank of "distinguished expert," a level of marksmanship very few officers (male or female) attain, she was sought as a partner by officers who valued force over finesse. This led to tensions. For example, during a felony stop with her first patrol partner, they pulled over a moving van. The officers stood behind the open doors of their cruiser and ordered the suspects out of the van. The driver came out on the left side, and Appleby's partner covered him, although the height of the van prevented Appleby from seeing him. Next, two men exited from the passenger side. One of them had a pistol and drew down on Appleby. She immediately ordered him to put the gun down, informing him that she had cover, and that he would be the loser in a shooting match. The suspect put the gun down, and all of the men were placed under arrest. Afterwards, Appleby's partner was incensed that she did not shoot the suspect the minute he drew his gun, lamenting that she had "passed up a perfect opportunity to kill some scum." He told her about some shootings he and other officers had been involved in and claimed it was simple for an officer to get away with "teaching people a lesson." He reminded her that "dead men don't talk." However, Appleby was not inclined to use deadly force when it was not necessary to resolve the problem. Under applicable rules, Appleby was clearly *permitted* to shoot (and kill) the suspect, so her refraining from doing so exhibited a value not captured by the rules: Shoot only when there is no alternative. Her partner, we might say, correctly believed that a suspect who draws a gun on a police officer loses immunity from deadly force, but he incorrectly inferred from the loss of immunity that the suspect deserved to be shot.[17]

I dwell on Appleby's experience in the HPD because it is important to keep in mind that there are two women featured in the case, not one. Some students, especially males, may seize upon Guinn-Shaver's story to confirm their prejudice that a man (as such, without identifying any specific qualities) would have handled the situation more satisfactorily. These students should be asked whether they think it would have been right for Appleby to "kill some scum" when she had the opportunity. If the answer is no, they may appreciate that the crucial factor is the attitude or value exhibited in Appleby's (and possibly Guinn-Shaver's) response, not gender. For this reason, among others, I usually begin the discussion of the main incident by asking what strengths and weaknesses Guinn-Shaver brought to policework and to the situation she found herself in. (Prior to the account of the shooting, the case briefly describes Guinn-Shaver's ten-year relationship with the HPD.) This reminds students that we are focusing on a specific person, not an abstract representative of a generic category. Nonetheless, though the debate about gender difference, as a general matter, is likely to be inconclusive, it offers the second possible explanation of why Guinn-Shaver hesitated so long to use her gun. (Even when she finally draws it, she uses it initially to hit the suspect.) It is of course highly provocative to suggest that she hesitated because she is a woman. Even the most ardent defenders of gender difference balk at that suggestion. However, that is why the case is an excellent vehicle for exploring the implications of the hypothesis of gender difference.

Returning to the class plan, let me say finally that a number of smaller questions can be posed along the way. For example: Should Guinn-Shaver have felt regret, as she did, at the suspect's death? Is it true, as she claims, that to use deadly force is to fail as a police officer? Should a male—or female—officer worry about having Guinn-Shaver as a partner? If it is true that women bring distinctive attitudes and commitments to policework, how should police departments exploit these differences? Should they be the basis for rewriting the rules of police conduct or for other changes in institutional design? All of these questions, and others, can be used to elaborate the two major themes of deadly force and gender difference.

REASONING IN AN ETHICS CASE

I hope I have now offered just enough details of the policewoman case to whet your appetite for learning more about it. However, in accordance with my assignment, my concerns here are primarily pedagogical. So I want to turn finally to another important aspect of case teaching—the kind of reasoning that one should expect to engage in. I shall offer some general remarks and illustrate them briefly by reference to the policewoman case.

The "class plan" I have sketched reveals that the function of a case teacher, in my view, is to facilitate discussion. It is not to expound doctrine or pet philosophical theories, not even necessarily to express a point of view. Facilitation is done primarily through asking a series of connected questions, so as to elicit opinions and arguments from students on the major issues raised by the case. The principal challenge for a teacher is so to structure class discussion that students are forced to reflect on and analyze the opinions they express. Sometimes I engage in brief Socratic colloquies, which are helpful for clarifying claims and dismissing ones that are clearly indefensible. But the most successful classes are those in which students challenge each other to clarify, defend, and give depth to their beliefs. The real art of case teaching lies in employing techniques to make that happen. The level of sophistication one can reach depends upon the students.

In managing an interactive, student-centered conversation about controversial ethical issues, there are two dangers to avoid: overestimating the amount of disagreement among members of the class, and underestimating the amount of disagreement. Which danger is the greater will depend on the case. In the policewoman case, the principal source of controversy —and tension—in the classroom is the gender question. In fact a typical class will mirror in miniature, but in a protected environment, the differences of opinion and attitude to be found in a contemporary police station. The controversy about gender difference, however, should not be allowed to obscure the deep moral agreement at the heart of the case which will emerge in the course of discussion if the conversation is conducted with appropriate foresight. The point of agreement is that deadly force should be used only as a last resort. Although Tinsley Guinn-Shaver may have exercised poor judgment in the way she pursued her suspect, what is so compelling—even noble—in her conduct is her exemplification of this idea. If students fail to achieve this insight, and fail to grasp it as a fixed point of agreement among them, the pedagogical exercise itself may have to be considered a failure.

How will this collective realization occur? Let me return to the subject of ethical reasoning. One task of moral reflection is to understand the basis of disagreement when it occurs and to survey the possibilities of agreement. This includes examining the forms of argument used in practical disputes, such as appeal to authority (including the law), appeal to intuition or "gut feeling," appeal to conventional or traditional belief, appeal to apt analogies, and so on. All of these forms of argument have a legitimate place in practical ethics, which is why case discussion does not lend itself easily to the application of general moral theories—what we could call the top-down method of reasoning.

The top-down method employs a theory—that is, a structure of abstract normative propositions—to justify specific rules, policies, or acts. The method is deductive; the paradigm is Euclidean geometry. At the top of the theory is an overarching goal (say, to maximize utility), or a set of fundamental rights (life, liberty, and property), or transcendent duties (to do justice, love mercy, and walk humbly with thy god). Other goals, rights, and duties are subordinate and derivative. Thus, in the policewoman case the top-down method will focus attention on deriving the idea of using deadly force only as a last resort from some abstract moral principle, perhaps the respect due human beings as independent, autonomous agents. Of course, the authority of the more abstract principle will also have to be established. And so by small but inevitable steps students are led to engage in an enterprise driven by strictly theoretical concerns.

In contrast, the bottom-up method is inductive. It begins with ongoing practices and judgments in particular cases—and moves beyond them only to the degree needed for resolution of the problem posed for discussion, or to connect a set of related cases. The idea is to uncover and to refine, and only sometimes to systematize, the moral perceptions, sentiments, or conventions that are salient for public officials. Many of these serve as "provisional fixed points," to borrow a term from John Rawls, and are employed in the formulation of heuristic middle-level principles.[18] If we go no farther than middle-level principles, it will be because the point in case discussion, after all, is to teach judgment not doctrine, sound practical reasoning not system. In the bottom-up method, ideas are in the service of problem solving.

To illustrate, let me draw your attention to one crucial dimension of the conversation in the policewoman case regarding the cultural and institutional context of decision making. We know that the problem of unnecessary use of force by police officers predates the events described in this case and indeed has a long history. One of the vital questions to explore is the extent to which this recurrent phenomenon may fairly be attributed to the nature of policework itself, even if only as an unwanted but unavoidable byproduct. The intriguing proposal made by the policewoman case is that the turning point in doing something about the problem of unnecessary force occurred not by a change in the rules of engagement (as we might call them), not by a change in management or organizational strategies (such as Lee Brown's innovative move to neighborhood policing), but by a change in personnel: that is, when a different type of person became a police officer—a person with different attitudes and values, as well as a different repertoire of skills—who, it turned out, was just as effective at the work that needed to be done.[19] This point about effectiveness is fundamental because a particular style or pattern of judgment in doing policework will not be acceptable unless it accords with the police function and what counts as success in carrying it out. The bottom-up method of reasoning keeps us focused on such practical criteria of moral acceptability.

It is worth noting that this point applies as well to the rules of engagement. Determining the most reasonable rule of conduct for situations in which a suspect is engaged in a life-threatening act will turn on such practical considerations as: (1) whether the rule can be readily followed in the kind of rapidly-evolving circumstances that officers encounter on the street; (2) whether the rule allows for officers' legitimate concerns for personal safety; (3) whether the rule is consistent with a routine process of accountability; and so on. My claim is that these practical considerations should not be thought of as requiring compromises with the "true" rule of conduct derived from abstract principles; they are valid criteria for determining which rule is the most reasonable. Thus, however sensible it may seem, abstractly, to have a rule that officers should shoot to wound rather than to kill, I am inclined to think that such a rule makes no practical sense and is therefore not a reasonable rule.[20]

To return to gender: I suppose one might think of the shift from male to female officers as a kind of experiment, testing whether gender difference is constitutional (that is, an inherent feature of the agent, whether biologically- or socially-rooted) or situational (that is, a variable feature elicited by activities engaged in). However, the experiment is actually unnecessary. Since the use of excessive force is not uniform among male officers, a test could be conducted with males alone. Then we could better determine whether unnecessary force is inherent in policework or attributable to a small band of cowboys and rogue officers.

In supporting the bottom-up approach, I do not mean to suggest that reasoning about principles has no part in moral reflection. If abstract principles are not the ultimate standards for evaluating specific decisions, they still may be useful as guidelines or rules of thumb, providing summaries of judgments made in particular cases in the past. If they have withstood critical reflection over time, they may even embody a certain collective social wisdom about practical affairs. But since they mirror only what has been seen before, they do not necessarily prepare us for novel, unanticipated happenings of the sort that the world tends constantly to throw at us. However nuanced their formulation may be, articulated standards rest on tacit assumptions and implicit expectations which often become evident only when some aberration occurs. In the usual case, the standards will be imprecise and fallible, and hence are not to be relied on anyway without testing them against one's own good sense—or the good sense, as Aristotle recommends, of the wise and virtuous person.[21]

If the judgments of a virtuous person were easily formulable as rules, and reliably took account of all the practical circumstances determining the reasonableness of conduct, ethical reasoning would consist in the cognitive exercise of getting the formulations correct and applying them to cases. But if, as I have suggested, they are not easily formulable, ethical conduct requires a preliminary educational process consisting of close observation of others, such as the narrative case method provides. In this respect, the policewoman case is especially apt because it reflects the two pedagogic motives for engaging in case discussion: eliciting imitation (Alice Appleby) and provoking reflection (Tinsley Guinn-Shaver). Teaching practical ethics, in this view, could perhaps be modeled on teaching someone how to play a musical instrument, where the student is initiated into a particular way of feeling and responding, mastering the local techniques, and eventually being able to improvise within settled practices when appropriate. In such learning, the considered judgments of experienced persons carry more weight than theoretical arguments.

Of course, the obstacles to reliable generalization—such as the mutability of the world and the indeterminacy of language—do not entirely defeat efforts to reach the common ground of universal principle. So the task in ethics may be to proceed dialectically, to attempt to balance the general and the particular, to test each against the other, aiming at an equilibrium between unshakable convictions in specific cases and the demands of reason. In this way, moral reflection retains a critical edge without becoming detached from the practices in which it is employed. But I want to emphasize that the theoretical enterprise of systematizing one's judgments can take on a life of its own and divert attention from the ethical problem at hand. Any comprehensive, integrated, overarching scheme may represent no more than the temporary victory of the intellect over good sense, which shows itself concretely, in particular cases.

ETHICAL KNOWLEDGE AND THE ROLE OF THE TEACHER

To close these remarks on case teaching, allow me to offer you an image which captures the differences in method I have been attempting to expound. In his *Discourse on Method,* René Descartes meditates on the difference between works produced by several persons and those produced by a single hand.[22] He thinks the latter are more likely than the former to be well constructed. For example, ancient towns which have developed only gradually and apparently haphazardly into great cities are ordinarily, he says, very badly arranged. With their crooked streets and odd assortment of houses, "one would rather suppose that chance and not the decisions of rational men had so arranged them." Such places stand in marked contrast to "the symmetrical metropolitan districts which a city planner has laid out on an open plain according to his own designs." (Keep in mind that Descartes was referring to Old World examples; he knew nothing of Boston or Washington, D.C.)

Descartes' aim in developing this image of two contrasting cities is to draw an analogy to two kinds of knowledge. The first has grown up little by little through the accumulation of the opinions of many different persons; the second consists in "the simple and natural reasonings" of a single person of ability, who rejects completely all received opinions and accepts only what is seen to fit into a rational scheme. The point of the analogy of course is to suggest that the reasonings of the single person of ability will be nearer to the truth.

This image has been attractive to philosophers ever since Descartes set it down. And there may well be some areas of inquiry where it has application. But Descartes himself recognized that it does not apply to the moral life, which closely resembles the haphazardly evolving city. It is a life of many accumulated opinions, reflecting the practice of many generations. Its pathways lead in unexpected directions and often expose unanticipated connections—or blind alleys. From the perspective of a single individual, part of the difficulty in attempting reconstruction (whether of a city or of the moral life) is the magnitude of the task: "large edifices are too difficult to set up again once they have been thrown down, too difficult even to preserve once they have been shaken, and their fall is necessarily catastrophic." And existing structures may embody a wisdom not easily discerned. "It is certain that many institutions have defects," Descartes says, even if custom has inured us to them. But custom has perhaps "found ways to avoid or correct more defects than prudence could have done." One thinks of the way urban renewal projects, in too many instances, ended up destroying vibrant, multi-ethnic communities, such as Boston's West End, only to be replaced by sterile enclaves for the well-to-do.

If the Cartesian image of the moral life is correct, it has implications for the role of the instructor in teaching practical ethics. It means, most importantly, that the moral life is a shared life; that student and teacher are in it together, exploring the place they have both resided all their lives. The teacher, perhaps, is more familiar with its general features, but not necessarily its details. So it would be a mistake for the teacher to take on the role of tourguide for visiting strangers. The enterprise is rather joint exploration of territory familiar to all parties, even if in varying degrees.

A tourguide gives lectures and answers questions. In an ethics case discussion, there may sometimes be information to impart through lecture —but not often. In general, it is not the teacher's function to be an oracle of some moral truth, let alone to elaborate general theories. In fact, depending on the issue, the teacher may not be in as good a position as some students to offer ethical instruction. In a discussion of the policewoman case, for example, it would be an enormous benefit to everyone if some members of the class were seasoned patrol officers or had engaged in comparable experiences, perhaps in the military. Their comments would not be epistemically privileged, but they would legitimately command everyone's attention as reports (for example) of ongoing practices and regulative norms—not readily available to outside observers. Of course, if the teacher were a representative human being whose moral sense, when analyzed, revealed the principles of sound ethical reasoning for every situation, the teacher would merit a special place in the classroom. But individuals have a reliable moral sensibility only if they have been well brought up and sufficiently immersed in the practices in which ethical judgment is exercised—and, regarding any given public role, such as policework, that is as likely to be true of one or more of the students as of the instructor.

In case discussion, therefore, the role of the teacher is not that of expert or source of knowledge; it is that of facilitator and intellectual foil, assisting students in their collaborative deliberations and attempting to nurture in them the ability to handle ethical conflict effectively on their own when the instructor is not around to monitor the conversation. The principal technique for realizing this aim is the reverse of the tourguide's; it is to *ask* questions. The questions, of course, must be carefully chosen so as to introduce students to a certain path of inquiry, to keep the inquiry moving in a productive direction, to press them to investigate areas not yet probed sufficiently, and so on. All with the outcome, one hopes, of mutual understanding, exploring their ethical life together.

NOTES

I am grateful to the conferees at John Jay College for their comments on the presented version of this paper, and especially to Gary Seay and John Kleinig for their written remarks.

1. My remarks on case teaching in this and subsequent sections draw upon my note, "Teaching Ethics by the Case Method," [N18-95-1304] (Cambridge: Kennedy School of Government Case Program, 1995). I should mention that I am wary of describing my attachment to narrative cases as "postmodern." My aim is not to displace discursive reasoning about ethics but to recast it in a practical form, using narrative cases in a way that learns from the work of Aristotle, Machiavelli, and other philosophers. In contrast, it often seems that the postmodernist preference for narrative over discursive styles has more to do with misology than a constructive search for alternative modes of ethical reflection.

2. Several Kennedy School faculty and staff members have written about the case method of teaching. The Case Program has usefully gathered together some of these pieces in "Five Notes on the Case Method," which includes Dorothy Robyn's "What Makes A Good Case?" [N15-86-673](Cambridge: Kennedy School of Government Case Program, 1986). Other items have appeared in professional publications, such as John Boehrer's "On Teaching A Case," *International Studies Notes* 19, no. 2 (1994).

3. Caroline Whitbeck addresses this aspect of practical ethics in "Ethics as Design: Doing Justice to Moral Problems," *Hastings Center Report* 26, no. 3 (1996), pp. 9-16.

4. On Cardozo's penchant for manipulating fact-descriptions in light of intended outcomes, see Richard Posner, *Cardozo: A Study in Reputation* (Chicago: Univ. of Chicago, 1990). On Cardozo's distancing strategies and its motivations, see John T. Noonan, Jr., "The Passengers of *Palsgraf*," in *Persons and Masks of the Law* (New York: Farrar, Straus and Giroux, 1976).

5. The opposing view has been defended by Frances Kamm, who prefers "unrealistic hypotheticals" because "real-life cases" involve "details inessential to a theoretical point." See Frances Myrna Kamm, "Ethics, Applied Ethics, and Applying Applied Ethics" in *Applied Ethics and Ethical Theory,* ed. David M. Rosenthal and Fadlou Shehadi (Salt Lake City: University of Utah Press, 1988), p. 164.

6. For the argument, see Kenneth I. Winston, "On Treating Like Cases Alike," *California Law Review* 62, no. 1 (1974), pp. 1-39, and "The Problem of Indeterminacy and Its Solution," *Archiv für Rechts- und Sozialphilosophie*, Beiheft 40 (1991), pp. 192-95.

7. The case is titled "A Policewoman's (Non)use of Deadly Force." It is available from the Kennedy School Case Program [C16-91-1040] and has been reprinted in *Gender and Public Policy: Cases and Comments*, ed. Kenneth Winston and Mary Jo Bane (Boulder: Westview Press, 1993).

8. Egon Bittner, "The Capacity to Use Force as the Core of the Police Role," *Moral Issues in Police Work*, ed. Frederick A. Elliston and Michael Feldberg (Totowa: Rowman and Allanheld, 1985), p. 21. John Kleinig argues that Bittner's characterization "feeds the image that police have of themselves as . . . working in a human jungle whose law is force," in *The Ethics of Policing* (Cambridge, UK: Cambridge University Press, 1996), p. 96. The jungle image surely does license such an inference, and Bittner appears to encourage the image when he observes that, as a practical matter, police authorization to use force "is essentially unrestricted" (ibid., p. 16). However, if we reject this last point, Bittner's formula seems perfectly compatible with regarding the use of force as, in Kleinig's words, "a last and regrettable option."

9. Malcolm K. Sparrow, Mark H. Moore, and David M. Kennedy, *Beyond 911: A New Era for Policing* (New York: Basic Books, 1990), p. 90.

10. Ibid.

11. David Elliston, "Ida Delaney Family Sues HPD, 3 Officers, City and Club," *The Houston Post*, December 5, 1989, p. A-1.

12. For an illuminating discussion of Brown's work at the HPD, and the lessons to be drawn from it, see Mark H. Moore, *Creating Public Value: Strategic Management in Government* (Cambridge: Harvard University Press, 1995), chs. 6 and 7.

13. See Jack Douglas, "Fatal Shootout on Freeway Brings Police Killings to 9," *The Houston Post*, November 2, 1989, p. A-19, and S. K. Bardwell and Andrew Kirtzman, "HPD's '89 Civilian Shootings Rise to 40," *The Houston Post*, January 11, 1990, p. A-23.

14. For references and a discussion of the issues, see Barbara Carson, "Women in Law Enforcement," in *Women and the Use of Military Force*, ed. Ruth H. Howes and Michael R. Stevenson (Boulder: Lynne Rienner Publications, 1993).

15. Carol Gilligan, *In A Different Voice: Psychological Theory and Women's Development* (Cambridge: Harvard Univ. Press, 1982). For a thoughtful assessment of the gender hypothesis, see Owen Flanagan, *Varieties of Moral Personality: Ethics and Psychological Realism* (Cambridge: Harvard University Press, 1991), chapters 7-11.

16. Sara Ruddick, *Maternal Thinking: Toward A Politics of Peace* (Boston: Beacon Press, 1989).

17. The governing law for this type of situation was formulated by the U. S. Supreme Court in Tennessee v. Garner, 471 U.S. 1 (1985). In this case, the Court

held that a necessary condition of the use of deadly force is that the officer has probable cause to believe that the suspect poses a significant threat of death or serious physical injury to the officer or others. During the discussion of my paper at John Jay College, William Heffernan captured Appleby's way of going beyond (but not against) the law by referring to her as a "*Garner*-plus cop"(*infra*, p. 193).

18. See John Rawls, *A Theory of Justice* (Cambridge: Harvard University Press, 1971), pp. 19-20. I hope I am not understood as suggesting that police officers—or public officials generally—should have a privileged status in determining which rules of conduct will regulate their activities. In my view, it is no more their prerogative to set such rules than it is for them to be exclusive determinants of their social function. These matters, especially in a democracy, are to be settled by the ongoing (and mostly informal) deliberations of all citizens. So, in this regard, I take issue with Michael Davis's defense of the autonomy of professional groups. See, e.g., Michael Davis, "Thinking Like an Engineer: The Place of a Code of Ethics in the Practice of a Profession," *Philosophy & Public Affairs* 20, no. 2 (1991), pp. 150-67.

19. Mark Moore observes that "the greater part of [a police department's] production process emerges from the particular way that individual officers do their work" (*Creating Public Value*, p. 222). But he does not consider the implications of gender difference in this regard.

20. Roger Wertheimer touches on some of these issues in "Regulating Police Use of Deadly Force," in *Ethics, Public Policy, and Criminal Justice*, ed. Frederick Elliston and Norman Bowie (Cambridge: Oelgeschlager, Gunn & Hain, 1982), pp. 93-109.

21. For Aristotle's view of rules, see Martha Nussbaum, "Rules and Practical Consistency" in *Aristotle's De Motu Animalium: Text with Translation, Commentary, and Interpretive Essays* (Princeton: Princeton Univ. Press, 1978), pp. 210-19. What I have called the bottom-up method of reasoning is defended in general terms by Nussbaum in *The Fragility of Goodness: Luck and Ethics in Greek Tragedy* (Cambridge, UK: Cambridge University Press, 1986). See also Annette Baier, "Theory and Reflective Practices" in *Postures of the Mind: Essays on Mind and Morals* (Minneapolis: University of Minnesota Press, 1985).

22. The quotations that follow are from René Descartes, *Discourse on the Method of Rightly Conducting the Reason and Seeking Truth in the Sciences*, trans. Laurence J. LaFleur (Indianapolis: Bobbs-Merrill, 1950), pp. 7-14.

Response to Winston

Gary Seay

In this paper I should like to look closely at some of Professor Winston's more general observations about the methodology of teaching ethics through the use of cases. My own experience has been mostly in teaching courses in moral philosophy for undergraduates at various levels, so my concern will be not with the very interesting police ethics case he discusses but with some equally interesting problems that I believe are inherent in teaching ethics by the case method.

Winston contrasts two alternative models of ethical reasoning, which in fact offer two very different views of the basis of justification in normative ethics. One is the familiar "top-down" or deductivist model, the other the "bottom-up" or inductivist model defended by Annette Baier, Martha Nussbaum, and others. Winston holds that it is natural for the case method to make use of the latter model, and he appears also to believe that that model (the inductivist model) is in any case adequate to show how practical moral judgments—of the sort met with in deliberations about cases—can be justified. But I have some doubts about that, which I shall outline briefly here.

Winston's account of why a "top-down," or deductivist, approach to ethical reasoning is inadequate for much of the practical moral thinking we do in deliberating about actual cases is surely correct: that because the rules generated by ethical theories are themselves at a certain level of abstraction, they turn out to be insufficiently adaptable to the nuances of real-life moral dilemmas. (In all the interesting cases, the problem of how to follow a moral rule seems to take the form, "I know I ought to do x in cases of type t, but is *this* case of that type?") Clearly, there are formidable problems with the deductivist model of moral reasoning, and I do not wish to defend such a model.

Furthermore, I believe that there is much to be said for using the case method in teaching practical ethics. No doubt Winston and other practitioners of that method are right that teaching with cases has great pedagogical value in its capacity to provoke lively discussions. Surely disputation does engage students as almost nothing else can, and is essential to any real philosophical understanding. Moreover, the use of cases affords students an opportunity to deliberate about moral dilemmas that are richly textured, with all the complexity, confusions, and subsidiary problems characteristic of moral quandaries in everyday life.

But I wonder whether students are really prepared to think seriously about these practical cases without having at least some exposure to ethical theory first. Winston asserts that the instructor's role in an ethics case discussion should not include the presentation of ethical theories. But without any theory at all, can we really expect that students will develop the capacity to think critically about the principles they discover by induction? Will they not be inclined, in their discussions, to fall back on their pre-reflective code moralities in ways that amount to question-begging? Furthermore, if we do think that some moral judgments are sound and others grounded only in irrational prejudice, how do we draw this distinction without appealing, at some level, to ethical theory? And what, exactly, is the *criterion* for determining whether an ethical deliberation is *getting anywhere*? If we have no independent standard of good reasons to appeal to—so that criticism of a contextual moral judgment can come only from *other pre-theoretical moral perceptions*—then how can we be sure that our moral deliberation is not just a contest between opposing prejudices? Inductivism, it seems to me, may well be stuck with the very problem that haunted W. D. Ross's ethical theory: when people differ in their intuitions about what prima facie duties there are—or about how to "weigh" prima facie duties to determine our actual duties—how do we resolve this? Is there some principle we can use to make this determination? Or must we fall back on some murky notion of being guided by one's "moral sense," or of trying to make a "conscientious judgment" (which, after all, sounds rather like Ross's famously mysterious answer)?

Now I think that what does often happen in moral reasoning is in fact something like that. People who are careful thinkers try to make a measured, dispassionate judgment, taking into account all they know about the circumstances of the case, as well as the competing evaluative principles that gave rise to the dilemma in the first place. And what "bridges the gap" between rules and their application is, as Winston says, nothing but the judgment itself. But it is not clear to me that this method is capable of generating moral decisions that we can truly have confidence in. For how do we know, in the end, that our decision was the right one?

Make no mistake, inductivists do think that we can distinguish good moral reasoning from bad—even though it is not always clear *how* we are supposed to do that. In Winston's view, the instructor's job in ethics case discussion is mainly to *ask questions*. But "the questions . . . must be carefully chosen so as to introduce students to a certain path of inquiry, to keep the inquiry moving *in a productive direction* . . . ."[1] But how does one know *which* direction *that* is, if not through an implicit appeal to normative ethical theory? Winston writes, "the role of a case teacher . . . is not to expound doctrine or pet philosophical theories . . . ",[2] yet he also believes that "the principle challenge for a teacher is so to structure class discussion that students are forced to reflect on and analyze the opinions they express."[3] But can they really analyze their opinions—can they examine and criticize them with sufficient acuity to enable some claims to be (as Winston says) dismissed as "clearly indefensible"—without at least *some* acquaintance with normative ethical theories?

Do not students need analytical tools to help them in this difficult undertaking? And is not that the very thing moral philosophy has always sought to provide? No doubt philosophers have tended to underestimate the analytical sophistication of ordinary nonphilosophers in deliberating about complex moral issues. Yet I make bold to suggest that even the cleverest adept in the case method of ethical analysis might profit by reading Mill, or John Rawls, or R. M. Hare. Some exposure to normative ethical theories might well be useful to students of the case method, since it could give them a conceptual apparatus for criticism of the rules and principles they develop inductively by analogy and generalization from contextual judgments.

But this seems not very different from what Winston himself suggests, toward the end of his paper, where he writes, ". . . the task in ethics may be to proceed dialectically, to attempt to balance the general and the particular, to test each against the other, aiming at an equilibrium between unshakable convictions in specific cases and the demands of reason."[4] On this point, Winston's argument appears to me correct. Yet, in moral thinking, "the demands of reason" must surely include more than just conformity with the principles of elementary logic. If it does not also include some consideration of normative theory, where will critical reflection get a foothold?

NOTES

1. Kenneth I. Winston, "Teaching With Cases," in this volume, p. 179 (my emphasis).

2. Ibid., p. 173.

3. Ibid.

4. Ibid., p. 177.

PART IV

Evaluating the Teaching of Criminal Justice Ethics

Chapter 6

Roundtable: Evaluating the Teaching of Criminal Justice Ethics

The participants were as follows: James Blashill, Joan Callahan, Charles Claxton, Michael Davis, James F. Doyle, William Heffernan, Mark Jones, Kate King, John Kleinig, Bruce MacMurray, Margaret Leland Smith, Zug B. Standing Bear, Cheryl Swanson, Elizabeth Welfel, and Kenneth Winston.

JK: How might we judge how well we do in teaching criminal justice ethics? It is a question that we cannot begin to answer without having some idea of what we are endeavoring to achieve as a result of that teaching. And, if nothing else is clear, it is at least clear that those who have presented papers have signaled markedly different ambitions in teaching criminal justice ethics.

On my reading, Professor Heffernan has probably expressed the most modest ambitions, and the ones that are most likely to be testable. He has said that what we wish to achieve on the part of our students is:

a familiarity with the literature;

an ability to contrast ideas and develop distinctions; and

an ability to analyze clearly the issues with which the course confronts them.[1]

At first blush, we should be able to get some rough assessment of how we are doing as teachers by seeing how students perform on exercises and tests designed to gauge these expectations.

But most of our presenters have expressed more ambitious aims. Professor Callahan probably comes closest to Heffernan, yet she also goes well beyond what he suggests. Speaking of the teaching of practical ethics in general, she says that we aim to:

help students to recognize moral issues;
develop their moral imagination;
sharpen their analytical/critical skills;
sort out disagreements; and
affect decisions and behavior.[2]

Some of these, it would seem, could be tested in the classroom setting; but others go beyond that and, given that, it might be wondered how, if at all, our teaching could be evaluated.

Professor Davis's list overlaps with Callahan's, but suggests aims that look even more difficult to assess—at least within the framework of a course. He suggests four goals:

increased ethical sensitivity;
increased knowledge of relevant standards of conduct;
improved ethical judgment; and
improved ethical will power.[3]

Although he has endeavored to show how these might be achievable in a course on criminal justice ethics, there still remains the question: How can we tell whether and to what extent we have advanced these four goals?

Professor Claxton, too, has ambitious and, it would seem, longer-term goals than those likely to be achievable within a single course. He, like Davis, suggests that we need an "ethically committed curriculum" (quoting Parks),[4] and not simply a fifteen-week course that engages students for a few hours each week. Claxton suggests that the role of criminal justice ethics education should be

> to support students' movement through interpersonal thought towards (or into) systemic thought so that they may deal more effectively with ethical issues in a criminal justice context.[5]

How can one test whether one is succeeding in this? Can a teacher test it?

Whatever strategies we adopt, we might also need to take heed of some observations of Amitai Etzioni:

> Curiously, the very effort—the desire to establish how we are doing and to find ways of improving if we are not doing as well as we ought to do—often has quite undesirable effects from the point of view of the organizational goals. Frequent measuring can distort the organizational efforts because, as a rule, some aspects of its output are more measurable than others. Frequent measuring tends to encourage overproduction of highly measurable items and neglect of the less measurable ones.[6]

This might seem to be particularly true of the teaching of criminal justice ethics. Some of the things that we may wish to aim at appear difficult to quantify, and, even if indirectly quantifiable, are measured only distortedly via the indirect measure.

What can we test/measure in evaluating the teaching of criminal justice ethics? And if we do test what we can, do we run the risk of distorting what we are trying to do?

MD: We should be careful that we do not expect more of professional ethics courses than we expect of other courses. If, for example, we do not ask calculus teachers to prove that their graduates will use calculus on the job, or will use it right, we should not ask ethics teachers to do that either. Much of the point of my paper[7] is that courses in professional ethics are not all that different from other college courses; hence, there is no reason to demand that they pass tests other courses cannot pass. Nevertheless, we at Illinois Institute of Technology did try to evaluate the effectiveness of our ethics courses. We have been teaching engineering ethics, business ethics, computer ethics, architecture ethics, and legal ethics since the late 1970s. In 1989, we got the last known addresses of the graduates of those courses (544) and wrote them, asking the following questions:

(1) Did you take any of the following courses while at ITT? Please circle the course(s) you took. [The list followed.]

(2) How often are you faced with a significant ethical decision in your professional work? [Alternatives were: every day, often, occasionally, rarely, never.]

(3) How well did the course in applied ethics prepare you to identify the ethical dimension in such decisions? [Alternatives were: very well, pretty well, adequately, poorly, not at all. There was an instruction to indicate, if the student took more than one applied ethics course, as some did, which course he was evaluating.]

(4) How well did the course in applied ethics prepare you to make the decision? [with the same alternatives as in (3)]

(5) Would you recommend this course to students if they asked your advice? [Alternatives: certainly, probably, not sure, probably not, certainly not.]

(6) Do you have any advice for the dean of the professional program from which you graduated about how ethics should be taught?

We received 132 responses (and 38 envelopes marked "returned to sender"). Highlights of the survey: 85 percent would certainly or probably recommend the course; 76 percent face significant ethical decisions *at least* occasionally; 54 percent thought the course prepared them pretty well or very well to *identify ethical decisions*; and 50 percent thought the course prepared them pretty well or very well to *make* the decisions.

CC: The way I would think about institutional effectiveness is in terms of outcomes. In recent years, accrediting agencies have turned their attention from a *resources* perspective to an *impact* perspective. So the expectation of some demonstrable outcome is no longer an exceptional one. It is now quite reasonable to expect colleges to follow up their alumni in an effort to gauge the impact of the courses they provide.

ZSB: It is arguable that courses in ethics are more important than other courses, and therefore an expectation that they be evaluated is reasonable. At Valdosta, Georgia we carried out several forms of evaluation: post-program evaluations; evaluations after one year out; ACJS review questionnaires; and the compilation of student letters.

EW: As part of our ACA accreditation process at Cleveland State University, we discovered that ethics courses were rated highest by the students and also considered the most practical or valuable. The ethics faculty are among the program's most enthusiastic. We plan to find out from employers and doctoral internship supervisors what is their view of the strengths and weaknesses of our graduate interns.

JB: We have carried out pre- and post-testing. We have done it partly out of curiosity. Sometimes students have regressed. Students claim that ethics is more important than anything else.

WH: Researchers often undertake pre- and post-testing to find out how much students learned in, say, history or chemistry courses. I doubt, though, that proponents of the guidance model would be willing to settle for so limited an inquiry. They would also want to find out whether ethics courses have changed dispositions; they might even want to find out whether these courses have changed behavior. I reiterate that I do not support efforts to change dispositions or behavior. However, because I also think that courses based on the guidance model are likely to encourage student hypocrisy—in other words, I fear that students in these courses are likely to undergo strategically valuable, and temporary, conversions to enhance their grades—I would be very interested to know whether methodologically sound research reveals changed dispositions and conduct.

JC: Other courses *do* expect behavioral change as an outcome. In expecting students to develop relevant skills, we have in mind the skills involved in dealing with ethical issues. What is additional in the case of ethics is an increased *disposition* to use these skills.

MD: I agree. Ethics courses are not exceptional in expecting a dispositional outcome. We want a dispositional outcome even in a course on calculus—we want students to be disposed to use calculus to solve problems when its use is appropriate.

BM: Outcomes assessment is an important part of a teaching-learning loop. Not only does it help us to assess what students have learned, but it also provides us with valuable information to enable us to modify our teaching.

JK: Our desire to affect outcomes may not be something we can test *in* a course. Some desired outcomes may be expected to manifest themselves only some time after the course is taken and, given that that is so, there will be no reason for a student to display the marks of "conversion," temporary or otherwise.

WH: I would like to make two brief points. The first is that we must distinguish between cognitive and conative outcomes. If one adheres to the contested issues model, only the former type of outcome needs to be considered; if one adheres to the guidance model, both must be considered. Second, I have a question for Professor Winston concerning his discussion of *Tennessee v. Garner*. Is it his intention in teaching this case study to suggest that police officers are better cops when they refrain from using deadly force even when they are legally permitted to do so?[8] I ask this question because I think the Supreme Court took considerable care in resolving *Garner* to consider the kinds of issues that concern Winston. If an officer were to refrain from using deadly force when this is legally permissible—"a *Garner*-plus officer," as we can call him—then that officer ignores the likelihood of deadly force being directed at himself or others. Does Winston believe an officer should ignore this likelihood of harm? That is, does he believe that an officer acts in a more commendable way when he fails to use deadly force to protect himself or others from deadly force than when he does offer that protection?

KW: It was not the aim of my case to claim that a *Garner*-plus cop is a better cop. The case truly does not take a position one way or the other. My purpose in writing it was to foster discussion about the readiness to use deadly force. Perhaps my expectation was that, in fostering discussion, something more would happen. But I did not presume to know what it would be. I guess that I *hope* there will be some improvement in conduct in the direction of a *Garner*-plus standard. However, it was not my *aim* to bring it about.

JK: Two comments. First, although there is a distinction between the cognitive and the conative, they are not always easily separable. In calculus, perhaps, you can teach people to solve problems using a certain technique without in any way affecting their disposition to use it. But in ethics, what one is exploring are *reasons for action*, and to the extent tthat people become more adept at that, they will be dispositionally affected. Second, in the very recognition that there is behavior properly characterizable as *Garner*-plus, students are brought to recognize that there is more to the decision whether to use deadly force than *Garner*. That very enterprise of seeing an additional option is behaviorally relevant.

MS: My aspiration for the ethics classroom is for growth of students' understanding in three areas: the complexity of ethical issues, the scope of professional standards, and the breadth of the discussion of justice in the community. I would argue that development of these critical skills of understanding support development in ethical decision making.

MD: Professor Heffernan has repeatedly raised a fundamental question about what we are trying to do. Here perhaps is the place to address it. The *Garner* standard for use of deadly force is a legal standard, the minimum for lawful conduct by police. If we wanted police to reach only that level of control in their use of deadly force, it would not be necessary to talk about ethics at all. The point of talking about *Garner*-plus, of considering its advantages and disadvantages as a standard of practice beyond what law requires, is to introduce a specifically ethical dimension into the discussion. Professor Heffernan's hostility to ethics thus seems to force him to try to solve every ethical problem by enunciating a new rule—or to do nothing.

Professor Heffernan's distinction between the guidance model and the contested issues model is therefore misleading. The guidance model includes both a thesis about ends (our purpose is to change conduct) and a thesis about means (certain means are effective in changing conduct). The contested issues model also includes both a thesis about ends and a thesis about means. Most of us accept (something like) the guidance model's thesis about ends: we want to do what we legitimately can to make OUR students *Garner*-plus police officers; but we reject the guidance model's thesis about means because psychologists have learned over the last few decades that the contested issues model's method, guided discussion of contested issues, is the most effective way to teach what we want to teach. We are not, therefore, committed to the guidance model's "brainwashing" (as Professor Heffernan has suggested). Even the devil could do well in our ethics class. Even the devil could demonstrate *ethical sensitivity* (that is, an ability to spot ethical issues), *ethical knowledge* (an ability to appeal to appropriate standards, to describe procedures he might use, and so on), and *ethical judgment* (an ability to use ethical sensitivity and ethical judgment to state and defend a reasonable response to the ethical problem he had diagnosed). We believe our students will be decent police officers, not devils, because we believe that they are already decent in motivation and need to learn only what decency requires.

WH: I must say I am astonished to hear Professor Davis speak of my "hostility to ethics." It is bad enough to be against motherhood and apple pie! But to be against *ethics*—well, I do not know quite how to put it—I guess this is to sink so low that I would be ranked with people like Richard Nixon and Bill Clinton.

Of course, my essay makes it clear that I do not oppose ethics but only a certain method of *teaching* ethics. Davis seems to have missed this distinction, and the fact that he has reinforces my misgivings about those instructors who claim the authority to guide students, for such instructors can convert disagreements with students into moral failings and award grades accordingly. Had Davis read my essay with care, he would have noted that I advocate what I call "the liberal approach to ethics instruction." This approach, I state,

> is not to be confused with moral nihilism. On the contrary, it provides morally significant reasons for employing morally neutral criteria in the evaluation of student work.[9]

Elsewhere in the essay, I argue that one of the aims of any ethics course should be the promotion of student autonomy.[10] Given these remarks, it is clear I believe that an ethical justification must be offered for the contested issues model of ethics instruction. The justification for this model will, of course, be less ambitious than the one that must be offered for the guidance model. The advocate of contested issues ethical education need show only why it is morally right to allow students to develop their own positions in ethics. By contrast, the advocate of the guidance model must show, first, why the moral principles he wishes to inculcate are substantively correct and, second, why it is morally proper to sanction students (through the mechanism of grades) for failing to adopt the moral principles offered for their edification. Perhaps my deepest reservation about advocates of the guidance model is that they do not address either of these points systematically. They assume that these points can readily be demonstrated when the history of ethics from Plato onwards reveals how deeply contested philosophers' answers to them have been.

JD: We should not lose sight of the fact that criminal justice ethics varies considerably from one place to another. I teach criminal justice ethics not to practitioners, but to criminology students. What our aims are likely to be will differ, depending on whether our students are from criminal justice, philosophy, or the social sciences. Also, we should remember that our students take what they learn with them into their other disciplinary studies: they begin to ask *ethical* questions in those studies. The fact that other faculty draw this to my attention constitutes some test of the effectiveness of what I teach. However, as far as the Department of Criminology is concerned, what is desired from me is the provision of an intellectual adventure—an expansion of my students' intellectual, cultural, and attitudinal appreciation.

MD: So what we have now are three different kinds of courses in criminal justice ethics: one that explores the ethical foundations of criminal justice, one that looks at institutional ethics, and one that explores issues in professional ethics. It is only in the latter two that our concern is with providing the means to carry out the good intentions students bring with them.

CS: I would like to speak in support of Professor Doyle's comments with respect to the scope of criminal justice ethics. In the Florida State University system, a large percentage of criminal justice majors do not pursue careers in criminal justice. They major in criminal justice because it is a field of interest to them, much as one might major in political science or history, with no specific career aspirations. For the students in our system, a focus on professional ethics would be too narrow. At Florida State, we have 1500 criminal justice majors.

MJ: We have found that including internships in the criminal justice major has been a powerful ethical tool. Students come back to us and say: "You know what we were talking about last week? Well, . . . " If we are not concerned with *Garner*-plus on the part of police, then we have no need for a criminal justice ethics class, only a criminal law class. The purpose of criminal justice ethics is rather more: it is to place an umbrella of civility over the law.

MS: Although I find case study/role play techniques to be valuable, I have reservations about the particular claims being made for their value. These stories are never expressions of the acting subject, but are invitations to evaluate or respond to a situation external to the subject. They are useful for intellectual skill building, but do not adequately mirror the context of decision making. Where there is clinical education, students have an opportunity to bring the uncertainties of the workplace back to the classroom.

KW: There is at least one similarity between an internship and the use of the case method: namely, each takes account of the institutional context of ethical decision making. One variant of the internship is "service learning," where students spend a number of hours each week doing volunteer work off campus and attempt to integrate that experience with their course work. In this regard, you may be interested to know about an experiment done by Judith Boss at the University of Rhode Island. She divided her ethics class into two sections; one had a straight academic course and the other had that plus a service-learning component. She used Rest's tests to measure ethical development over the semester and found that the section with the service component scored higher. I cannot vouch for the results, but it would be an interesting finding if true.

MS: There is an important difference between an internship and the case method. The case study method invites students to recognize in stories the possibility of intervention through ethical understanding, and gives explicit support to the elaboration of alternatives. Although field experiences may also stimulate this task of understanding, the articulation of the problem intersects with the desire of the student to be liked, to fit in, and to appear competent—in short, to produce a much more complex subjective field for ethical decision making. Having parallel field and classroom experiences will allow a student to practice thinking in the classroom about the desires, discontinuities, and conflicts of the field.

KK: Internships can be quite problematic. We found that in some cases students were confronted with real ethical dilemmas—where, for example, they witnessed police brutality, and were then pressured not to inform on them. When the teacher learns of this, what is the teacher to do? What is the teachers' ethical duty in such a case.

ZSB: At Valdosta we took the view that since students on internships were not paid, they were protected from institutional reprisals.

EW: One of the things we have been assuming is that our students want to do what is right. That no doubt is true of the majority. But not all of them do. For these, we cannot appeal to their good will.

MD: I agree. Ethics is for students who mean well. The criminal law is for those few who do not. I cannot recall ever having had a student who did not mean well, but I am sure that I must have had some. Of course, even they may behave better if they can recognize ethical issues, know what standards apply, and have learned from classroom experience how much of what they want to do will seem indefensible to others. Even *they* do not want to do wrong because they were insensitive to it, because they did not know what was expected of them, or because they exercised poor judgment. A devil without some virtue is impotent.

WH: Professor King's example is very troubling. I am reminded of Allan Bloom's remark on a student's essay: "Brilliant but evil." I have no idea what grade Bloom gave the student; I do not know whether he focused exclusively on what he considered brilliant, exclusively on what he considered evil, or both. I do know that Bloom's comment provides a helpful way of thinking about a theme relevant to this conference. Professor Callahan wants to make students "morally astute";[11] Professor Kleinig wants them "morally conscientized."[12] Given Bloom's comment, I suppose this means that Callahan and Kleinig are prepared to say of a student's paper: "analytically sharp but morally obtuse." I, for one, would be troubled by such a comment. First, I am troubled, as I noted earlier, about the way in which teachers such as Callahan and Kleinig have assumed what needs to be demonstrated: they have assumed that they have identified authoritatively valid moral propositions when in fact these are exactly what need to be demonstrated. Needless to say, polling will not suffice on this point. Callahan and Kleinig are philosophers; their professional training should have taught them that they cannot simply invoke the norms of their community but that they must be able to demonstrate through rational analysis that the propositions they are propounding are morally valid. And second, I am troubled by the ease with which instructors employing the guidance model can dress up highly contested ideological positions as authoritative moral insights. Once an instructor claims to be offering guidance to her students, she could well claim that students who disagree with her position on, say, abortion or welfare rights are "morally obtuse" and so deserve Cs.

MD: Once again, I think we need to separate out the issue of moral motivation, a good will, from what we can in fact teach in a college class. "Brilliant but evil" seems to me an overly dramatic characterization of a certain kind of student and perhaps even of an essay such a student might write. I have in mind, for example, a student in engineering ethics who seemed wholly indifferent to safety but had a gift for philosophy. I gave him the A (he earned it), but took him aside and advised him to get out of engineering. The chances are that he would not be happy spending his life around people committed to safety, would not be nearly as good as they at engineering, and might eventually get in serious trouble for not paying attention to safety issues. Such a student can nonetheless write a good essay in engineering ethics, that is, one in which he identifies all the relevant issues in a situation (including the safety issues), the relevant standards (including those relevant to safety), and then proposes a course of action which, though ignoring the safety issues, makes intellectually respectable arguments for so doing. Although there is a motivational component to acting ethically, acting ethically has a large intellectual component as well—and ethical sensitivity is part of the intellectual component. It is that intellectual component that Professor Heffernan seems to me systematically to ignore in his critique of "moral sensitivity."

JC: We *should* be aiming for sensitivity. What is wrong with saying that people are analytically strong but morally weak?

MS: I am troubled by the individualist characterization of much of this discussion. Ethics education is concerned with the development of communications skills. Ethical action is social action.

KW: Professor Heffernan's remarks remind me of the quip that everyone else is political. Is his position more neutral than anyone else's?

WH: Perhaps the best answer to this is that the informing principle of the contested issues model is pedagogical neutrality in evaluating student work while the informing principle of the guidance model is the inculcation of virtue according to supposedly authoritative moral principles. I am not contending, of course, that contested issues instructors invariably employ neutral criteria in evaluating students' work, nor am I claiming that guidance instructors invariably stifle student dissent. I think, though, that it is a safe bet that instructors following the contested issues model are more likely to employ neutral criteria than are instructors following the guidance model. Because most of the people sitting in this room have been trained as philosophers, it is ironic, I think, that the history of moral philosophy is best summarized in terms of contests over what is good and valuable. Yet it is the philosophers here who are arguing for evaluative criteria such as "morally astute" and "morally sensitive." I suspect I share with these philosophers a commitment to human rights, yet I would not reject as "morally insensitive" a student who took the Marxist position that the concept of human rights is a fiction whose primary function is to preserve bourgeois hegemony. I suspect I also share with the philosophers here a commitment to reducing torture, yet I would not lower a student's grade because the student commented favorably on the relish Nietzsche expresses in *The Genealogy of Morals*, for boiling certain people in oil. I ask the adherents of the guidance model: would they brand as "morally obtuse" students taking Marxist and Nietzschean positions concerning ethics? And, perhaps even more important, what justification can they offer for their decisions? That is, if Professors Callahan and Kleinig each conclude that the Marxist and Nietzschean positions are not morally obtuse, why could not some other instructor using exactly the same criterion reach the opposite conclusion?

JK: The problem with Professor Heffernan's distinction is his assumption that the contested issues model is neutral. It is not. It is my claim that the tasks of identifying issues as moral, of making morally relevant distinctions, and of drawing conclusions from morally relevant considerations are themselves normatively laden, and that they are so without it also being assumed, as Heffernan's account of the guidance model suggests, that there is some single acceptable moral point of view known to the teacher and able to be imposed on the students. But neither does it follow from that that it is not possible to exclude certain kinds of arguments and certain categories of reasons.

NOTES

1. William C. Heffernan, "The Aims of Criminal Justice Ethics Education," in this volume, p. 4.

2. Joan Callahan, "Teaching Criminal Justice Ethics: Freestanding, Pervasive, and Combined Approaches," in this volume, pp. 92-96.

3. Michael Davis, "Teaching Police Ethics: What to Aim at?" in this volume, p. 41.

4. Charles S. Claxton, "Teaching and Learning in Criminal Justice Ethics," in this volume, p. 72, quoting Sharon Daloz Parks, "Is It Too Late? Young Adults and the Formation of Professional Ethics," in T. R. Piper, M. C. Gentile, and S. D. Parks, *Can Ethics Be Taught? Perspectives, Challenges, and Approaches at Harvard Business School* (Boston, MA: Harvard Business School, 1993), p. 63.

5. Ibid., p. 62.

6. Amitai Etzioni, *Modern Organization* (Englewood Cliffs, NJ: Prentice Hall, 1964), p. 9.

7. Davis, "Teaching Police Ethics," pp. 35-58.

8. Kenneth I. Winston, "Teaching with Cases," in this volume, pp. 166-73.

9. Heffernan, "The Aims of Criminal Justice Ethics Education," p. 8.

10. Ibid., p. 7.

11. Callahan, "Teaching Criminal Justice Ethics," p. 95.

12. John Kleinig, "Response to Heffernan: Moral Neutrality in Criminal Justice Ethics Education," in this volume, p. 20.

APPENDICES

Appendix I

Survey of Criminal Justice Ethics Education: A Research Report

Margaret Leland Smith

BACKGROUND

The Institute for Criminal Justice Ethics was founded in 1981 to foster discussion of the normative dimension of criminal justice—issues such as the uses of deception and force to police and punish, the parameters of discretionary decision making by police and prosecutors, the defense of the accused—and to assist in the development of principles to undergird professional standards in criminal justice. The Institute, through its biannual journal *Criminal Justice Ethics* and its scholarly conferences, emphasizes the importance of confronting ethical issues in the course of criminal justice education. Ethical inquiry and elaboration have long been considered the foundation for learning and more recently as a necessary component of professional preparation.

In 1982, William Heffernan, then Director of the Institute, conducted a study of ethics teaching in police academies and graduate and undergraduate programs. Drawing on published course listings and responses to a questionnaire mailed to 199 academic institutions, Professor Heffernan was able to identify 94 courses that offered criminal justice ethics instruction in academic programs. In the spring of 1995, the Institute undertook to reexamine the state of criminal justice ethics education through an extended bibliographic search, an updated survey, and, in June of 1996, a two-day intensive workshop. The survey was expected to provide participants in the workshop with a sense of the distribution and orientation of ethics courses in criminal justice programs, and an opportunity to hear about the prospects and problems of such courses.

A two-part questionnaire, the Survey of Criminal Justice Ethics Education,[1] was mailed to a total enumeration of 528 baccalaureate-granting colleges and universities in the United States which offer a major in criminal justice or criminology. The survey asked about the institutional framework for the study of criminal justice and the inclusion of courses specific to (or related to) ethical issues in criminal justice, and requested an assessment of those courses. The first part of the survey included questions about the administration of the criminal justice major, the number of majors offered and the type of degree, the provision for the discussion of ethical issues in the curriculum, as well as the number of students majoring in criminal justice. The second part of the survey inquired about six possible problem areas in the teaching of courses oriented to criminal justice ethics and about the most pressing issues found in those problem areas. Additionally, the Institute invited respondents to suggest questions for special emphasis at the June 1996 Workshop on Criminal Justice Ethics Education and to list products of the study that would be useful.[2]

METHODOLOGY

The design of the study called for surveys to be completed by the program director for the criminal justice major in each academic institution. The initial source list of United States colleges and universities offering criminal justice majors was drawn from a commercial college guide[3] and program listings of professional criminal justice associations.[4] In order to ensure that the surveys were being mailed to the faculty member currently responsible for the criminal justice program, and at the correct address, every tenth listing was verified before mailing. When multiple listings were available for directors of graduate and undergraduate programs at a single school, surveys were mailed to both. In all, 577 surveys were mailed to 528 academic institutions.

Surveys from 203 institutions were returned by mail. In October 1995, the Institute began to make calls to nonresponders: 85 program directors were interviewed to complete the first part of the survey. When more than one individual at a single institution returned a survey, responses were combined into a single record for the school. A comparison of these three subsets (the mail-in response subset, the telephone response subset, and the 10% subset) shows no significant differences in the likelihood that, for any of the independent variables used, a course related to criminal justice ethics will be offered, or required. In this report, the combined responses are used and no further subset listing will be made. To ensure that the results are unbiased, a simple random sample of 52 nonresponding programs was surveyed by telephone in early 1996. In addition to the questions from the first part of the survey, additional questions were asked about the issues at stake in deciding whether to offer an ethics course, and for those who did have a course, about its objectives, content, and etiology. For the 27 institutions from the random sample whose curriculum included an ethics course, questions about the course were addressed to the faculty member currently teaching the course.

This multi-stage survey process has returned three discrete kinds of information: (1) demographic and institutional data from part one of the survey on criminal justice programs at 340 colleges and universities; (2) an assessment of the problems of teaching ethics from part two of the survey from faculty in 130 programs; and (3) interviews with 52 faculty members about the choices involved in deciding whether to include an ethics course in the criminal justice curriculum, and the objectives and focus of 27 of the courses already offered.

INSTITUTIONAL FRAMEWORK

For Undergraduate Programs

It was anticipated that characteristics of the institutional framework—whether a program was administered by a criminal justice or a social or behavioral science department, and the type and variety of degree offered—would be associated with significant differences in the likelihood that a course in criminal justice ethics would be offered or required. All departments which are identifiable as devoted primarily to criminal justice concerns, whether they are called criminal justice, justice and public safety, or administration of justice departments, are categorized as criminal justice departments. Departments which are identified as social or behavioral science and departments of an individual discipline such as sociology or political science are categorized as social science. In cases in which the disciplines are mixed, such as a department of political science and criminal justice, the department was classified according to the answer to the first question on the survey.

The type of degree further distinguishes those programs which give a baccalaureate in criminal justice from those which give a social science degree. The analysis of majors was provided to consider whether departments which had developed several courses of study in criminal justice would be any more likely to require a course offering in criminal justice ethics. Courses relevant to ethics instruction in a criminal justice curriculum have been classified as *REQUIRED, EXCLUSIVE,* and *RELATED.* Required and exclusive courses are courses devoted to ethical issues in criminal justice; related courses are criminal justice courses that include discussion of ethical issues. All required courses are also counted as exclusive courses; no course listed as required or exclusive is included in the count of related courses.

A number of respondents (47) noted that criminal justice majors were required to take ethics or a similar course in a department of philosophy and/or religion. Such courses are not classified as criminal justice ethics courses. However, if the course which was required or offered by the department of philosophy was *Ethical Issues in Criminal Justice,* it has been included in this tally. A small number of program directors replied that *all* courses in their departments are taught in ways which take account of the ethical issues presented by the subject matter. This pervasive approach to teaching ethics has not been explicitly addressed in this study.

Undergraduate criminal justice programs that are administered by a department of criminal justice, rather than by a social or behavioral science department, are almost twice as likely to offer a course in ethical issues specific to criminal justice. It may be that departments of criminal justice have more resources to mount a course and are, perhaps, more receptive to the value of such a course than are interdisciplinary programs administered by social science departments. The number of majors was not found to reveal statistically significant differences among the respondents.

Figure 1. Frequencies of Criminal Justice Ethics Courses, By Type of Department

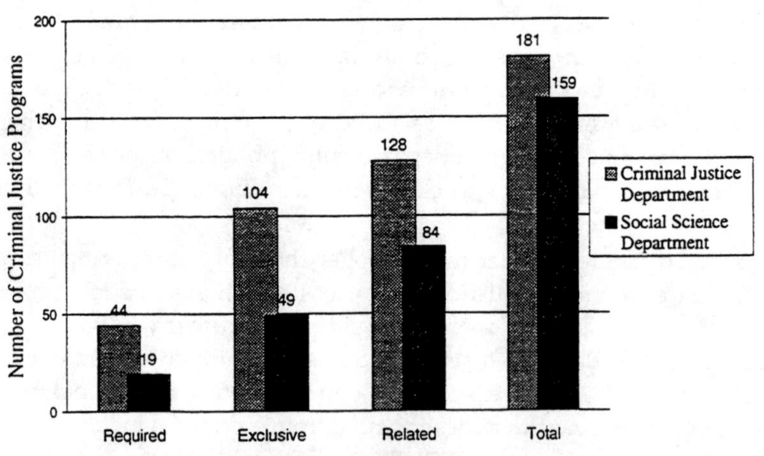

The Survey of Criminal Justice Ethics Education recorded the enrollment of undergraduate majors and graduate students for the fall semesters of academic years 1993, 1994, and 1995. The 1995 enrollment in undergraduate criminal justice programs ranged from 15 to 1,700, with a median size of 207. (John Jay College, with 9,108 criminal justice majors, lies outside this range.) A comparison of enrollments, based on information from those programs that reported enrollments for all three years, shows an increase of 4% from 1993 to 1994 and a further increase of 6% from 1994 to 1995 in the aggregate number of students majoring in criminal justice.[5] Masters programs ranged from 4 to 650 (median=30) students in 1995, and doctoral programs from 2 to 90 (median=15). As Figure 2 shows, the size of an undergraduate program does not seem to be associated with an increased likelihood that a course specific to ethical issues would be offered or required at the graduate or undergraduate level. *However, the top 10%, or programs with the largest enrollment (not shown in Figure 2), are most likely, at 65%, to have an ethics course specific to criminal justice concerns.*

Figure 2. Precent of Programs Offering or Requiring a Criminal Justice Ethics Course, by Fall 1995 Enrollment[6]

Type of Criminal Justice Ethics Course	Number of Criminal Justice Majors Enrolled for the Fall 1995 Semester				
	15-75	76-160	161-275	276-400	401-9,000
Required for Undergraduates	15% (10)	18% (12)	16% (11)	18% (12)	25% (17)
Exclusively CRJ Ethics	37% (25)	34% (23)	41% (28)	46% (31)	60% (41)
Including Discussion of Ethical Issues	45% (31)	66% (45)	63% (43)	54% (37)	72% (49)
(N)	68	68	68	68	68

For Graduate Programs

Graduate study in criminal justice was reported by 140 of the respondents to the survey, with 118 institutions granting only a masters degree and 21 conferring both masters and doctoral degrees. One respondent institution offers only a doctoral program. As shown in Figure 3, 19 (16%) of the masters programs require a graduate course in criminal justice ethics, compared with only one (4.7%) of the Ph.D.-granting programs. Institutions providing advanced study in criminal justice are not more likely to require undergraduates to take a course devoted to ethical issues. By contrast, respondents from programs with *undergraduate and masters-level study only* indicated that they were twice as likely to include a course exclusively devoted to ethical issues in criminal justice in their curricula as were those who had doctoral programs or only undergraduate programs.

Figure 3. Comparison of Criminal Justice Ethics Courses, By Type of Degree Granted

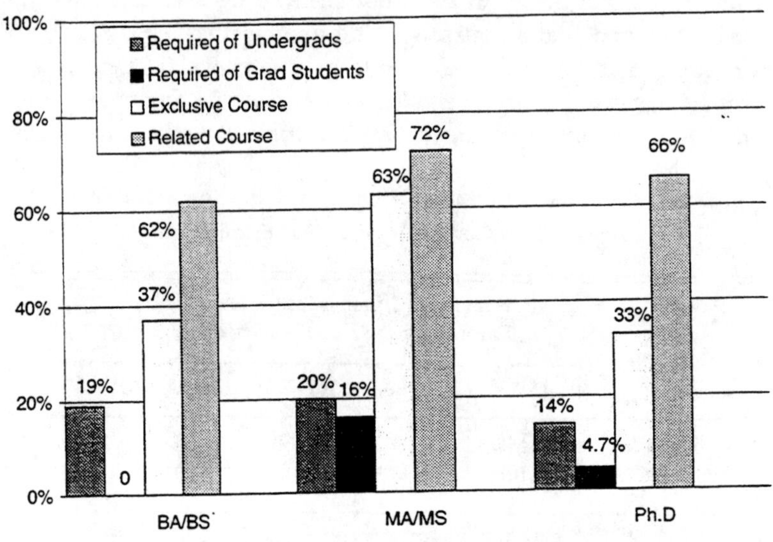

INSTITUTION TYPE AND REGION

All academic institutions were classified by type (independent, state-supported, affiliated to a religious body)[7] and by region (East, South, Midwest, and West).[8] Using these categories to compare respondents does not reveal any statistically significant differences. Although it might be expected that colleges and universities with formal religious affiliation would be more likely to include courses on ethics in their criminal justice curricula, the survey results show that they are as likely to report that all courses have an ethical component, or that students are required to take one or more courses in departments of philosophy and/or religion.

The regional distribution of criminal justice programs with ethics courses shows two minor variations. Respondents in the East are less likely to require an ethics course, and respondents in the West are slightly more likely to offer a course exclusively in criminal justice ethics. The survey results suggest that local influences may affect the likelihood of having an ethics course in the criminal justice curriculum. For example, West Virginia's public colleges and universities work together on the criminal justice curriculum, and they have established a required course in ethics for undergraduates from Fall 1995.

Figure 4. Frequencies of Criminal Justice Ethics Courses, By Region of the United States

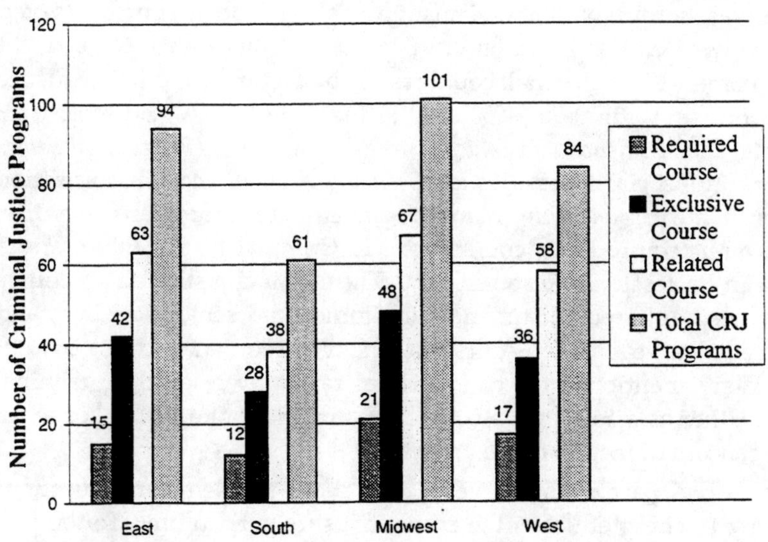

SUMMARY OF KEY FINDINGS

- A course devoted to ethical issues in criminal justice is offered by 45% of responding programs.
- A course that addresses ethical issues in criminal justice is *required* in 19% of undergraduate programs, as well as in 15% of graduate programs.
- Of the 340 programs surveyed, 181 were administered by departments of criminal justice or justice studies, and 159 by social or behavioral science departments. In 1995, these criminal justice departments enrolled 66,583 undergraduate majors as compared to the social science departments, which listed 40,420.

- Criminal justice departments are *almost twice* as likely as social science departments to offer a course exclusively devoted to criminal justice ethics or to require such a course.
- Schools with Ph.D.-granting programs are significantly less likely to require criminal justice ethics, or to offer a specific course, than those which offer only a Masters program.

THE CONTENT OF CRIMINAL JUSTICE ETHICS COURSES

The variety of courses structured to address ethical issues in criminal justice was impressive. Of 154 institutions that had a course devoted exclusively to ethical issues in criminal justice, there were 65 different course names. More than half could readily be classified as criminal justice ethics courses, with about 10% each in the areas of law and ethics (for example, *Law, Evidence, and Ethics*), professional ethics (*Professional Ethics and Liability*), social issues (*Justice, Society and Law*), and administration (*Administrative Responsibility*). Many programs offered more than one course, and several required two courses, one in Criminal Justice Ethics and a second in Professional Responsibility. The criminal justice ethics course was typically offered to students with junior and senior standing, and often called a "capstone" course or a senior seminar. Almost 10% of respondents mentioned the ethical issues raised by research in criminal justice, either as a focus for a course, a component of a course, or as an active concern of faculty in the program.

The second part of the survey asked about problems and questions posed by teaching ethics in the criminal justice curriculum. To the first survey question, asking whether problems had been encountered in teaching courses related to criminal justice ethics, 75% of the respondents said *NO*. Despite this initial response, the majority of these went on to check one or more of a list of problems, perhaps indicating that these were *concerns*, albeit ones which had not become problems. The tally of responses to the checklist of problems is presented in Figure 5, which displays both the total responses and the subset from schools that offered a course, for six areas of concern. Despite the comments of teachers who found the available material difficult for students, dissatisfaction with the course by students did not appear to be a significant problem. On the contrary, many respondents affirmed the value of the course and said that their course was popular with students.

Figure 5. Affirmative Responses to Problems or Concerns Presented by Teaching Criminal Justice Ethics

Problems/Concerns in Teaching Ethics	All Responses	Programs with Courses
Availability of Materials	33% (43)	31% (25)
Focus (Practical vs. Philosophical)	22% (29)	23% (19)
Course Content	17% (22)	18.5% (15)
Finding Instructors	15% (20)	17% (14)
Student Dissatisfaction	6% (8)	6% (5)
Course Evaluation	.8% (1)	1.3% (1)
(N)	(130)	(81)

Responses to the question that asked participants to describe the issues of greatest concern in the teaching of ethics split into two groups: the first referred to the *substantive* issues to be highlighted in an ethics course, the second identified problematic issues in the *process* of teaching ethics. One issue, which may be seen as a feature of teaching ethics—the integration of theoretical explanations or justifications for behavior with practical criminal justice dilemmas—was mentioned by a majority of those who noted problems. The challenge of teaching ethics to students who have little preparation in philosophy was expressed as the difficulty of "getting students to appreciate abstract theories." The curriculum questions—(1) whether criminal justice ethics is to be a single course, a component of a series of courses, or a part of all courses; (2) whether the course should be required; (3) whether the course should be taught by faculty trained in philosophy—reflected broad debate about the integration of ethics into the criminal justice program. The responses were sufficiently wide-ranging and individualized so as to discourage generalization about their pattern, but it appears that faculty from social science departments find the role of ethics in the criminal justice curriculum to be more problematic than faculty from criminal justice departments. A number of respondents highlighted areas of ethical uncertainty within the academic environment or specific to the relationship of faculty to students.

The most frequently noted general substantive issues for an ethics course were the following:

(1) Social inequalities; unequal access to justice;

(2) Corruption, bribery, and influence peddling;

(3) The integrity of evidence; truthful testimony;

(4) Plea-bargaining;

(5) Use of force, weapons, and coercion;

(6) The death penalty;

(7) Ethical responsibility and the "Rule of Law."

TEACHING OBJECTIVES IN CRIMINAL JUSTICE ETHICS

Despite the discovery of an array of courses distributed through programs of all sizes, the factors which helped to shape the decision to include ethics in the criminal justice curriculum, and, more importantly, the aspirations of ethics teachers, were not yet clear to us. In the spring of 1996, additional questions about the goals and development of criminal justice ethics courses were added to the survey for a random sample of 52 of the nonresponding criminal justice programs.[9] Debate about the character of ethics teaching, specifically about the question of whether it is to be *instruction*, or *direction*, in the ways of correct action, is a regular occurrence when criminal justice ethics teachers meet at professional conferences. William C. Heffernan's discussion of the status of guidance as a goal of ethics teaching opened the Workshop on Criminal Justice Ethics Education and is reprinted in this volume.[10] It was anticipated that faculty might be somewhat unsure about how to go about answering the question, "What are the objectives of your course?" Concern about the difficulties of summarizing a wide range of responses to this question prompted the Institute to suggest three possible answers to faculty members who were interviewed.[11]

The following alternative responses were read to faculty who taught criminal justice ethics courses, with the introduction, "For instance, would you say

(a) that your course develops students' understanding of justice in this society? If yes, do you use a constitutional framework or a more general moral framework for your discussions of justice?

(b) that the course is directed to improve discretionary decision making among practitioners in criminal justice?

(c) that your course is intended to enhance your students' disposition to do that which is good?"

These examples allow a comparison of the responses of teachers who use an "issues" perspective in their classes with those of teachers who use a professional ethics perspective on the question of guiding their students' behavior. The largest group of respondents who shared a response (7) affirmed all three objectives. Five teachers gave the understanding of justice as the goal of their course, and three endorsed the improvement of moral action. Interestingly, no one chose improving decision making as a single goal. Twelve teachers chose two of the three objectives: (1) five selected objectives (a) and (b); (2) two selected objectives (a) and (c); and (3) five chose (b) and (c). Although the number of teachers interviewed was small (27), the teachers who affirmed the second objective of improving discretionary decision making were twice as likely to affirm the third objective of improving moral action as well. The second part of the first objective, the question about constitutional framework versus moral framework was not well understood by respondents.

Faculty trained in philosophy were teaching the ethics courses in 14 of the 27 criminal justice programs that offered a course. The balance of 13 teachers had backgrounds in sociology, political science, business and psychology. Almost half of the faculty interviewed (13) said that their courses were issue-oriented. Six said that their courses were oriented to practitioners, and eight said that their courses covered both issues and the concerns of practitioners.

The history of the discussions in criminal justice departments about whether and how to introduce a criminal justice course was not easily captured in the interviews. Not all faculty knew how their courses had come to be offered, and others were unwilling to give a great deal of detail about the discussions within their programs or department. Two features of the responses stand out: In this sample, as in the written responses to part two of the survey, financial resources and the energy and persistence of individual teachers are often cited a crucial factors in the development of a criminal justice ethics course.

SURVEY of CRIMINAL JUSTICE ETHICS EDUCATION

Questionnaire

Part 1

1 Does your College/University have a Department of Criminal Justice, or a Department which includes Criminal Justice as well as other disciplines?

Department of Criminal Justice Y/N School of Criminal Justice Y/N

Department Name ______________________________

If you do not have a Department of Criminal Justice, what Department administers the Criminal Justice majors?

2 What Criminal Justice majors are offered by your College/University?

3 Do you offer a graduate degree in Criminal Justice? Y/N

Please list graduate degrees offered:

4 Do you require undergraduate Criminal Justice majors to complete a course in ethical issues related or specific to criminal justice? Y/N Graduate students? Y/N

If yes, Course Name(s):______________________________

5 Do you offer courses that deal exclusively with ethical issues related to criminal justice? Y/N

If yes, Course Name______________________________

6 In addition to the courses listed in (5), are there other courses in which the discussion of ethical issues is a significant component? Y/N

If yes, Course Names______________________________

7 Who among your faculty have criminal justice ethics as a major teaching interest?

8 If you are able to find out, without undue difficulty, approximately how many students major in criminal justice related programs in your college/university?

Undergraduate, by first semester registration:
1993__________ 1994__________ 1995__________

Masters, by first semester registration:
1993__________ 1994__________ 1995__________

Doctoral, by first semester registration:
1993__________ 1994__________ 1993__________

Part 2

1 Has your department or program encountered problems in the teaching of courses relating to criminal justice? Y/N

Have any of the following issues been troublesome for your department or program?

Course content (e.g., breadth)__________
Focus (philosophy vs. practical concerns)__________
Availability of suitable course materials__________
Finding instructors__________
Course evaluation__________
Student dissatisfaction__________

Please use the space below to describe the issues you have found to be of greatest concern.

2 Based upon your experience with a course/courses in the general area of criminal justice ethics, what questions do you feel deserve emphasis in our workshop on criminal justice ethics education?

3 What products of our study would be of use to your department or program?

Part 3

FOR PROGRAMS WHICH DO TEACH COURSES

1 What are the objectives of your course?

[If respondent asks for direction, say: For instance would you say:

(1) that your course develops students' understanding of justice in this society?

If yes, do you use a constitutional framework or a more general moral framework for your discussions of justice?

(2) that your course is directed to improve discretionary decision-making among practitioners in criminal justice?

(3) that your course is intended to enhance your student's disposition to do that which is good?]

2 Which faculty member teaches the course? Background?

3 Would you describe your course as issues-oriented or more oriented to the needs of practitioners?

4 How did you come to offer or require this course?

5 What factors were important to your faculty?

FOR PROGRAMS WHICH DO NOT TEACH COURSES

1 Have you discussed the inclusion of an ethics course in your program? Y/N

2 What were some of the issues that came up in those discussions?

3 What overall decision was reached?

4 Have you considered other ways of incorporating ethics into the curriculum?

NOTES

1. See pp. 214-15, in this Appendix.

2. Preparation and distribution of the questionnaires, coding and data entry of the responses, and telephone surveys were done by Valerie West, with the assistance of Tara Becker and Amy Martterer. The design of the survey, the coding scheme, and the data analysis was done by the author in consultation with John Kleinig and William Heffernan.

3. *Peterson's Guide to Four-Year Colleges, Twenty-fifth Edition* (Princeton, NJ: Petersons, 1995).

4. American Society of Criminology, Academy of Criminal Justice Sciences.

5. Program directors from 197 academic institutions returned enrollment information for the fall semesters of 1993, 1994 and 1995.

6. Numeric values for each cell entry are given in parentheses. Courses which are required are also listed as exclusively criminal justice ethics courses; neither required nor exclusive courses are counted in the category of courses which include discussion of ethical issues.

7. *Peterson's Guide to Four-Year Colleges, Twenty-fifth Edition* (Princeton, NJ: Petersons, 1995).

8. George P. Gallup, *The Gallup Poll, Public Opinion 1934-1971, Vol. 1, 1935-1948* (New York: Randon House, 1972) pp. vi-vii. The division of states into regions used by Gallup (East, Midwest, South and West) are used in this survey. East: ME, NH, VT, MA, RI, CT, NY, NJ, PA, MD, DE, WV, DC; Midwest: OH, MI, IN, IL, WI, MN, IA, MI, ND, SD, NE, KS; South: VA, NC, SC, GA, FL, KY, TN, AL, MS, AK, LA, OK, TX; West: MT, AZ, CO, ID, WY, UT, NV, NM, CA, OR, WA, HI, AK.

9. See pp. 215-16, in this Appendix.

10. See William C. Heffernan, "The Aims of Criminal Justice Ethics Education" in this volume, pp. 3-14.

11. The interviews were conducted by Mary Hapel, who graciously contributed time, energy, and patience to the survey and the Workshop on Criminal Justice Ethics Education during the spring of 1996, and by the author.

Appendix II

Teaching Criminal Justice Ethics: A Working Bibliography

INTRODUCTION

Because the teaching of criminal justice ethics is still fragmented, with newly assigned faculty and a slowly evolving literature, we have endeavored to assist those with responsibility for developing courses that are oriented to ethical issues encountered within the criminal justice system.

This task has been complicated by the fact that criminal justice ethics may be taught to different groups of students—to liberal arts students, for whom the criminal justice system is a social institution to be examined and critiqued like any other social institution; to social science students, for whom the criminal justice system offers an arena for research hypotheses and experimentation; and to aspiring and active practitioners, for whom the criminal justice system is a career opportunity and personal practical challenge.

Despite the natural overlaps fostered by each of these interests, significant divergences are also likely to be encountered. There is a fair chance that liberal arts students will be more interested in theories of punishment than in sentencing, more interested in the relation between policing and democratic theory than in the discretionary authority of police; that social science students will be more interested in the ethical issues surrounding the use of human subjects or the effects of social programs than the treatment of informants or the use of taser guns; and that practitioners will be more interested in the role of a professional code or limits of loyalty than the social sources of crime or right to bear arms. Of course, there is nothing hard and fast about these distinctions, but their somewhat different emphases make the task of bibliographic construction more difficult.

To some extent, the bibliography that follows seeks to cater to each of these interests, though—perhaps as a reflection of the predominant concern in criminal justice education—it is geared rather more to the needs of practitioners. It does not pretend to be exhaustive; it endeavors only to familiarize those who wish to teach criminal justice ethics with a groundwork which they can then build on for themselves.

The materials have been arranged to address first the *teaching* of ethics—ethics in general, then criminal justice ethics and research ethics, followed by corrections, the judiciary, law, police, and prosecution—and then the ethics *syllabus*—textual materials for courses in criminal justice ethics, whether of a general nature or directed more specifically at research, corrections, forensic science, the judiciary, law, police, or prosecution. Occasionally we have indicated works that will be of particular value to teachers in the field.

GENERAL WORKS ON THE TEACHING OF ETHICS

Note: The works cited here represent only a few of the many that address this topic.

Bok, Derek "Can Higher Education Foster Higher Morals?" *Business & Society Review*, no. 66 (summer 1988), pp. 4-9.
A call for structural, program, and course incentives to moral growth.

Callahan, Daniel and Bok, Sissela (eds.) *Ethics Teaching in Higher Education* (New York: Plenum, 1980).
A multi-authored comprehensive review.

Eisele, Thomas D. "Must Virtue be Taught?" *Journal of Legal Education*, 37, no. 4 (December, 1987), pp. 495-508.

Gee, Elizabeth D. "Legal Ethics Education and the Dynamics of Reform," *Catholic Lawyer*, 31, no. 3 (summer 1987), pp. 203-39.
A critical review of legal ethics education in the United States.

Ignelzi, Michael G. "Ethical Education in a College Environment: The Just Community Approach," *NASPA Journal*, 27, no. 3 (spring 1990), pp. 192-98.
Moral education as a product of college community structure.

Kasachkoff, Tziporah (ed.) Special Issue on Teaching Practical and Professional Ethics, *American Philosophical Association Newsletter on Teaching Philosophy*, 90, no. 1 (fall 1990), pp. 27-80.
Defenses and course outlines.

Kernaghan, K. and Mancino, S. "Approaches to Ethics Education," *Canadian Public Administration*, 34, no. 1 (spring 1991), pp. 184-91.
Workshop strategies for public servants.

Link, David T. "The Pervasive Method of Teaching Ethics," *Journal of Legal Education*, 39, no. 4 (December 1989), pp. 485-89.
The University of Notre Dame's law program.

McDowell, Banks "The Ethical Obligations of Professional Teachers of Ethics," *Professional Ethics*, 1, nos. 3-4 (fall-winter 1992), pp. 53-75.
The ethical dimensions of teaching practices.

Penn, W. Y. T. Jr. "Teaching Ethics: A Direct Approach," *Journal of Moral Education*, 19, no. 2 (1990), pp. 124-38.
A critique of teaching ethics via moral dilemmas.

Piper, Thomas R., Gentile, Mary C. and Parks, Sharon Daloz *Can Ethics Be Taught? Perspectives, Challenges, and Approaches at Harvard Business School* (Boston, MA: Harvard Business School, 1993).

Preston, Noel (ed.) *Ethics for the Public Sector: Education and Training* (Annandale, NSW: Federation Press, 1994).
Australian initiatives in public sector ethics education.

Rest, James R. "Why Does College Promote Development in Moral Judgment?" *Journal of Moral Education*, 17, no. 3 (1988), pp. 183-94.
The college environment as a stimulus to development of moral judgment.

Rest, James R. and Narváez, Darcia (eds.) *Moral Development in the Professions: Psychology and Applied Ethics* (Hillsdale, NJ: Lawrence Erlbaum Associates, 1994).

Rhode, Deborah "Professional Ethics and Professional Education," *Professional Ethics*, 1, nos. 1-2 (spring/summer 1992) pp. 31-72.
An argument for pervasive and continuing legal ethics education.

Silverman, Mitchell, Blount, William R., and Johnson, Marson H. "Teaching and Demonstrating Ethics in the Classroom," *International Journal of Offender Therapy and Comparative Criminology*, 36, no. 3 (fall 1992), pp. 169-72.

Solomon, Robert A. "Teaching Morality," *Cleveland State Law Review*, 40, 3-4 (summer-fall 1992), pp. 507-11.
Teaching ethics in a law school setting.

Weil, Vivian. "How Can Philosophers Teach Professional Ethics?" *Journal of Social Philosophy*, 20, no. 1&2 (spring/fall 1989), pp. 131-36.

Weinstein, Mark *Critical Thinking and Moral Education*, Institute for Critical Thinking, Resources Publication Series 1, No. 7 (Upper Montclair, NJ: Montclair State College, 1988).
Examines relevance of critical thinking strategies for moral education in high schools.

Whitbeck, Caroline "The Trouble With Dilemmas: Rethinking Applied Ethics," *Professional Ethics*, 1, nos. 1-2 (spring/summer 1992), pp. 119-42.

Willingham, Mark and Tucker, Melvin L. "Ethics and Values Training: A Multifaceted Approach," *Police Chief*, 55, no. 11 (November 1988), pp. 70, 72.
Strategies for a police department.

WWW Ethics Center for Engineering & Science, at http://web.mit.edu/ethics/www/.
Web site for teaching professional and practical ethics, containing case studies, articles, syllabi, etc.

Wynne, E. A. "The Great Tradition in Education: Transmitting Moral Values," *Educational Leadership*, 43, no. 4 (December 1985/January 1986), pp. 4-9.
A defense of normative moral education.

GENERAL WORKS ON THE TEACHING OF CRIMINAL JUSTICE ETHICS

Cederblom, Jerry, and Spohn, Cassia "A Model for Teaching Criminal Justice Ethics," *Journal of Criminal Justice Education*, 2, no. 2 (fall, 1991), pp. 201-17.
Discussion of a course outline, structured around the utilitarian-contractualist debate.

Delaney, H.R. "Teaching the Applied Criminal Justice Ethics Course," in F.A. Schmalleger (ed.) *Ethics in Criminal Justice: A Justice Professional Reader* (Bristol, IN: Wyndham Hall Press, 1990), pp. 148-63.
The debate over absolutism-relativism used as the fulcrum for discussion.

Emmons, David and Nutt, Larry "Values Education and the Criminal Justice Curriculum," *Journal of Criminal Justice Education*, 6, no. 1 (spring, 1995), pp. 147-52.
Incorporating values education into an introductory criminal justice course.

Felkenes, George T. "Ethics in the Graduate Criminal Justice Curriculum," *Teaching Philosophy*, 10, no. 1 (March 1987), pp. 23-36.

Fishman, Ethan "'Falling Back' on Natural Law and Prudence: A Reply to Souryal and Potts," *Journal of Criminal Justice Education*, 5, no. 2 (fall 1994), pp. 189-203.

Galligan, Ann M. "Using Courtroom Video in the Classroom: The Rodney King Case," *Journal of Criminal Justice Education*, 5, no. 2 (fall 1994), pp. 265-70.

Hyatt, W.D. "Teaching Ethics in a Criminal Justice Program," *American Journal of Police*, 10, no. 2 (1991), pp. 77-86.

Pollock, Joycelyn M. "Ethics and the Criminal Justice Curriculum," *Journal of Criminal Justice Education*, 4, no. 2 (fall 1993), pp. 377-90.
Aims and methods discussed.

Pring, Robert K. "Logic and Values: A Description of a New Course in Criminal Justice and Ethics," *Justice Professional*, 3, no. 1 (1988), pp. 94-106.
Basic ethical theory as a starting point.

Schmalleger, Frank (with Robert McKenrick) *Criminal Justice Ethics: Annotated Bibliography and Guide to Sources* (Westport, CT: Greenwood Press, 1991).

Schmidt, D.P. and Victor, J. L. "Teaching Ethics in Criminal Justice," in Roslyn Muraskin (ed.), *Issues in Justice: Exploring Policy Issues in the Criminal Justice System* (Bristol, IN: Wyndham Hall Press, 1990), pp. 105-18.

Sherman, Lawrence W. *Ethics in Criminal Justice Education* (Hastings-on-Hudson, NY: Hastings Center, 1982).
Overview of the requisites for ethics teaching in criminal justice.

Silverman, Mitchell, Blount, William R., and Johnson, Marson H. "Teaching and Demonstrating Ethics in the Classroom," *International Journal of Offender Therapy & Comparative Criminology*, 36 , no. 3 (fall 1992), pp. 169-72.
The ethical responsibilities of criminal justice teachers.

Souryal, Sam S. and Potts, Dennis W. "'What Am I Supposed to Fall Back On?' Cultural Literacy in Criminal Justice Ethics," *Journal of Criminal Justice Education*, 4, no. 1 (spring 1993), pp. 15-41.
A call to incorporate study of the classical philosophers into the criminal justice ethics curriculum.

Warwick, Donald P. *The Teaching of Ethics in the Social Sciences* (Hastings-on-Hudson, NY: Hastings Center, 1980).
Comprehensive overview.

TEACHING RESEARCH ETHICS (FOR CRIMINAL JUSTICE)

Beins, Bernard C. "Using the Barnum Effect to Teach about Ethics and Deception in Research," *Teaching of Psychology*, 20, no. 1 (February 1993), pp. 33-35.
Teaching by experience.

Elliott, Deni. "Case Studies for Teaching Research Ethics," *Professional Ethics*, 4, nos. 3-4 (1996), pp. 179-98.
Laboratory-oriented.

Korn, James H. "Coverage of Research Ethics in Introductory and Social Psychology Textbooks," *Teaching of Psychology*, 11, no. 3 (October 1984), pp. 146-49.
What do students learn from being used as research subjects?

Murray, Thomas H. "Learning to Deceive," *Hastings Center Report*, 10, no. 2 (April 1980), pp. 11-14.
Educating social psychologists.

Rosnow, Ralph, L. "Teaching Research Ethics Through Role-Play and Discussion," *Teaching of Psychology*, 17, no. 3 (October 1990), pp. 179-81.

Strohmetz, David B. "The Use of Role-Play in Teaching Research Ethics: A Validation Study," *Teaching of Psychology*, 19, no. 2 (April 1992), pp. 106-08.
Follow-up to Rosnow.

Swazey, Judith P. and Bird, Stephanie J. "Teaching and Learning Research Ethics," *Professional Ethics*, 4, 3-4 (1996), pp. 155-78.
Overview, with emphasis on the value of case studies.

ETHICS TEACHING IN SPECIFIC AREAS OF CRIMINAL JUSTICE

1 Corrections

Silvester, D. B. "Ethics and Privatization in Criminal Justice: Does Education Have a Role to Play?" *Journal of Criminal Justice*, 18, no. 1 (1990), pp. 65-70.
Privatization as a stimulus for teaching ethics in a correctional context.

2 Judiciary, Law and Prosecution

Note: The literature on teaching legal ethics is substantial. The works represented below constitute only a small portion of what is available.

Ackerman, Robert M. "Law Schools and Professional Responsibility: A Task for All Seasons," *Dickinson Law Review*, 88, no. 2 (winter 1984), pp. 202-20.
Defense of the pervasive approach as a way of overcoming student resistance.

Burger, Warren "The Role of the Law School in the Teaching of Legal Ethics and Professional Responsibility," *Cleveland State Law Review*, 29, nos. 3-4 (summer-fall 1980), pp. 377-95.
The responsibility of the law school to teach a professional ethic.

Burns, Susan "Teaching Legal Ethics," *Legal Education Review*, 4, no. 1 (spring 1993), pp. 141-63.
An overview from Australia.

Chemerinsky, Erwin "Pedagogy without Purpose: An Essay on Professional Responsibility Courses and Casebooks," *American Bar Foundation Research Journal,* no. 1 (1985), pp. 189-99; reply by Ted Schneyer in no. 4 (1985), pp. 943-58; rejoinder in no. 4 (1985), pp. 959-69.
Critical review (and defense) of three code-based texts in legal ethics.

Collins, John W. "Experience-Based Ethics Study: The Implications for Business Law Teachers," *Journal of Legal Studies Education,* 10, no. 1 (winter-spring 1992), pp. 107-20.
Argument for combining personal experience with realistic case studies.

Elkins, James R. "The Pedagogy of Ethics," *Journal of the Legal Profession,* 10 (1985), pp. 37-83.
Ethics as *being,* and not merely *doing.*

Esau, Alvin "Teaching Professional Responsibility in Law School," *Dalhousie Law Journal,* 11, no. 2 (March 1988), pp. 403-70.
Canadian frustration with teaching professional responsibility.

Fitzpatrick, Collins "Misconduct and Disability of Federal Judges: The Unreported Information Responses," *Judicature,* 71 (1988), pp. 282ff.

Gee, Elizabeth D. and Elkins, James R. "Resistance to Legal Ethics," *Journal of the Legal Profession,* 12 (1987), pp. 29-48.
Why legal ethics education fails, and what can be done about it.

Hall, Timothy L. "Moral Character, the Practice of Law, and Legal Education," *Mississippi Law Journal,* 60, no. 3 (winter 1990), pp. 511-54.
Legal ethics as character development, rather than as an intellectually oriented exercise.

Hartwell, Steven "Moral Development, Ethical Conduct, and Clinical Education," *New York Law School Law Review,* 35, no. 1 (spring 1990), pp. 131-67.
Kohlberg in clinical education.

Kelly, Michael J. *Legal Ethics and Legal Education* (Hastings-on-Hudson, NY: Institute of Society, Ethics and the Life Sciences, 1980).
Overview.

Moliterno, James E. "An Analysis of Ethics Teaching in Law Schools: Replacing Lost Benefits of the Apprentice System in the Academic Atmosphere," *University of Cincinnati Law School,* 60, no. 1 (summer 1991), pp. 83-134.
An analytic framework and programmatic model.

Sacks, Howard, "Student Fieldwork as a Technique in Educating Law Students in Professional Responsibility," *Journal of Legal Education,* 20 (1968).

Spader, Dean J. "Teaching Due Process: A Workable Method of Teaching the Ethical and Legal Aspects," *Journal of Criminal Justice Education,* 5, no. 1 (spring, 1994), pp. 81-101.
Legal ethics in a criminal justice curriculum.

Symposium: "Legal Education and the Pedagogy of Ethics," *The Legal Studies Forum*, 10, no. 3 (1986), pp. 265-324.
Papers by Elkins, Gee, Stanford, Foster, and LaRue.

"Teaching Legal Ethics: A Symposium," *Journal of Legal Education*, 41, no. 1 (March, 1991).

3 Police

Cohen, Howard "Teaching Police Ethics," *Teaching Philosophy*, 6, no. 3 (July 1983), pp. 231-43.
Describes and provides rationale for a course directed to police training instructors.

Das, Dilip "Police Training in Ethics: the Need for an Innovative Approach in Mandated Programs," *American Journal of Criminal Justice*, 11, no. 1 (fall 1986), pp. 62-80.

Doyle, Edward and Olivet, George D. "An Invitation to Understanding: Workshop in Law Enforcement Integrity," *Police Chief*, 39, no. 5 (May 1972), pp. 34-36, 38, 41-42, 44.
Academy-based program.

Elliston, Frederick A. *Police Ethics: Source Materials* (Washington, DC: Police Foundation, n.d. [1983]).

Heffernan, William C. "Two Approaches to Police Ethics," *Criminal Justice Review*, 7, no. 1 1982), pp. 28-35.
Developing integrity v. discussing hard cases.

Jones, D. M. "Using the 'Unfinished Story' as a Mechanism for Exploring Ethical Dilemmas in Criminal Investigation," *The Justice Professional*, 2, no. 2 (fall 1987), pp. 64-77.

Jordan, Trevor, "Teaching Police Ethics," in Noel Preston (ed.), *Ethics for the Public Sector* (Annandale, NSW: Federation Press, 1994), pp. 247-58.
An Australian perspective.

Kleinig, John "Teaching and Learning Police Ethics: Competing and Complementary Approaches," *Journal of Criminal Justice*, 18, no. 1 (January 1990), pp. 1-18.
A comparative overview of aims and approaches.

Lynch, Gerald W. "The Contribution of Higher Education to Ethical Behavior in Law Enforcement," *Journal of Criminal Justice*, 4, no. 4 (winter 1976), pp. 285-90.
A liberal arts education as developmental of empathy, tolerance, and judgment.

Massey, David "Why Us and Why? Some Reflections on Teaching Ethics to Police," *Police Studies*, 16, no. 3 (fall 1993), pp. 77-83.

McGarry, William, Doyle, Edward, and Olivet, George "Invitation to Understanding," *Police Chief*, 38, no. 6 (June 1971), pp. 20-27.
Ethical awareness workshop for police officers.

Miller, Larry S. and Braswell, Michael C. "Teaching Police Ethics: An Experiential Model," *American Journal of Criminal Justice*, 10, no. 1 (fall 1985), pp. 41-54.

Pollock, Joycelyn M. and Becker, Ronald F. "Law Enforcement Ethics: Using Officers' Dilemmas as a Teaching Tool," *Journal of Criminal Justice Education*, 6, no. 1 (spring 1995), pp. 1-20.
An argument for short, limited-issue dilemmas. Many examples.

Sherman, Lawrence W. "Learning Police Ethics," *Criminal Justice Ethics*, 1, no. 1 (winter/spring 1982), pp. 10-19.
Argument for college-based training.

Tyre, Mitchell and Braunstein, Susan "Higher Education and Ethical Policing," *FBI Law Enforcement Bulletin*, 61, no. 6 (June 1992), pp. 6-10.

GENERAL TEXTS IN CRIMINAL JUSTICE ETHICS

Braithwaite, John and Pettit, Philip *Not Just Deserts: A Republican Theory of Criminal Justice* (Oxford: Clarendon Press, 1990).
An integrated theory of criminal justice.

Braswell, Michael C., McCarthy, Belinda R., and McCarthy, Bernard J. (eds.) *Justice, Crime and Ethics*, 2nd ed. (Cincinnati, OH: Anderson Publishing Co., 1996).
Good selection of articles.

Close, Daryl and Meier, Nicholas (eds.) *Morality in Criminal Justice: An Introduction to Ethics* (Belmont, CA: Wadsworth, 1994).
Wide ranging, but more heavily weighted to law enforcement.

Elliston, Frederick A. and Bowie, Norman (eds.) *Ethics, Public Policy, and Criminal Justice* (Cambridge, MA: Oelgeschlager, Gunn & Hain, 1982).
Early and eclectic conference proceedings.

Gorr, Michael J. and Harwood, Sterling (eds.) *Crime and Punishment: Philosophic Explorations* (Boston: Jones and Bartlett, 1995).
Broad-ranging undergraduate text.

Kittrie, Nicholas N. and Susman, Jackwell (eds.) *Legality, Morality, and Ethics in Criminal Justice* (New York: Praeger, 1979).
Broad-ranging and eclectic.

Malloy, Edward A., C.S.C., *The Ethics of Law Enforcement and Criminal Punishment* (Lanham, MD: University Press of America, 1982).
Essays on the use of force, corruption, and punishment, influenced by Roman Catholic tradition.

Muraskin, Roslyn (ed.) *Issues in Justice: Exploring Policy Issues in the Criminal Justice System* (Bristol, IN: Wyndham Hall Press, 1990).

Pennock, J. Roland and Chapman, John W. (eds.) *Criminal Justice*, NOMOS XXVII (NY: Columbia University Press, 1985).
Original, sophisticated, yet narrowly-focused papers.

Pollock, Joycelyn M. *Ethics in Crime and Justice: Dilemmas and Decisions*, 2nd ed. (Pacific Grove, CA: Brooks/Cole Publishing Co., 1994).
One of very few single-authored texts.

Schmalleger, Frank A. (ed.) *Ethics in Criminal Justice: A Justice Professional Reader* (Bristol, IN: Wyndham Hall Press, 1990).
A collection extracted from the pages of *The Justice Professional.*

Schmalleger, Frank A. and Gustafson, Robert (eds.) *The Social Basis of Criminal Justice: Ethical Issues for the 1980's* (Washington, DC: University Press of America, 1981).
Eclectic.

Souryal, Sam S. *Ethics in Criminal Justice: In Search of the Truth* (Cincinnati, OH: Anderson, 1992).
Links criminal justice ethics to classical philosophy.

TEXT MATERIALS FOR RESEARCH ETHICS (IN CRIMINAL JUSTICE)

Note: The number of textbooks in this area is limited, and teachers might find it more productive to construct their own from some of the articles that have been published on various problems in research ethics.

Arboleda-Flórez, J. "Ethical Issues Regarding Research on Prisoners," *International Journal of Offender Therapy and Comparative Criminology*, 35, no. 1 (1991), pp. 1-5.
Editorial.

Baumrind, Diana "Research Using Intentional Deception: Ethical Issues Revisited," *American Psychologist*, 40, no. 2 (February 1985), 165-74.

Baunach, Phyllis Jo "Random Assignment in Criminal Justice Research: Some Ethical and Legal Issues," *Criminology*, XVII, 4 (February, 1980), pp. 435-44.

Beauchamp, Tom L. "Ethical Issues in Funding and Monitoring University Research," *Business & Professional Ethics Journal*, 11, no.1 (spring 1992), pp. 5-16.

Bebeau, Muriel J., Pimple, Kenneth D., Muskavitch, Karen M., Smith, David H., and Borden, Sandra L. (eds.) *Moral Reasoning in Scientific Research* (Poynter Center, Indiana University, 1995).
Focuses mostly on scientific research. Some reference value for criminal justice.

Bennett, L. "Ethics in Research and Evaluation," in F.A. Schmalleger and R. Gustafson (eds.) *The Social Basis of Criminal Justice: Ethical Issues for the 1980's* (Washington, DC: University Press of America, 1981), pp. 257-86.
Explicitly linked to criminal justice.

Bloomberg, Seth Allan and Wilkins, Leslie T. "Ethics of Research Involving Human Subjects in Criminal Justice," *Crime & Delinquency*, 23, no. 4 (October 1977), pp. 435-44.
Overview.

Bulmer, Martin (ed.) *Social Research Ethics: An Examination of the Merits of Covert Participant Observation* (New York: Holmes & Meier Publishers, 1982).
Includes criminal justice-related material.

Cassell, J. "Ethical Principles for Conducting Fieldwork," *American Anthropologist*, 82, no. 1 (1980), pp. 28-41.
Broad focus, though some relevance to criminal justice-related fieldwork.

Cook, Stuart W. "Ethical Issues in the Conduct of Research in Social Relations," in Claire Sellitz, Lawrence Rightsman and Stuart Cook (eds.) *Research Methods in Social Relations*, 3rd ed. (New York: Holt, Rinehart & Winston, 1976).

Davidson, Paul *Ethical Dilemmas and Social Science Research* (San Francisco: Jossey-Bass, 1979).

Diener, E. and Crandall, R. *Ethics in Social and Behavioral Research* (Chicago, IL: University of Chicago Press, 1978).

Fisher, Celia B. "Reporting and Referring Research Participants: Ethical Challenges for Investigators Studying Children and Youth," *Ethics and Behavior*, 4, no. 2 (1994), pp. 87-95.

Goodman, Gail S. "Ethical Issues in Child Witness Research," *Child Abuse & Neglect*, 18, no. 3 (March 1994), pp. 290-93.

Homan, Roger "The Ethics of Open Methods," *British Journal of Sociology*, 43, no. 3 (September 1992), pp. 321-32.
The manipulation of consent.

Kelling, George L. "Justifying the Moral Propriety of Experimentation: A Case Study," in W.A. Geller (ed.), *Police Leadership in America* (New York: Praeger, 1985).
The Kansas City Preventive Patrol Experiment.

Kimmel, Allan J. *Ethics and Values in Applied Social Research* (Newbury Park, CA: Sage, 1988).

Klockars, Carl B. and O'Connor, Finbarr W. *Deviance and Deviancy: The Ethics of Research with Human Subjects* (Beverly Hills, CA: Sage, 1979).
Substantial criminal justice focus.

Lee, Raymond M. *Doing Research on Sensitive Topics* (London: Sage, 1993).
Overview with practical as well as ethical focus.

Longmire, Dennis R. "Ethical Dilemmas in the Research Setting: A Survey of Experiences and Responses in the Criminological Community," *Criminology*, 21, no. 3 (August 1983), pp. 333-48.

McCarthy, Belinda R. "Ethics and Criminal Justice Research," reprinted in Braswell, Michael C., McCarthy, Belinda R., and McCarthy, Bernard J. (eds.) *Justice, Crime and Ethics* (Cincinnati, OH: Anderson Publishing Co., 1991), pp. 297-319.

Renzetti, Claire M. *Researching Sensitive Topics* (Thousand Oaks, CA: Sage Publications, 1993).

Scarr, Sandra "Ethical Problems in Research Behaviors and Risky Populations," *Ethics and Behavior*, 4, no. 2 (1994), pp. 147-55.

Schiltz, Michael E. (ed.) *Ethics and Standards in Institutional Research* (San Francisco: Jossey-Bass, 1992).

Shapard, J.E. "The Ethics of Experimentation in Law Enforcement," in W.A. Geller (ed.), *Police Leadership in America* (NY: Praeger, 1985), pp. 418-29.
With responses by Kelling, Elliston, Rice, and Bergstrom.

Shuy, Roger W. "Ethical Issues in Analyzing FBI Surreptitious Tapes," *International Journal of the Sociology of Language*, 62 (1986), pp. 119-28.

Sieber, Joan E. *Planning Ethically Responsible Research: A Guide for Students and Internal Review Boards* (Newbury Park, CA: Sage, 1992).

Sieber, J. E. and Stanley, B. "Ethical and Professional Dimensions of Socially Sensitive Research," *American Psychologist*, 43, no. 1 (1988), pp. 49-55.

Smith, A.B. "The Ethics of Criminological Research with Children as Subjects," in R. Muraskin (ed.), *Issues in Justice: Exploring Policy Issues in the Criminal Justice System* (Bristol, IN: Wyndham Hall Press, 1990), pp. 132-39.

Westcott, Helen "On Sensitivity and Ethical Issues in Child Witness Research," *Child Abuse & Neglect*, 18, no. 3 (March 1994), pp. 287-90.

Wolfgang, Marvin "Confidentiality in Criminological Research and Other Ethical Issues," *Journal of Criminal Law & Criminology*, 72, no. 1 (spring 1981), pp. 345-61.

TEXT MATERIALS FOR SPECIFIC FIELDS IN CRIMINAL JUSTICE ETHICS

Note: The absence of available textbooks will sometimes make it necessary that instructors compile their own set of readings.

1 Corrections

AIMS Instructional Media *The Correctional Officer: Ethics and Conduct* (Glendale, CA: AIMS Instructional Media, 1987).
VHS video-cassette, 20 mins.

Arboleda-Flórez, J. "Ethics of Psychiatry in Prison Society," *Canadian Journal of Criminology*, 25, no. 1 (1983), pp. 47-54.
The fine line between treatment and punishment, and the problem of consent.

Becker, J. V. and Abel, G. G. "Methodological and Ethical Issues in Evaluating and Treating Adolescent Sexual Offenders," in M. O. Emeline, et al. (eds.) *Adolescent Sex Offenders: Issues in Research and Treatment* (Rockville, MD: National Institute of Justice, 1985), pp. 109-29.

Bedau, Hugo Adam "Prisoners' Rights," *Criminal Justice Ethics* 1, no. 1 (winter/ spring 1982), pp. 26-41.
Useful ethical overview.

Bonnie, Richard. "Dilemmas in Administering the Death Penalty: Conscientious Abstention, Professional Ethics, and the Needs of the Legal System," *Law and Human Behavior*, 14, 1, (1990), pp. 67-90.
Determining competence for execution. Response by Stanley Brodsky (pp. 91-97).

Braswell, Michael C., Fletcher, Tyler and Miller, Larry. *Human Relations and Corrections*, 3rd ed. (Prospect Heights, IL: Waveland Press, Inc., 1996).
Collection of case studies.

Carroll, Leo, "AIDS and Human Rights in the Prisons: A Comment on the Ethics of Screening and Segregation," in C. Hartjen and E. E. Rhine (eds.) *Correctional Theory and Practice* (Chicago: Nelson-Hall Publishers, 1992), pp.162-77.

Dickens, Bernard M. "Legal and Ethical Considerations in 'Enforced Therapy,'" in R. J. Freeman, et al. (eds.) *Treatment of Sexual Aggression: Legal and Ethical Issues* (Burnaby, BC: Simon Fraser University, 1988), pp. 23-52.
A Canadian perspective.

Duff, R. A. *Trials and Punishments* (Cambridge: Cambridge University Press, 1986).
Rich discussion of the ethics of punishment.

Duff, R. A. "Penal Communications: Recent Work in the Philosophy of Punishment," in Michael Tonry (ed.), *Crime and Justice: An Annual Review of Research* (Chicago: University of Chicago Press, 1996), vol. 20, pp. 1-97.
Excellent overview.

Erez, Edna "Randomized Experiments in a Correctional Context: Legal, Ethical and Practical Concerns," *Journal of Criminal Justice*, 14 (1986), pp. 389-400.

Geis, Gilbert "Ethical and Legal Issues in Experiments with Offender Populations" (1967), reprinted in Susette Talarico (ed.), *Criminal Justice Research: Approaches, Problems, and Policy* (Cincinnati, OH: Anderson, 1980), pp. 221-30.

Gordon, Robert, and Verdun-Jones, Simon N. "Ethics and Ethical Dilemmas in the Treatment of Sex Offenders," in S.N. Verdun-Jones, et al. (eds.), *Sexual Aggression and the Law* (Burnaby, BC: Simon Fraser University, 1983), pp. 73-96.

Haas, Kenneth C. and Alpert, Geoffrey P. *The Dilemmas of Corrections*, 3rd ed. (Prospect Heights, IL: Waveland Press Inc., 1996).

Kantor, Jay E. "Psychiatry in the Service of the Criminal Punishment System: Some Conceptual and Ethical Issues," in R. Rosner and R.B. Harmon (eds.) *Correctional Psychiatry* (New York: Plenum Press, 1988), pp. 169-195.

Kleinig, John and Lindner, Charles "AIDS on Parole: Dilemmas in Decision Making," *Criminal Justice Policy Review*, 3, no. 1 (1989), pp. 1-27.

McCarthy, Bernard J. "Keeping an Eye on the Keeper: Prison Corruption and its Control," reprinted in Braswell, Michael C., McCarthy, Belinda R., and McCarthy, Bernard J. (eds.) *Justice, Crime and Ethics* (Cincinnati, OH: Anderson Publishing Co., 1991), pp. 239-52.

Miller, David B., Noury, Mostafa M., and Tobia, Joseph J. "Questions of Ethics in Prison Systems in America," in F.A. Schmalleger and R. Gustafson (eds.) *The Social Basis of Criminal Justice: Ethical Issues for the 1980's* (Washington, DC: University Press of America, 1981), pp. 217-39.

Newell, J. David "Ethics and Prison Administrators: Learning to Articulate the Reasons for Your Decisions," *Federal Prisons Journal*, 2, 1, (1991) pp. 38-44.

Overholser, James C. "Ethical Issues in Prison Research: A Risk/Benefit Analysis," *Behavioral Sciences & the Law*, 5, no. 2 (spring 1987), pp. 187-202.

Pollock-Byrne, Joycelyn M. "Moral Development and Corrections," reprinted in Braswell, Michael C., McCarthy, Belinda R., and McCarthy, Bernard J. (eds.) *Justice, Crime and Ethics* (Cincinnati, OH: Anderson Publishing Co., 1991), pp. 221-38.
The impact of imprisonment on moral development.

Scheurell, Robert "Social Work Ethics in Probation and Parole," in A.R. Roberts (ed.) *Social Work in Juvenile and Criminal Justice Settings* (Springfield, IL: Charles C Thomas, 1983), pp. 241-51.

Scott, N. A. "Counseling Prisoners: Ethical Issues, Dilemmas and Cautions," *Journal of Counseling and Development*, 64, no. 4 (1985), pp. 272-73.

Silverman, Mitchell "Ethical Issues in the Field of Probation," *International Journal of Offender Therapy & Comparative Criminology*, 37, no. 1 (spring 1993), pp. 85-94.

Stevens, Carolynne H. "Correctional Ethics: The Janus View," in F.A. Schmalleger and R. Gustafson (eds.) *The Social Basis of Criminal Justice: Ethical Issues for the 1980's* (Washington, DC: University Press of America, 1981), pp. 181-215.

Ten, C. L. *Crime Guilt and Punishment* (London: Oxford University Press, 1987).
Readable text on the philosophy of punishment.

Thomas, Charles W. "Prisoners' Rights and Correctional Privatization: A Legal and Ethical Analysis," *Business & Professional Ethics Journal*, 10, no. 1 (Spring 1991), pp. 43-45.

Tonry, Michael " Prediction and Classification: Legal and Ethical Issues," in D. M. Gottfredson and M. Tonry (eds.) *Prediction and Classification: Criminal Justice Decision Making* (Chicago: University of Chicago Press, 1987), pp. 367-413.

von Hirsch, Andrew "The Ethics of Selective Incapacitation: Observations on the Contemporary Debate," *Crime and Delinquency*, 30, no. 2 (April 1984), pp. 175-94.

von Hirsch, Andrew and Ashworth, Andrew (eds.) *Principled Sentencing* (Edinburgh: Edinburgh University Press, 1992).
Comprehensive text on sentencing ethics.

Weinberger, Linda E. and Sreenivasan, Shoba "Ethical and Professional Conflicts in Correctional Psychology," *Professional Psychology: Research and Practice*, 25, no. 2 (1994), pp. 161-67.

Whitehead, John T. "Ethical Issues in Probation and Parole," reprinted in Braswell, Michael C., McCarthy, Belinda R., and McCarthy, Bernard J. (eds.) *Justice, Crime and Ethics* (Cincinnati, OH: Anderson Publishing Co., 1991), pp. 253-71.

Williams, Brian (ed.) *Probation Values* (Birmingham, UK: Venture Press, 1995).
Ethical dimensions of the tension between social welfare and managerial models of probation.

Williams, P. C., et al. "Ethical Problems: Cases and Commentaries: Health vs. Safety—Receiving Needed Care," *Journal of Prison Health*, 1, no. 1 (1981), pp. 44-55.

2 Forensic Sciences

Note: We know of no single text on ethical issues in the forensic sciences, though the symposium edited by Joseph L. Peterson in *Journal of Forensic Sciences*, 34, no. 3 (May 1989), pp. 717-93, might well be used for such purposes.

Ashford, N. A. and Gregory, K. A. "Ethical Problems in Using Science in the Regulatory Process," *National Resources &Environment*, 2 (fall 1986), pp. 13-16, 55-57.

Biasotti, Alfred A. "The Role of the Forensic Scientist in the Application of Chemical Tests for Alcohol in Traffic Law Enforcement," *Journal of Forensic Sciences*, 29, no. 4 (October 1984), pp. 1164-72.

Brunelle, R. L. and Cantu, A. A. "Training Requirements and Ethical Responsibilities of Forensic Scientists Performing Ink Dating Examinations," *Journal of Forensic Sciences*, 32, no. 6 (November 1987), pp. 1502-1506.
Letter in response to technical article.

Curran, W. J. "Ethical Standards," in W. J. Curran, A. L. McGarry and C. S. Petty (eds.) *Modern Legal Medicine, Psychiatry and Forensic Science* (Philadelphia, PA: F. A. Davies, 1980), pp. 29-48.
Review of forensic science Code requirements.

Frankel, Mark S. "Ethics and the Forensic Sciences: Professional Autonomy in the Criminal Justice System," *Journal of Forensic Sciences*, 34, no. 3 (May 1989), pp. 763-71.

Giannelli, Paul C. "Evidentiary and Procedural Rules Governing Expert Testimony," *Journal of Forensic Sciences*, 34, no. 3 (May 1989), pp. 730-48.
Formal constraints on forensic scientists in sworn testimony.

Lucas, Douglas M. "The Ethical Responsibilities of the Forensic Scientist: Exploring the Limits," *Journal of Forensic Sciences*, 34, no. 3 (May 1989), pp. 719-29.

Peterson, Joseph L. "Promises, Compromises, and Commitments: The Protection of Confidential Research Data," *American Behavioral Scientist*, 27, no. 4 (1984), pp. 453-80.
Dilemmas confronting research into the practices of forensic science laboratories.

Peterson, Joseph L. "Ethical Issues in the Collection, Examination and Use of Physical Evidence," in G. Davies (ed.) *Forensic Science*, 2nd ed. rev. (Washington, DC: American Chemical Society, 1986), pp. 35-48.

Peterson, Joseph L. and Murdock, John E. "Forensic Science Ethics: Developing an Integrated System of Support and Enforcement," *Journal of Forensic Sciences*, 34, no. 3 (May 1989), pp. 749-62.

Saks, Michael J. "The Prevalence and Impact of Ethical Problems in Forensic Science," *Journal of Forensic Sciences*, 34, no. 3 (May 1989), pp. 772-93.

Schroeder, Oliver C., Jr. "Ethical and Moral Dimensions in Forensic Science," in G. Davies (ed.) *Forensic Science*, 2nd ed. rev. Washington, DC: American Chemical Society, 1986.

Starrs, James E. "The Ethical Obligations of the Forensic Scientist in the Criminal Justice System," *Journal of the Association of Official Analytical Chemists*, 54 (1971), pp. 906-14.

3 Judiciary

Abramson, Jeffrey. *We, The Jury System and the Ideal of Democracy* (New York: Basic Books, 1994).

Barbark, Stephen B. and Player, S. Jay "Disciplining the Federal Judiciary: The Law of Federal Judicial Discipline and the Lessons of Social Science," *University of Pennsylvania Law Review*, 192 (1993), pp. 1ff.

Copple, R.F. "From the Cloister to the Street: Judicial Ethics and Public Expression," *Denver University Law Review*, 64, no. 3 (1988), pp. 549-78.

Cunningham, Richard P., Nagel, Robert F., and Lomasky, Loren E. "Ethics in Context: The Selling of Jury Deliberations," *Criminal Justice Ethics*, 8, no. 1 (winter/spring 1989), pp. 26-34.

Forer, Lois G. "When Should Judges be Whistle Blowers?" *The Judge's Journal*, 27, no. 3 (1988), pp. 5-9, 39-41.

Fretz, D. R. *Ethics for Judges*, 2nd ed. (Reno, NV: National College of the State Judiciary, 1975).

Gallas, G. and Lampasi, M. "A Code of Ethics for Judicial Administrators," *Judicature*, 61, no. 7 (February 1978), pp. 311-17.

Henderson, S.A. *Canons of Judicial Ethics* (Chicago, IL: American Judicature Society, 1969).

Juries on Trial (Available from Films for the Humanities and Sciences, PO Box 2053, Princeton, NJ, 08543)
Video, color, 23 mins.

Lubet, S. *Beyond Reproach: Ethical Restrictions on the Extrajudicial Activities of State and Federal Judges* (Chicago: American Judicature Society, 1984).

Noonan, John T., Jr. and Winston Kenneth I. (eds.) *The Responsible Judge* (Westport, CT: Praeger, 1993).

Plea Bargains: Dealing for Justice (Available from Films for the Humanities and Sciences, PO Box 2053, Princeton, NJ, 08543)
Video, color, 28 mins.

Scott, C.F. "Reconciling Conflicts in Illinois Judicial Ethics," *Loyola University of Chicago Law Journal*, 19, no. 3 (1988), pp. 1067-95.

Shaman, Jeffrey M., Lubet, Steven, and Alfini, James J. *Judicial Conduct and Ethics*, (Charlottesville, VA: Michie, 1990).

Thoron, G. "Report on Judicial Ethics," *Annals of the American Academy of Political and Social Science*, 363 (January 1966), pp. 36-43.

Twentieth Century Fund Task Force *The Good Judge*, Report on Judicial Responsibility (New York: Priority Press, 1989).

4 Law

Note: Many texts for legal ethics courses are available. Those listed below are representative. In addition, there is substantial journal literature covering different aspects of lawyers' work.

Bloom, Murray Teigh (ed.) *Lawyers, Clients and Ethics: Using the Law School Clinic for Teaching Professional Responsibility* (NY: Council on Legal Education for Professional Responsibility, 1974).
Cases and comments.

Buckingham, Donald E., Bickenbach, Jerome E., Bronaugh, Richard, and Wilson, Bertha (eds.) *Legal Ethics in Canada: Theory and Practice* (Toronto: Harcourt Brace/Canada, 1996).
Wide-ranging.

Davis, Michael and Elliston, Frederick A. (eds.) *Ethics and the Legal Profession* (Buffalo, NY: Prometheus Books, 1986).
Wide-ranging collection, suitable for criminal justice programs.

Elliston, Frederick A., and van Schaick, Jane *Legal Ethics: An Annotated Bibliography and Resource Guide* (Littleton, CO: Fred B. Rothman, 1984).

Lawyers on Trial (Available from Films for the Humanities and Sciences, PO Box 2053, Princeton, NJ, 08543)
Video, color, 29 mins.

Luban, David "Are Criminal Lawyers Different? (Criminal Defense Ethics)," *Michigan Law Review*, 91, no. 7 (June 1993), pp. 1729-66.

Luban, David (ed.) *The Good Lawyer: The Lawyers' Roles and Lawyers' Ethics* (Totowa, NJ: Rowman & Allanheld, 1983).
Collection of scholarly essays.

Rhode, Deborah L. *Legal Ethics* (Westbury, NY: Foundation Press, 1992).
Standard law school text.

Rotunda, Ronald D. *Professional Responsibility*, 4th ed. (St. Paul, MN: West, 1995).
Standard law school text.

Schrader, David E. *Ethics and the Practice of Law* (Englewood Cliffs, NJ: Prentice Hall, 1988).
Standard law school text.

5 Police

Note: This listing focuses mainly on texts. There is, however, a substantial journal literature that can be drawn upon.

Bad Cops or Cops Getting a Bad Rap? (Available from Films for the Humanities and Sciences, PO Box 2053, Princeton, NJ, 08543)
Video, color, 28 mins.

Barker, Tom *Police Ethics: Crisis in Law Enforcement* (Springfield, IL: Charles C Thomas, 1996).
Law Enforcement Code of Ethics as a framework for practitioner training.

Burke, Francis V., Jr. "Lying During Crisis Negotiations: A Costly Means to Expedient Resolution," *Criminal Justice Ethics*, 14, no. 1 (winter/spring 1995), pp. 49-62.

Cohen, Howard S. "Exploiting Police Authority," *Criminal Justice Ethics*, 5, no. 2 (summer/fall 1986), pp. 23-31.

Cohen, Howard S. "Overstepping Police Authority," *Criminal Justice Ethics*, 6, 2 (summer/fall, 1987), pp. 52-60.

Cohen, Howard S. and Feldberg, Michael *Power and Restraint: The Moral Dimension of Police Work* (New York: Praeger, 1991).
Text for professional ethics course.

Delattre, Edwin J. *Character & Cops: Ethics in Policing*, 2nd ed. (Washington, DC: AEI Press, 1994).
Practitioner-oriented.

Dunham, Roger G. and Alpert, Geoffrey P. *Critical Issues in Policing*, 2nd ed. (Prospect Heights, IL: Waveland Press, Inc., 1996).

Elliston, Frederick A. and Feldberg, Michael (eds.) *Moral Issues in Police Work* (Totowa, NJ: Rowman & Allanheld, 1985).
Early classroom collection.

Gilbert, J. N. *Investigative Ethics* (Cincinnati, OH: Anderson, 1984).

Heffernan, William C. and Stroup, Timothy (eds.) *Police Ethics: Hard Choices in Law Enforcement* (New York: John Jay Press, 1985).
Scholarly collection.

IACP Bureau of Operations and Research *Police Ethics—ACP Training Key No. 295* (Gaithersburg, MD: IACP, 1980).
Academy-oriented.

Insight Media *Ethics and Conduct*, New York, NY: Insight Media, 1987
VHS video-cassette, 20 mins.

Insight Media *Ethics in Law Enforcement*, New York, NY: Insight Media, 1989
VHS video-cassette, 19 mins.

Kania, Richard R. E. "Should We Tell the Police to Say 'Yes' to Gratuities?," *Criminal Justice Ethics*, 7, 2 (summer/fall, 1988), pp. 37-49.

Kleinig, John *The Ethics of Policing*, Cambridge: Cambridge University Press, 1996.

Kleinig, John (ed.) *Handled with Discretion: Ethical Issues in Police Decision Making*, Lanham, MD: Rowman & Littlefield, 1996.

Marx, Gary T. *Undercover: Police Surveillance in America*, Berkeley, CA: University of California Press, 1988.
Study of all aspects of undercover work.

Miller, Larry S. and Braswell, Michael C. *Human Relations and Police Work*, 4th ed. (Prospect Heights, IL: Waveland Press, 1997).
Collection of short case studies, with instructor's manual.

NIJ/Program in Criminal Justice Policy and Management, John F. Kennedy School of Government, *Perspectives on Policing*, 1988-93.
Series of 17 papers on various initiatives in policing, several with a focus on ethical questions.

Skolnick, Jerome "Deception by Police," *Criminal Justice Ethics* 1, 2 (summer/fall, 1982), pp. 40-54.

Skolnick, Jerome H. and Leo, Richard "The Ethics of Deceptive Interrogation," *Criminal Justice Ethics*, 11, 1 (winter/spring, 1992), pp. 3-12.

The Tarnished Shield: When Cops Go Bad (Available from Films for the Humanities and Sciences, PO Box 2053, Princeton, NJ, 08543)
Video, 52 mins.

6 Prosecution

Alschuler, Albert "Courtroom Misconduct by Prosecutors and Trial Judges," *Texas Law Review*, 50 (April 1972), pp. 629-735.
An overview.

Aron, C. "Prosecutorial Misconduct: A National Survey," *De Paul Law Review*, 21 (1971), pp. 422-84.

Burke, Alafair S. R. "Reconciling Professional Ethics and Prosecutorial Power: The Non-Contact Rule Debate," *Stanford Law Review*, 46, no. 6 (July 1994), pp. 1635-75.

Corrigan, Carol A. "On Prosecutorial Ethics," *Hastings Constitutional Law Quarterly*, 13, no. 3 (spring 1986), pp. 537-43.

Cross, John J., III, "Prosecutorial Vindictiveness: An Examination of Divergent Lower Court Standards and a Proposed Framework for Analysis," *Vanderbilt Law Review*, 34, no. 2 (March 1981), pp. 431-60.

Daugherty, D. A. "Separation of Powers and Abuses in Prosecutorial Discretion," *Journal of Criminal Law and Criminology*, 79, no. 3 (1988), pp. 953-96.

Donahue, Kara S. "Prosecutorial Ethics: The Case for the Per Se Rule," *Fordham Urban Law Journal*, 18, no. 2 (winter 1991), pp. 407-35.

Douglass, J. J. *Ethical Issues in Prosecution* (Houston, TX: National College of District Attorneys, 1988).

Feldman, S. W. "Ethics Workshop: Prosecutorial Interference with Defense Access to Prospective Witness," *Criminal Law Bulletin*, 21, no. 4 (July - August 1985), pp. 353-63.

Gershman, Bennett L. "Why Prosecutors Misbehave," *Criminal Law Bulletin*, 22, no. 2 (March-April 1986), pp. 131-43; reprinted in Braswell, Michael C., McCarthy, Belinda R., and McCarthy, Bernard J. (eds.) *Justice, Crime and Ethics* (Cincinnati, OH: Anderson Publishing Co., 1991), pp. 163-73.

Green, Bruce A. "The Ethical Prosecutor and the Adversary System," *Criminal Law Bulletin*, XXIV, 2 (Mar-Apr, 1988), pp. 126-45.

Green, Bruce A. "'Package Plea Bargaining and the Prosecutor's Duty of Good Faith," *Criminal Law Bulletin*, 25, no. 6 (November-December 1989), pp. 507-49.

Jonakeit, R. N. "Ethical Prosecutor's Misconduct," *Criminal Law Bulletin*, 23, no. 6 (November - December 1987), pp. 550-67.

National College of District Attorneys, *Ethical Considerations in Prosecutions: Roles and Functions of the Prosecutor* (Houston, TX: National Council of District Attorneys, 1977).

Uviller, H. Richard "The Virtuous Prosecutor in Quest of an Ethical Standard: Guidance from the ABA," *Michigan Law Review*, 71, no. 6 (May 1973), pp. 1145-68. Selective prosecution, prejudgment of credibility, and conflict of interest.

Wright, T. P. "Prosecutorial Ethics and Values in Plea Bargaining," *Prosecutor*, 21, no. 3 (winter 1988), pp. 23-28.

Zacharias, Fred C. "Structuring the Ethics of Prosecutorial Trial Practice: Can Prosecutors Do Justice?" *Vanderbilt Law Review*, 44, no. 1 (January 1991), pp. 45-114.

The Institute for Criminal Justice Ethics is currently constructing a web site at **http://www.lib.jjay.cuny.edu/cje**. As this develops, new resources for teaching criminal justice ethics will be posted.

Indexes

Names

References to the Working Bibliography (pp. 217-35) are not included

Subjects

Notes on Contributors

JOAN C. CALLAHAN is professor of philosophy at the University of Kentucky, where she is also a member of the women's studies faculty. She has served on the editorial board of *Professional Ethics*, and currently serves on the editorial board of *Race, Gender, and Class*. She is author of numerous journal and encyclopedia articles on practical ethics and social and political philosophy. Her books include *Ethical Issues in Professional Life* (1988); *Preventing Birth: Contemporary Methods and Related Moral Controversies* (with reproductive physiologist, James W. Knight, 1989); *Menopause: A Midlife Passage* (1993); and *Reproduction, Ethics and the Law: Feminist Perspectives* (1995).

CHARLES S. CLAXTON is professor of higher education in the Department of Leadership and Educational Studies at Appalachian State University in Boone, North Carolina. He was the founding director of the Leadership Institute in Judicial Education, a national project concerned with strengthening continuing education for judges and other court personnel. Among his publications is *Education for Development: Principles and Practice in Judicial Education*. He serves each summer as a faculty member at the Institute for the Management of Lifelong Education at Harvard University. He has been a workshop leader and consultant at over 100 colleges and universities throughout the United States on effective teaching and learning, deepening the sense of community in academe, and new approaches to educational leadership.

MICHAEL DAVIS is Senior Research Associate at the Center for the Study of Ethics in the Professions, Illinois Institute of Technology. Before coming to IIT in 1986, he taught at Case-Western Reserve, Illinois State, and the University of Illinois at Chicago. For 1985-86, he held a National Endowment for the Humanities fellowship. He has received a number of grants, including two from the National Science Foundation to integrate ethics into technical courses (1991-95 and 1996-98). Davis has published more than eighty articles, authored two books—*To Make Punishment Fit the Crime* (1992) and *Justice in the Shadow of Death* (1996)—and co-edited two others—*Ethics and the Legal Profession* (1986) and *AIDS: Crisis in Professional Ethics* (1994). Davis received his Ph.D. from the University of Michigan in 1972.

ROBIN FLATON is an adjunct associate professor of psychology at Hofstra University. She received a J.D. from St. John's School of Law and an M.A. in social service administration from the University of Chicago. She is currently completing her Ph.D. in Human Development at Teachers College, Columbia University. Her research interests include the development of informal reasoning, juror reasoning, and the jury process.

WILLIAM C. HEFFERNAN is associate professor of law at John Jay College of Criminal Justice and the Graduate Center of the City University of New York. His articles on constitutional criminal procedure have appeared in numerous law reviews. He is also an editor of *Criminal Justice Ethics,* a journal published by John Jay's Institute for Criminal Justice Ethics.

FRANCIS M. KAMM is professor of philosophy and adjunct professor of law at New York University, and Visiting Professor of Philosophy at UCLA. Her research and teaching is in the area of ethical theory and practical ethics. She is the author of *Creation and Abortion* (1992), *Morality, Mortality,* Vol. 1 (1993) and Vol. 2 (1996), and numerous articles on theoretical and practical ethics.

JOHN KLEINIG is professor of philosophy in the Department of Law and Police Science, John Jay College of Criminal Justice, City University of New York, executive director of the Institute for Criminal Justice Ethics, and an editor of *Criminal Justice Ethics.* He is author of *The Ethics of Policing* (1996), and editor of *Professional Law Enforcement Codes: A Documentary Collection* (with Yurong Zhang, 1993) and *Handled with Discretion: Ethical Issues in Police Decision Making* (1996). He is currently writing a book to be titled *Loyalty and Loyalties.*

DOROTHY E. ROBERTS is a professor at Rutgers University School of Law–Newark, where she teaches courses on criminal law, family law, and civil liberties. Professor Roberts received her B.A. from Yale College and her J.D. from Harvard Law School. She has written and lectured extensively on the interplay of gender, race, and class in legal and ethical issues. Her articles include "Punishing Drug Addicts Who Have Babies: Women of Color, Equality, and the Right to Privacy" (*Harvard Law Review* 1991), "The Genetic Tie" (*University of Chicago Law Review* 1995), and "Welfare and the Problem of Black Citizenship" (*Yale Law Review* 1996). She recently completed a book entitled *Killing the Black Body: Race, Reproduction, and the Meaning of Liberty* (fall, 1997), which she began during a fellowship at Harvard University's Program in Ethics and the Professions.

GARY SEAY is assistant professor of philosophy at Medgar Evers College of The City University of New York. His articles and book reviews on moral philosophy and its applications to contemporary controversies have appeared in philosophical journals and in periodicals devoted to higher education. He is especially interested in ethical controversies in medicine and in civil liberties issues.

MARGARET LELAND SMITH, who is completing a doctorate in criminal justice at Rutgers School of Criminal Justice, has taught criminal justice ethics courses at Rutgers/Newark and John Jay College. She studies the experience of punishment, and the representations of the impact of incarceration.

ELIZABETH REYNOLDS WELFEL received her doctorate in counseling psychology from the University of Minnesota in 1979. She has served on the faculties of Boston College and Cleveland State University, where she is professor and coordinator of the counselor education programs. She is also a licensed psychologist in Ohio with competency in psychotherapy with adults. Dr Welfel has authored more than a dozen articles on ethics in counseling and psychotherapy, and her book on that subject will be published in January, 1998. Her research has focused on the ethical decision-making process and on strategies to help ethics educators develop effective ethics education programs in the professions.

CAROLINE WHITBECK is a philosopher of science, technology, and medicine, and has published widely in these areas and related areas of ethics. A major theme in her recent work is trust and trustworthiness, and she recently edited a special issue of *Science and Engineering Ethics* on Trustworthy Research. She held a fellowship in medical ethics at the Hastings Center, was a Phi Beta Kappa Scholar in 1994-95, and was elected Fellow of the AAAS for her work in engineering ethics. Whitbeck serves on the advisory board of *Professional Ethics* and on the editorial board of *Science and Engineering Ethics,* and is director of the WWW Ethics Center for Engineering and Science. Her book, *Ethics in the Works: Understanding Ethical Problems in Engineering Research and Practice,* will appear in fall, 1997.

KENNETH I. WINSTON is professor of philosophy at Wheaton College in Massachusetts. He was a visiting professor in ethics at Harvard's Kennedy School of Government from 1986 to 1991 and 1994 to 1996. He has written on issues in legal philosophy and political theory as well as in practical ethics, and edited *The Responsible Judge: Readings in Judicial Ethics* (1993, with John T. Noonan, Jr.) and *Gender and Public Policy: Cases and Comments* (1993, with Mary Jo Bane).